The Imprisoned Traveler

TRANSITS

LITERATURE, THOUGHT & CULTURE, 1650–1850

Transits is a series of scholarly monographs and edited volumes publishing beautiful and surprising work. Without ideological bias the series seeks transformative readings of the literary, artistic, cultural, and historical interconnections between Britain, Europe, the Far East, Oceania, and the Americas between the years 1650 and 1850, and as their implications extend down to the present time. In addition to literature, art and history, such "global" perspectives might entail considerations of time, space, nature, economics, politics, environment, gender, sex, race, bodies, and material culture, and might necessitate the development of new modes of critical imagination. At the same time, the series welcomes considerations of the local and the national, for original new work on particular writers and readers in particular places in time continues to be foundational to the discipline.

Since 2011, sixty-five *Transits* titles have been published or are in production.

Recent titles in the *Transits* series:

The Imprisoned Traveler: Joseph Forsyth and Napoleon's Italy
Keith Crook

Fire on the Water: Sailors, Slaves, and Insurrection in Early American Literature, 1789–1886
Lenora Warren

Community and Solitude: New Essays on Johnson's Circle
Anthony W. Lee, ed.

The Global Wordsworth: Romanticism Out of Place
Katherine Bergren

Cultivating Peace: The Virgilian Georgic in English, 1650–1750
Melissa Schoenberger

Jane Austen and Comedy
Erin M. Goss, ed.

Intelligent Souls? Feminist Orientalism in Eighteenth-Century English Literature
Samara Anne Cahill

For a full list of *Transits* titles go to https://www.bucknell.edu/script/upress/series.asp?id=33

TRANSITS

The Imprisoned Traveler

JOSEPH FORSYTH AND NAPOLEON'S ITALY

KEITH CROOK

Bucknell University | UNIVERSITY PRESS

LEWISBURG, PENNSYLVANIA

Library of Congress Cataloging-in-Publication Data

Names: Crook, Keith, author.
Title: The imprisoned traveler : Joseph Forsyth and Napoleon's Italy / by Keith Crook.
Description: Lewisburg, Pennsylvania : Bucknell University Press, 2019. | Series: Transits: literature, thought & culture, 1650–1850 | Includes bibliographical references and index.
Identifiers: LCCN 2019011883 | ISBN 9781684481637 (cloth : alk. paper) | ISBN 9781684481620 (pbk. : alk. paper)
Subjects: LCSH: Forsyth, Joseph, 1763–1815. Remarks on antiquities, arts, and letters during an excursion in Italy, in the years 1802 and 1803. | Forsyth, Joseph, 1763–1815—Travel—Italy.
Classification: LCC DG425 .F735 2019 | DDC 945/.082—dc23
LC record available at https://lccn.loc.gov/2019011883

A British Cataloging-in-Publication record for this book is available from the British Library.

♾ The paper used in this publication meets the requirements of the American National Standard for Information Sciences—Permanence of Paper for Printed Library Materials, ANSI Z39.48-1992.

www.bucknell.edu/UniversityPress

Distributed worldwide by Rutgers University Press

Manufactured in the United States of America

For Nora

CONTENTS

ILLUSTRATIONS

Figures 5.2, 6.10, 6.11, and 6.12 are by the author. Except where stated, all other images are in the public domain.

PREFACE

Twenty years ago, Nora Crook drew my attention to Joseph Forsyth's *Remarks on Antiquities, Arts and Letters during an Excursion in Italy in the Years 1802 and 1803*, first published in 1813. She suggested that students of Romanticism needed a modern edition of a book that had become rare and expensive. This set me on a path that resulted in my editing an annotated edition in 2001 for the University of Delaware Press. It was not a facsimile but a reset text of the second edition of 1816. It preserved the original index and page numbers and recorded corrected typographical errors and variant readings of substance from the first edition. The annotations included translations of passages in Greek, Latin, Italian, and French; a glossary of architectural terms; and a biographical index. My research took me to Forsyth's roots in Elgin, the principal town of Morayshire, in the north of Scotland. At the Moray Local Heritage Centre, I found copies of Forsyth's letters from prison to his brother Isaac thanks to the assistance of Graeme Wilson. I wish to pay tribute to the excellence of the service given by him, his staff, and volunteers in helping me access this invaluable resource. In subsequent years, the idea for another book took shape, one that would place the story of Forsyth's making of his *Italy* and the writing of these letters within the context of the grim conditions under which he wrote it, one that would bring to light the buried, coded political comment underlying his ostensibly neutral and objective narrative. It would also account for the substantial additions made to his later edition, which Forsyth began to revise once he was a free man. This present work tries to fulfill those desiderata. The translations, except where stated otherwise, are my own.

Keith Crook
Cambridge

ABBREVIATIONS

1813	Joseph Forsyth, *Remarks on Antiquities, Arts, and Letters during an Excursion in Italy, in the Years 1802 and 1803* (London: Cadell & Davies, 1813). Where an edition is not explicitly mentioned, *1816* may be assumed to be the source.
1816	Joseph Forsyth, *Remarks on Antiquities, Arts, and Letters during an Excursion in Italy, in the Years 1802 and 1803*, 2nd ed. (London: John Murray, 1816). Where an edition is not explicitly mentioned, *1816* may be assumed to be the source. Pages 357 to 462 of *1816* contain the portion added by Isaac Forsyth.
BLJ	George Gordon Byron, *Byron's Letters and Journals*, ed. Leslie A. Marchand, 13 vols. (London: John Murray, 1973–1982).
CHP	George Gordon Byron, *Childe Harold's Pilgrimage*, in *CPW*, vol 4.
CPW	George Gordon Byron, *The Complete Poetical Works*, ed. Jerome J. McGann, 7 vols. (Oxford: Clarendon, 1980–1993).
L	Letters exchanged between Joseph and Isaac Forsyth (transcribed from photocopies).
MF	George Gordon Byron, *Marino Faliero*, in *CPW*, vol. 4, 296–446, 547–564.
Murray Archive	John Murray Archive, National Library of Scotland, Edinburgh.

The Imprisoned Traveler

1
THE HISTORICAL MOMENT OF *FORSYTH'S ITALY*

IN 1803, ITALY WAS THE wrong place to be for the Scotsman Joseph Forsyth (1763–1815). A civilian traveler in Italy for eighteen months, he had committed no crime, but as an enemy alien, he was thrown into a French dungeon by Napoleon's troops and, in following years, transferred to other prisons, an ordeal of eleven years. Seeking his release on the grounds that he was a man of learning, he wrote a book of his observations on the artworks and literature of Italy. It was designed to convince the authorities of his credentials. Its long title, *Remarks on Antiquities, Arts and Letters during an Excursion in Italy in the Years 1802 and 1803*, later often shortened to *Forsyth's Italy*, was the work of an attractive and original mind. It became a classic in the literature of continental travel. His appreciation of the people he met and the works of art that he saw is delightful and thought-provoking. His book draws upon a wealth of literary and aesthetic sources. Although scholarly, it is easy to read. Written in a style that is urbane, witty, and understated, there are nevertheless hidden meanings that passed by his contemporary readers or that have been lost on later ones. Little attention has been given to it as a piece of prison literature or to its politics.

Another story is revealed by using evidence from the letters Forsyth wrote to his brother Isaac Forsyth from prison, which are printed here for the first time. Prison letters of this period are rare. They give us a key to understanding how Forsyth managed his conditions as a civilian in French prisons, which differed from those of a combatant, and also a chronology that enables us to understand the nature of the passages that he excised in the first edition. When they are reinstated, they reveal a first draft that was probably therapeutic for him to write. It gives voice to his vigorous protest at Napoleon's looting of Italian treasures. He understood the oppression felt in Italy at the beginning of the Napoleonic wars. It shows him networking with Italians opposed to the occupation, and moved to sympathy by the misery of the people. His observations were based on the political and cultural life of a wide range of Italians he met, for he had an excellent facility in speaking and reading Italian and French and a particularly inquiring frame of mind, a testament to the Scottish Enlightenment. He made keen inquiries of many Italians and found that different cities reacted in different ways to the occupation. Uncovering what lies behind Forsyth's reticence, which was partly temperamental and partly to avoid compromising himself as a prisoner of war, we find a personality both congenial and other, whose appraisal of Italian works of art became an appreciation of the Italian people, clear-eyed, unsentimental, and overall, approving.

The journey to Italy that led to the arrest of Forsyth came about during the brief period of the Treaty of Amiens, when war between France and Britain ceased. On the first of October 1801, Britain and revolutionary France had fought each other to a standstill, and peace was declared (see figure 1.1). Within twelve days, Forsyth, aged thirty-eight, set off to Italy "and stopped some weeks at Paris, engaged by the great museum, and the revolutions which that capital had undergone since my former visit" (1).[1] This museum became the Musée du Louvre but was then the Musée central des arts, which in 1803 was renamed the Musée Napoléon. It had been supplied with treasures looted from Italy since 1796. The plunder continued to come in until 1811,[2] but "in July 1798, the bulk of the pictures and antiquities" required by the Treaty of Tolentino had reached Paris.[3] For the next

FIGURE 1.1 Jules Ziegler, 1853: Peace of Amiens, 1801

nineteen months, Forsyth journeyed through Italy via Lyon and Marseille, staying for months at important cities, getting to know and like Italians in each community. He went to study their works of art (the portion that had not gone to Paris) and architecture and to learn about their literary writings. He went intellectually prepared, for he had been a precocious classics undergraduate at Aberdeen University before becoming the young principal of an academy in the village of Newington Butts, south of the River Thames, now part of the London Borough of Southwark. Much of his spare time he spent in improving his language skills in Latin, Greek, French, Italian, and probably German, since his brother Isaac mentions German literary works in his library (see chapter 5). He read the latest plays of Schiller and Alfieri and the writings of Johan Joachim Winckelmann, and he pored over the engravings of Piranesi in readiness for the expedition he had longed for.

In 1803, the states of Italy were occupied by the French and divided as shown in the map (see figure 1.2) on which Forsyth's route has been superimposed in blue. He traveled south on the Mediterranean side to Paestum, returning to Rome. He then crossed over to the Adriatic to take in Bologna and Venice before turning toward Turin, intending to go home through Switzerland. He had to quicken his pace toward the end and avoid France because war between Britain and France had broken out again in May 1803. All the British, including civilians, had been declared potential enemies of France. He was captured in Turin and imprisoned until 1814. Forsyth originally had no "intention of sporting my pen on so beaten a field as Italy" but was encouraged to write a book in the hope that it would win his release. So his book was from the outset an appeal to Napoleon and a demonstration that the author was both a noncombatant scholar and a man of learning. He wrote for people who had already been to Italy, "chiefly for those who have already examined the objects I review" (v). His manuscript, sent from his place of detention in Valenciennes, France, was submitted to the respectable London firm of Cadell & Davies, which published it in 1813.

On publication, *Forsyth's Italy* was well received in Britain. It became even better known when a revised edition came out from John Murray in 1816, after the war was over and Napoleon had been sent to exile in St. Helena. Reviews in Britain across the political spectrum admired and commended it. It became, briefly, embroiled in a politically motivated war of words. Literary figures wrote of it with appreciation—people such as Byron, Percy Bysshe Shelley, Mary Shelley, Claire Clairmont, Leigh Hunt, Stendhal, and Henry James. For over one hundred years, guidebooks drew upon it as an arbiter of taste. Today, art historians discuss Forsyth's views and regard him as a significant witness of his times. For example, Francis Haskell and Nicholas Penny note how Forsyth "acutely pointed out" a feature of classical sculpture: "The ancient artists seldom aimed at mixt passion,

FIGURE 1.2 Italian states, 1803, with Forsyth's journey

they knew practically the limited powers of art; they were content to bring forth one strong sentiment, and left us to the amusement of analyzing that in into fifty."[4]

But as early as 1817, Francis Cohen (later Palgrave) was warning in the *Edinburgh Review* that *Forsyth's Italy*—together with Eustace's *Classical Tour*,[5] the contemporary travel guide with which it was regularly coupled and to which it was often compared—were both in need of replacement: "Even the excellent tours of Forsyth and Eustace, perhaps the most intelligent travellers who ever visited these countries, are already out of date and unsatisfactory."[6] An 1825 review of John Bell's *Observations on Italy* in the *Edinburgh Magazine* makes much the same point but gives additional reasons for this perception and differentiates Eustace from Forsyth:

> When Eustace's Tour first appeared, the avidity with which it was read proved not only the long suspension of intercourse with Italy but the comparative degree of ignorance which prevailed among us regarding that country. . . . It contains much exaggerated description, and it is deficient in candor. Since the publication of the author's Tour . . . observations

> on Italy have poured in upon us from every quarter. . . . Forsyth, unlike Eustace, is accurate in all he observed, and original in every view which he takes of the subjects. But the inadequate and desultory notices with which he favored the public may serve to excite our regret that an author of such spirit and talent, and so admirably qualified to execute the task of delineating Italy, did not put forth a work of greater length and more systematic character.[7]

Later in this review, the writer regrets that even Bell does not, in 1825, address the "political aspect of Italy[, which] is alone sufficient to excite our most intense regard" and wishes to know "the modification which the manners and opinions of its population must have undergone during the existence of a foreign regime."[8] Both Palgrave and the reviewer of Bell desire a publication that combines the requirements of an accurate, practical, and comprehensive tourist guidebook with up-to-date political commentary on Italy and the Italians in post-Napoleonic Europe. Palgrave, the future author of the first edition of Murray's *Hand-Book for Travellers in Northern Italy* (1843), is particularly concerned with the change in the political situation after the Napoleonic wars. Neither critic remarks on the fact that Forsyth had described the beginning of the political reaction to the French occupation in 1803–1804; they are concerned (understandably) with its effects from a post-Napoleonic perspective only.

Forsyth's early reviewers came from the same background as he. They were steeped in classical culture. They were able to appreciate his erudition and wide reading;[9] some had visited Italy. They were able to engage with him on his level and endorse or challenge his interpretations. But by the 1820s, the number of tourists on the Continent had grown, and the readership was changing. This can be seen from the fortunes of Eustace's *Classical Tour*. The sixth edition of Eustace (1821) announced on the title page that it was "with an additional preface, and translations of the various quotations from ancient and modern authors." Mawman, Eustace's publisher, wished to broaden the appeal of Eustace with the translations—which were perhaps intended as a gesture toward female readers, insofar as Latin and Greek were involved. The sixth edition was the last that he issued. Pirated editions of Eustace, published in Leghorn, added material on Pompeii in order to make it a more comprehensive guidebook. The next edition of Eustace, printed in Paris in 1837 by Baudry's European Library, kept the translations but cut out the polemical and embattled preface—the record of a fight long out of date.[10]

The restricted nature of a classically educated readership had been raised as a matter of concern even when Isaac Forsyth was seeking advice from an Edinburgh bookseller, Michael Anderson, concerning where to publish the second edition. Anderson wrote back, "The Book is excellent—I have read it, but unless the notes were translated it never will be so generally read as it deserves—it is, at any rate confined to the learned, and to conneiseurs in the fine arts."[11] But for Forsyth, there had been no reason to translate the classical allusions, which he had supposed would be read in the first place by French scholars and then, perhaps, by his peers. Unlike Eustace, he had not been a traveling tutor (or *bear leader*, to use the common term) who accompanied and instructed tourists in Italy. His original motive in publishing his book had been to get his release by demonstrating to the French authorities that he was a scholarly man, a *savant Anglais*. It had been necessary to impress with his learning any official body or influential person who might bring about his release, as another *savant Anglais* (discussed in the next chapter) had succeeded in doing. As it turned out, encouraged by Michael Anderson and with the added good fortune that a former apprentice, George Smith, was then a clerk at John Murray's famous publishing house at Albemarle Street, his brother Isaac successfully placed the book with the most prestigious publishing house in Britain.[12] Murray, who was also Byron's publisher, issued four editions. It was also reprinted in Geneva in 1818 and 1820. But by the late 1830s, *Forsyth's Italy* was about to go out of print; Murray's fourth edition in 1835 was issued in a run of two thousand copies, but that was the last. From 1838 onward, Murray invested in the famous Murray Guides, in which *Forsyth's Italy* continued to live—excerpted. It could not fulfill the demand for a guidebook but became a source for anthologies and quotation. However, there are other ways in which the legacy of Forsyth's intense focus on detail, underpinned by the best historical information available to him, lived on into Victorian period. One of the purchasers of a copy of the 1835 edition was John Ruskin's father, prior to his son's visit to Italy, which set the younger Ruskin on the path to his career as a critic of Italian art.[13]

In one sense *Forsyth's Italy* had never been up to date. Writing about the first edition, Henry Brougham in the *Edinburgh Review* considered that Forsyth's imprisonment meant that readers should make allowances: "The unfortunate termination of the author's travels in France, where he was detained, and from whence he dates his work in the tenth year of his captivity, adds a claim to forbearance of critics, more especially in those points where the want of acquaintance with recent productions might otherwise have been noticed. He appears to have been kept in ignorance of the works published in this country during the greater part of his detention."[14] It is worth pausing here to ask this question: If *Forsyth's Italy* was regarded as neither an adequate guidebook nor even as particularly up to date, in what did its appeal consist? What the reviews remark on enthusiastically are the author's exceptional intelligence and his power of conveying impressions succinctly. The *Edinburgh Review* praised his "mind of no ordinary strength and originality" and his language, which had "the vigour of epigram and point."[15] Writing of the second (1816) edition in 1817, the *British Critic* spoke of his going to Italy "with a mind of prompt and active powers" and welcomed his "happy faculty of conveying his impressions to the mind of his reader, in few and forcible words."[16] In 1819, the *Monthly Review* said that he had "an enlarged and comprehensive mind" and "a terseness in his mode of expression which has struck us as peculiarly happy, and, considering the taste of modern times, peculiarly rare."[17] In the phrase "considering the taste of modern times," we can see the warning that Forsyth's qualities are getting rarer and that his text might in the future need explication just as he would need translation.[18]

Personal reticence was another factor that recommended his book to reviewers. In a period when magazines eagerly printed the wartime heroics of individuals, the same *Monthly Review* article particularly praised Forsyth's reluctance to intrude himself. That readers only occasionally get a glimpse of the author was regarded as one of the merits of *Forsyth's Italy*: "He does not dwell on things of trifling interest: we have no hair-breadth escapes, no tedious journeyings more tedious still in narration, no sad vicissitudes of wind and weather: it is seldom that we are again introduced to the traveller after we have taken leave of him at the commencement of the tour, but we are from that time indulged only with more interesting observations of the antiquary, the scholar and the man of the world."[19] It was only with the second edition that the reading public learned—through his brother Isaac, in his introduction to *Forsyth's Italy*—the details of Forsyth's capture and his death seventeen months after his release. There was much that Isaac held back. He explained that Forsyth had been revising the text but did not say that it was he who, in his role as editor, had added material to the end of the book. This material had been written by Forsyth, evidently before the 1813 edition, and amounts to about a quarter of the second edition. *Forsyth's Italy* is advertised (fittingly enough) at the back of Byron's 1816 *The Prisoner of Chillon, and Other Poems*, among a list of "May 1818. Books printed for John Murray," as though Forsyth had put in the additions himself: "With numerous and important corrections and additions, made by the Author previous to his recent Decease, and a Life of the Author. 8vo. 15s." There was no credit to Isaac as his ghost editor—nor, of course, did it say that Isaac had negotiated with Murray a higher fee for enlarging his brother's work.

The *Monthly Review*, in the article just quoted, was puzzled by these additions: "The plan of the work, also, not being a continued narrative, gives it a miscellaneous character; to which we should not object, if due care were observed in preventing it from assuming a desultory and unfinished appearance.—Towards the end of the volume, a kind of appendix or supplement is almost unnecessarily introduced. At page 400. we find ourselves again at Rome, and at p. 406. again at Naples, of which we conceived that we had long taken our final leave."[20] It seems likely that the unfortunate effect of the extra material being shoved in as "a kind of appendix" made reviewers overlook the significance of these passages and so to undervalue Forsyth's political stance. That he kept these passages (which might have been in his original notes, earlier drafts, or penultimate draft) suggests he valued them and might have returned at least some of them to their original positions once the need for discretion, patent in 1813, had passed. As we shall see, Isaac's placing of this material affects the thrust of the narrative.

A vigorous, original, and cultivated mind; the power of pithy expression; and an abstention from intruding the self under circumstances in which the writer might be excused for doing so—these are the merits that secured the reviewers' praise. Where they had reservations, it was because Forsyth could be unduly fastidious, a little affected, and quaint. But not only did *Forsyth's Italy* please reviewers. It made a singular impression upon major Romantic writers of the post-Napoleonic period, all of whom had a particular investment in the idea of Italy. Two examples, Leigh Hunt and Byron, illustrate this. Although neither wrote anything on the subject of Forsyth's ordeals, it is hard not to speculate that both had an instinctive fellow feeling for him because of his unjust imprisonment for political reasons. The experience of Forsyth, unjustly held captive for eleven years of the Napoleonic Wars, bore a resemblance to Byron's own prisoner of Chillon, while Leigh Hunt had been sentenced to two years in jail in 1812 for a libel against the prince regent, where his determination to flourish, not languish, gained him Byron's sobriquet "the wit in the dungeon."[21] In an article for the *Liberal*—the short-lived periodical that Hunt, Byron, and Shelley cofounded in 1822, bringing the three briefly together in Italy just before Shelley drowned—Hunt praised Forsyth as a guide for his perceptions while noting the different set of values Forsyth adhered to, some of which he emphatically disagreed with: "Mr. Forsythe, a late traveller of much shrewdness and pith, (though want of ear, and an affectation of ultra good sense, render him sometimes extremely unfit for a critic on Italy,—as where he puts music and perfumery on a level,) has been beforehand with the spot itself in putting this idea in my head."[22] As a result of reading Forsyth's description of Pisa, Leigh Hunt sought out the Campo Santo. In his own account, he compared what he read with what he saw, noting his agreements with Forsyth and triumphing at something Forsyth overlooked. He turned to the frescoes, including the *Triumph of Death* and echoed Forsyth's enthusiasm. Like Forsyth, he saw in them "the germs of beauty and greatness, however obscured and stiffened, the struggle of true pictorial feeling with the inexperience of art." As he explored their detail, his prose imitated his thinking aloud, for his appreciation grew warmer. He developed parallels with Dante and with Chaucer (whom he, nevertheless, saw as bookish and quaint) until the accumulation of admiration brought to his lips high praise for a "super abundance and truth of conception in all this multitude of imagery." Such a judgment reaches beyond his initial careful placing to give great force to his comment that they are the "the real inspirers as well as the harbingers of Raphael and Michael Angelo."[23] Forsyth had "been beforehand," as Leigh Hunt said, "in putting the idea in my head." The direction of Forsyth's remarks spurred this intelligent and critically alert reader to see more. And this was at a time when a high valuation of the frescoes was not general in England. Indeed, they were hardly known. Giovanni Rosini, professor of eloquence at Pisa during the post-Napoleonic period, had published a laudatory descriptive account of them in 1810,[24] and Carlo Lasinio, the *conservatore* (custodian) of the Campo Santo frescoes, began to make engravings of them in 1812 as a precaution against losing a record of them should they be damaged by Napoleon's troops.[25] But it was not until Alexis-François Rio's *Poésie Chrétienne* (1836), with its revaluation of the so-called Italian Primitives, that the *Triumph of Death* began to be appreciated as a masterpiece of its age.[26]

Byron valued *Forsyth's Italy* initially because it helped him see Italy for the first time. However, the book became increasingly more important to him. When, in 1817, he paid his first visit to Rome, he wrote that Rome delighted him but added, "I can't describe [it], because my first impressions are always strong and confused, and my memory selects and reduces them to order, like distance in the landscape, and blends them better, although they may be less distinct."[27] If his close friends wanted to share in his feelings, he said, they should read his guidebook, *Forsyth's Italy*. He was so pleased with the book that he said this on three occasions to different people: to his publisher John Murray, to his half sister Augusta Leigh, and to his friend Thomas Moore.[28] Three years later, in 1820, he approved it even more, for he extended his praise to include Forsyth's political sense of the Italian people. He bracketed the book with the recently published *Diary of an Invalid* by Henry Matthews and "part" of John Hobhouse's *Historical Illustrations*. (Both Matthews and Hobhouse admired Forsyth and were friends of Byron.) These three, Byron said, were "all we have of truth or sense upon Italy."[29] He contrasted with them Jane Waldie's recently published *Sketches Descriptive of Italy*, judging that "she evidently don't know the Italians—or rather don't like them—and forgets the *causes* of their misery and profligacy (*Matthews* and *Forsyth* are your men of truth and tact)."[30] Part of Forsyth's value for Byron lay in his knowledge of and liking for Italians and his understanding "the *causes* of their misery."

Byron's liking for Forsyth was no flash in the pan. For three years, the man stayed in his mind. He appreciated both the aesthetic and the political aspects of Forsyth—a keen observer with a sophisticated eighteenth-century taste and an Enlightenment love of liberty. His aesthetic judgments, Byron said, were "very accurate." He told Moore to read Forsyth on the Colosseum, the Pantheon,

St. Peter's, the Vatican, and the Palatine. Byron's own Augustanism was another source of his admiration for Forsyth, whose aestheticism has elements of Burke and of Addison while being characteristically individual, whose commentary dwells on the actual, and whose criticism is marked by sharp observation, shrewd judgment, and a multivalent response. Forsyth combines an intelligent sympathy for art with Gibbon's erudition and David Hume's skeptical wit. His delightful mixture of learning and elegant expression may well have encouraged Byron to focus on works of art in the poem he composed soon after, *Childe Harold's Pilgrimage, Canto the Fourth* (1818).[31]

Byron conceived the fourth canto as taking a new direction, away from the metaphysics of the third.[32] It would be about works of art and have a learned apparatus of notes. He told Murray in July 1817 that his own "notes are to come, of which it will require more than the *third* Canto, as it necessarily treats more of works of art than of nature."[33] In the event, the majority of the notes were done by Hobhouse but approved by Byron, so they have their place in the experience of the poem. As Stuart Curran has suggested, the romance of *Childe Harold* has something of the medieval technique of interlace,[34] where the learned notes offer glimpses of other terrains and stories. Entertaining, erudite, sometimes self-serving and sometimes laborious, these notes direct attention both toward and away from the poem. Occasionally Forsyth is used to illuminate one of Byron's stanzas or to justify it. Sometimes Forsyth is present in the turn of phrase that Byron has in his verse, for the fourth canto incorporates many literary voices.

Peter Vassallo has remarked that "it was Byron's reading rather than the physical actuality of being in a foreign country which was the primary source of his inspiration."[35] Vassallo gives an extended examination of the echoes of Germaine de Staël's *Corinne*. It is in these areas that Forsyth may also be heard. As with de Staël, and just as it does in Byron's *Childe Harold*, the name of Cornelia—mother of the Gracchi, type of the noble austere republican Roman matron—occurs to him at the tomb of Caecilia Metella.[36] But the most striking parallel occurs when Forsyth, in a panegyric on the Pantheon, draws attention to the efficiency and strength of the illumination from the *single aperture* to the sky: "Here a flood of light falling through one large orb was sufficient for the whole circle of divinities below, and impartially diffused on *all*." Byron makes the same emphasis in "Glory sheds / Her light through thy sole aperture," and Hobhouse annotated it with Forsyth's remark.[37]

Byron fuses both de Staël and Forsyth at St. Peter's. De Staël gives him the musical harmony of the building, and Forsyth provides the response to the dome. Forsyth has a sense of heightened appreciation, where de Staël's Corinne is overwhelmed. She exclaims, "Even seen from below, the dome arouses a feeling of terror. Abysses seem to be suspended over one's head. Everything beyond certain proportions inspires in man, in that limited being, an unconquerable terror."[38] But not so for Forsyth, who is released into a larger dimension: "The cupola is glorious. Viewed in its design, its altitude, or even its decoration; viewed either as a whole or as a part, it enchants the eye, it satisfies the taste, it expands the soul. The very air seems to eat up all that is harsh or colossal, and leaves us nothing but the sublime to feast on" (180). It is this note Byron sounds twice. He enters the cathedral but

> its grandeur overwhelms thee not;
> And why? it is not lessen'd; but thy mind,
> Expanded by the genius of the spot,
> Has grown colossal.[39]

The greatness of the dome gives him increased stature, for it

> defies at first our Nature's littleness,
> Till, growing with its growth, we thus dilate
> Our spirits to the size of that they contemplate.[40]

Forsyth's presence elsewhere in the poem is less obvious, more a matter of Byron using him to endorse the direction of his writing. He recommends Forsyth's several pages of particular observation and reflection on the Colosseum. Forsyth admires the robustness of its engineering and the elegance of its Vitruvian design and discriminated between the fine and hasty elements of its execution. On its purpose for gladiatorial combat, he expresses a vigorous morality and poignant sympathy, noting the watercourses that washed away the blood. Byron's reflections on the Colosseum follow Forsyth: the triumphant design, the bloody slaughter, the watercourses metaphorically present in the crowd roaring as a mountain stream, the "ruin—yet what [a] ruin," ending in "Rome and her Ruin" mirroring each other as "past Redemption's skill."

Although Byron, like any creative artist, transformed what he selected, he took pride in being more accurate than other writers. For example, he wrote in 1820 to Murray, asking him to add to his notes of *Marino Faliero* that Benintende's membership in "the ten" was "an arbitrary alteration of mine" and that doges before Faliero were buried in St. Mark's, not St. John's and St. Paul's. He said, "As I make such pretensions to accuracy—I should not like to be *twitted* even with such trifles on that score."[41] This did not prevent him from taking poetical license elsewhere. Here, he uses Forsyth as a secure base from which to create his poetry. Neither Byron nor Forsyth saw the later evidence that suggested the watercourses might have facilitated the spectacle of sea fights. It was not until the great excavations of 1874 and 1875 that a mechanism for the naumachia using the underground channels was proposed (see chapter 6). Forsyth saw only a level arena. The upperworks of the channels exposed by the excavation of 1810–1814 were filled in before Byron's visit.

Byron showed Forsyth's praise of Ippolito Pindemonte's poetry to the poet himself, who in return expressed his pleasure.[42] He discussed Forsyth with Hobhouse when talking over the notes to *Childe Harold* in August 1817. Hobhouse had obtained favorable opinions of its accuracy from Italians of his acquaintance, including one who had known Forsyth, and wrote enthusiastically to John Murray in December 1817,

> What is chiefly admirable in Mr Forsyth is the address with which he seizes the picturesque part of a sight or a subject and presents just as much, and no more as serves to present the intended image to the reader—A small but strong instance occurs of this in his mention of a village in the Apennines seen from the road to Naples, which he touches off by saying "where they have vipers for sale" or some such phrase—I declare that when I passed that road & saw that village perched amongst bare sunburnt rocks looking blacker than the stone on which it was built, I thought they could have no other trade or means of subsistence.[43]

Hobhouse wrote to Murray proposing that he himself might amplify a future edition of Forsyth.[44]

It is in the tragic drama *Marino Faliero*, however, that the congeniality of Forsyth's political outlook with that of Byron is most manifest. This play was germinating in his mind in 1817, when he first praised Forsyth,[45] and was written in 1820, when he said that he particularly admired Forsyth's understanding of the causes of Italian misery. Byron believed that what stood in the way of a rebellion against the Austrians was the fatal disunity of Italians. Byron wrote, "For the Italians are *not*—like any other nation. . . . *Would* they—or *could* they but unite—they would soon scatter the Barbarians.—But that is difficult—each province and district has all the prejudices of it's past history."[46] While this was a common enough view, Forsyth documented the differences between states and also noted signs of resistance to French hegemony, which I will discuss in more detail in the next chapter. There is much that validates Byron's judgment that Forsyth does "know the Italians," does "like them," and "analyses . . . the *causes* of their misery and profligacy." He was in contact with various individuals engaged in different forms of resistance, but the demoralized society lacked leadership. Good government, Forsyth believed, was a prerequisite for a society to achieve its potential. If the citizens of Rome had lost some of their glorious character, "men in the mass are what governments make them, and who can now calculate the powers of the present race if differently directed? they inherit at least one characteristic of their republican ancestors, that local pride which Rome has always excited in its natives" (400). Forsyth's theme here is the dependence of national character upon government. Mary Shelley, who read *Forsyth's Italy*, makes a similar comment in her review of J. P. Cobbett's *Journal of a Tour in Italy*: "It is our faith that bad governments are the parents of the crimes of their subjects."[47] The theme is one that Byron examines in *Marino Faliero*. In this poem, the "sovereign" doge of Venice, Marino Faliero, is the only hope of a rebellion against the aristocracy, who do not listen to the needs of the people. Byron altered Marino Sanuto's history, making it a people's rebellion and not Faliero's self-motivated attempt to gain despotic control over a corrupt establishment. This has the effect of identifying Faliero, in Byron's words, as "a prince with the Commons against the aristocracy" in a drama, which he admitted to Kinnaird, was "full of republicanism."[48] Faliero, a once noble defender of the state but as flawed as Napoleon,[49] is betrayed by a patrician. He is condemned to be beheaded, and the people's cause is lost. They are left to endure a future under slavish senates and beggarly nobles.

> [Venice] shall be bought
> And sold, and be an appanage to those
> Who shall despise her!—She shall stoop to be
> A province for an empire, petty town
> In lieu of capital, with slaves for senates,
> Beggars for nobles, pandars for a people![50]

Marino Faliero illustrates the danger of resting the hope for the well-being and civic greatness of a state on a single man, however enlightened, or however much he may seem to embody the will of the people if that will is not de facto enshrined in the laws of that country. In this, there is a striking parallel with Forsyth's analysis of the career of Pietro Leopoldo, Grand Duke of Tuscany (1747–1792). The liberal reforms of this benevolent despot, he observed, were too dependent on his absolute hereditary power and his will. Since Leopoldo's death, the Church and the Florentine aristocracy were actively undoing all his good work. So effective were they that later, in 1816, Sismondi was to observe that the Tuscans were forgetting what they owed to this remarkable prince. His view had the benefit of reading Forsyth. Volume 16 of his *Histoire des républiques italiennes du moyen âge* [History of the Italian republics in the middle ages] came out in January 1818, after Sismondi received *Forsyth's Italy* from Murray on March 10, 1817. In both Forsyth's and Byron's histories, when the commons and the prince cannot act together, the outcome for the people is, in Faliero's words,

a sense of woe
'Gainst which thou wilt not strive, and dar'st not murmur.[51]

Forsyth argued that the state of Tuscany had been weakened by the aristocracy; once it had been overrun by the French, independence of action had been crushed and replaced by a kind of servitude, resembling the "slaves for senates, beggars for nobles" in Faliero's prophecy.

Whereas Byron's assimilation of Forsyth into his republican-inflected drama was not overt, Hobhouse used Forsyth as a spearhead.[52] His notes to canto 4 of *Childe Harold* elevated *Forsyth's Italy* above Eustace's *Classical Tour*, which had come out at the same time as Forsyth's first edition of 1813. His preference for Forsyth over Eustace turned into a cause of contention and a political issue. How this affected the fortunes of the two travelogues shows how politicized literary criticism was during and after the Napoleonic wars and how it forced a coterie spirit on writers by their association with authors praised or execrated. There had been a previous division of opinion between the reviews on the merits of these two. But these did not follow simple party lines until Hobhouse entered the arena.

Eustace's *Tour* was from the first caught between the *Edinburgh Review* and the *Quarterly Review*. The *Edinburgh Review*—edited by Frances Jeffrey from its foundation on October 10, 1802—was initially an independent and mild political quarterly, allowing both Whig and Tory contributions, but in 1809, Jeffrey's Whiggish review of Walter Scott's *Marmion* led to a rupture with him and other Tory contributors. The *Quarterly Review* was founded in February 1809 by John Murray following a proposal by Walter Scott to provide a Tory and anti-Jacobin answer to the *Edinburgh Review*. It was edited by William Gifford (chief editor also for the publishing house of John Murray).

In July 1813, the *Edinburgh Review* praised Eustace's *Tour*: "This is one of the best books of travels that have appeared since we began our labours, and consistently with our high sense of its value, we cannot delay bringing it before our readers."[53] Eustace was a Roman Catholic priest. His book might have been expected to receive an adverse review for that reason alone, yet Brougham, his reviewer in the *Edinburgh*, declared that his "manly avowal" of his persuasion disarmed the reader and his perspective lent "animation and interest." This liberality toward Eustace's Catholicism was, to be sure, balanced by reservations about his style: "It is rather free from great faults, than distinguished by any striking excellences. It is somewhat monotonous, and by no means either close or concise. It is certainly sufficiently easy and copious, but frequently a little heavy and feeble."[54] Nevertheless, it continued, "Mr Eustace seems to be not only a very learned and well-informed man, but an amiable and an honest one—which is a far better thing." His happiest gift was in "his descriptive performances," that of Vallombrosa being the best. In common with the other major reviews, these judgments were supported by extensive quotation.

There were, however—again a common feature of the reviews—"strictures" to be made. (The experience of reading such reviews is generally that the reviewer knows more than the author and that the articles have the power to make or break reputations.) Eustace had praised the king of Naples as having the most suitable intellect for his position, "without either defect or excellency," and the *Edinburgh Review* retorted with the sarcastic agreement that "if his talents are of the most ordinary description, his accomplishments base and grovelling, his manners, habits, and propensities disgusting in the eyes of his people, and his vices fitted to secure their hatred, then is the state safe."[55] Because Eustace retraced his route, journeying back, he returned to issues discussed earlier. This resulted, according to the reviewer, in "observations which would certainly have been more conveniently placed in the former part of his work. Indeed, there is nothing more defective in his book than the arrangement; and the consequence is, frequent repetition, and considerable indistinctness of statement."[56] Eustace also wrote a long dissertation on the national character of Italy and France, which the *Edinburgh Review* saw as one-sided, for he "proposes for his object to praise and magnify Italy, and to cry down France. Much of what he says is undoubtedly true; and no one can blame his partialities, who reflects on the warmth of his religious and classical enthusiasm. . . . But the question, after all, is not one of feeling," and the dissertation "fails in its object, and is, as a piece of reasoning or statement, materially defective."[57]

In the October 1813 number of the *Quarterly*, which appeared five months after the *Edinburgh Review* notice, Eustace was slashed. The reviewer had lived in Italy. He attacked Eustace on his classical knowledge in a way that shows classical history could still stir passion. Eustace had praised the Roman Emperor Augustus as a "republican prince"; the *Quarterly* replied, "Yes, of the school of Buonaparte! What a perversion of ideas have we here! For what act is he entitled to this exaggerated praise, which would sound ridiculous even from the lips of Mecænas?—for destroying the liberties of his country?—for consenting to the murder of Cicero, the friend and benefactor of youth?—for transmitting his authority to Tiberius, in hopes that the crimes and vices of that execrable monster might serve as a shade to his own?"[58] The *Quarterly* continued with the complaint that Eustace inconsistently praised Romans for policies he condemned in the French. Despite his opening remarks, he had not looked closely enough at the political institutions of Italy: "It would be extremely difficult to find in any author, possessing the candour and information of Mr. Eustace, opinions less supported by facts." His anti-French remarks showed little power of discrimination. His taste was unsound. Praising Italian drama above the French, he had ignorantly placed "the vulgar buffoonery of

Goldoni upon a level with the wit and discriminating genius of Molière." To "our unspeakable astonishment, we find him selecting the intellectual mediocrity of [Naples's] uneducated sovereign, as the model for a royal understanding."[59] He was mistaken to ascribe popular discontent with his government as proceeding from the "the late French invasion." And here the *Quarterly* showed that despite its ferocity against anything smacking of Jacobinism and Bonapartism, it had no fondness for knee-jerk xenophobia. The Neapolitan people, in its view, were oppressed by the king:

> Mr. Eustace, however, has assumed as an established principle, that nothing hostile to the French can possibly be wrong; nor any thing accomplished by their intervention, conducive to the happiness of mankind. Now, in spite of our contempt for the philosophy and the republicanism of the GREAT NATION, and all our abhorrence for the character of its despot, we cannot but flatter ourselves that some eventual benefit may possibly arise out of the confusion and chaos of the revolution itself; not one iota of which, however, is ascribable to the wisdom or the benevolence of those diabolical agents by whose instrumentality it was produced.[60]

Forsyth's Italy now had its turn. In January 1814 came Brougham's piece in the *Edinburgh Review*, quoted earlier in this chapter. (This, of course, like all pre-1816 reviews, dealt with the first edition, which does not have Isaac's memoir explaining how his brother hoped to secure release by its publication nor the supplementary chapters.) Brougham, after praising Forsyth's "mind of no ordinary strength," elaborated on this, but as with his previous review of Eustace's *Classical Tour*, he balanced undiluted praise with a few "strictures": "Mr Forsyth is evidently a man of observation and reflection: He brings to his task, a very respectable knowledge of the subjects which ought to occupy an Italian traveller; and he is for the most part both liberal and original in his remarks. He expresses himself shortly and with force, though he does not always steer clear of affectation, and not unfrequently takes dogmatical and even extravagant views of things." Brougham's review was also exercised by the range of reference: "He writes, too, rather for those who have examined the subject, or are engaged in surveying it, than for the uninformed; and this often gives his statements and observations an air of obscurity, which the initiated will be content to take for the sake of their shortness and substantial qualities."[61] The *Edinburgh* took the opportunity to assert its Whig credentials, slapping down Forsyth for his defense of Charles I against the defamation of the Italian dramatist, Alfieri: "An Englishman in these times must have lived abroad, until he has forgotten the blessings of a limited and constitutional monarchy, before he could whine in favour of the Stuarts."[62] In its zeal to remind readers of its Whiggish alignment with the constitutional settlement of 1688 and with the Hanoverian succession, it seems unaware of the possibility that Forsyth was a Scot. Not that this would have excused him in the eyes of the *Edinburgh*—it would have laid him open to the charge of being a latter-day Jacobite. As it happens, although a Scot, Forsyth frequently wrote of himself as English.

In spite of these reservations, the *Edinburgh*'s review of *Forsyth's Italy* was, overall, warmly respectful and ample. It did not, however, examine his work in such minute detail as the *Classical Tour*, explaining this as due to "the length to which our account of Mr Eustace's book extended." The *Edinburgh* was thus able to reassert the "valuable" qualities of Eustace without an invidious comparison between the two and to praise *Italy* as a distinctively different work: "His book is, indeed, in all respects a contrast to Mr Eustace's valuable work; for it is full of vigour—always displays an active reasoning mind free from prejudice—more prone at all times to argue than to feel, and occupied with the matter rather than the language—or only careful about the latter, with the view of condensing it, and giving it the vigour of epigram and point. Frequently he is very happy in description."[63] The *Edinburgh*'s review of Forsyth (January 1814) quickly followed the *Quarterly*'s hatchet job on Eustace (published December 1813) but there is no internal evidence that it was a direct response to the earlier review, and indeed, the timing of the two makes it exceedingly unlikely that it could have been. The *Quarterly* did not answer with a critique of Forsyth, though Robert Southey read the first edition and made an adverse comment in a review of a life of Alfieri (January 1816—four months before Murray published the enlarged and revised edition of Forsyth). He picked up Forsyth's censure of Alfieri's character as having "more asperity . . . than would result from a fair estimate of his good and evil qualities" but chiefly criticized Forsyth's high estimate of Alfieri's dramatic power. Referring to the "admirable translation by Mr Coleridge" of Schiller's *Wallenstein*, he replied, "The question where lives his tragic equal? might have been triumphantly answered, in Germany and in England: Schiller, Goethe, Joanna Baillie, are all superior to him. His verse, indeed, is constructed more skilfully than Miss Baillie's; and the character of his dramas is perfectly original; but in poetry, in thought, in feeling, they leave him far behind."[64] Coleridge was favored by the *Quarterly*, and Joanna Baillie was a favorite of Scott's. In all this, it is Forsyth's literary taste that is being challenged by Southey, not his political alignments.

Two other reviews had espoused Eustace. The *Monthly Review*, founded in 1803, was Whig and Nonconformist and, as might be expected, controverted the *Quarterly*. It devoted a long article to Eustace's *Tour* over three issues (March, April, May 1814): "In perusing and reflecting on the work of this learned, dispassionate, and energetic writer, we know not whether to bestow the greatest share of commendation on those talents for description which place the reader on the very spot, and surround him by every *admonitus locorum* [local associations], or on the many profound remarks and discussions respecting historical, political, literary, and religious subjects, which are scattered in different parts of his volumes." A somewhat disingenuous footnote to this very passage on the same page remarked a "rather large" table of errata, and despite the review proclaiming its classical qualities "by a strange fatality the errors are of a description that should seem to indicate an inattention to prosody."[65]

Contemporaneously with this three-part article appeared another review (in March and April 1814) in the *British Critic*, founded in 1793 as a High Church and ultra-Tory monthly. This was the periodical that Byron was later to mock as "my grandmother's review—the British" in the first canto of *Don Juan* (1819).[66] More than all others, this reviewer appears to be highly knowledgeable about traveling in Italy, commenting on the soundness of certain routes; the best seasons to visit, according to climate; the management of floods; the state of modern Italian music and literature; and the whereabouts of paintings, as well as distinguishing Veronese dialect from "general Italian." He is also an Italophile, looking to a united Italy, in his opening remarks using the current war to show how vulnerable the country is from "the dangerous effects produced by a composition of dismembered states, which alienates every patriotic attachment from the whole, produces a hostile collision of independent interests, and lays bare the frontier to every ambitious invader. Had Italy been an united and compacted whole, she might have been, perhaps, the arbiter of the balance of Europe."[67] The second article returns to the theme: "There are perhaps no two countries [such as Italy and England], whose mutual interests would be more actively promoted by a firm alliance."

The review is a meticulous survey, in which the reviewer finds errors in Eustace. Examples of misplaced birthplaces, confused names, poor ancient history, and inaccurate classical references jostle with talk of Eustace's weak political analysis, such as his ascribing worldly prosperity as a benefit of religion: "We much wish Mr Eustace would omit all political disquisition, as we are persuaded that our readers will have already perceived that he is but ill adapted for such a task." His repeated defense of Roman justice and magnanimity approaches the "turgid declamation of a fifth-form school boy" and will provoke the "quiet, complacent smiles of our readers." He catches at a rumor like "a child with a new rattle." Like the writer in the *Quarterly*, the reviewer is reminded of the betrayal of Cicero and denies that Augustus was "modest, just and magnanimous." Similarly, he attacks Eustace's praise for the person and regime of the King of Naples as support for what is "worthy of only of the contempt of his subjects." Showing more liberal taste, he will not allow Eustace to cast slurs on the "illustrious Boccaccio."[68]

It is surprising, therefore, to find how little this affected the favorable verdict, which accepted Eustace's excuse for the many errors, "especially in Italian orthography," as owing to a weakness in his eyes. The reviewer forgave Eustace's shortcomings and almost all his Catholicism, impressed by the sincerity of his faith: "The observations upon Religion do equal honour to Mr. Eustace's head and heart, and breathe throughout a spirit of candour and benevolence." As a High Churchman, he reminded Eustace that "the Protestant *cannot* believe in the very mystery, which the Catholic considers as the very corner-stone of his faith" and that the concept of the pope as a "common father of Christians" is a pleasing but utopian idea.[69] But faced by the godless condition of Napoleon's empire, religion united rather than divided High Tories and Catholics. This instance shows how far critical judgments were subordinated to a Christian agenda and indicates the strength of the opposition that one might expect to be given to any work smacking of irreligion. The *British Critic*'s review concluded,

> Seldom have our labours been employed in an occupation so gratifying to ourselves, as in tracing Mr. Eustace's steps through Italy. We have travelled in idea with a man of sound principles, of elegant taste, of extensive literary information, who adheres to truth, which is the most necessary, but perhaps the least regarded accomplishment of a traveller. Partiality, we will not call it prejudice, has sometimes allured him from strict fidelity in the representation of facts, of historical facts in particular, but this is the less reprehensible, as the reader here can judge for himself, and use his own eyes in traversing a field laid open before him by past records. The political opinions of the author are sometimes singular, and sometimes shallow, as we have found reason to remark in the course of our strictures.[70]

Judging from the familiarity with and enthusiasm for Italy, it is probably the same reviewer of the *British Critic* who reviewed the second edition of *Forsyth's Italy* in January 1817. The tone is quite different; it is respectful, enters into the detail of the routes, is entertained by the episodes, and admires the intelligence of the author: "With a large proportion of the best qualifications for a traveller in Italy, full possession of the language, and of the attainments of a scholar, with a mind of prompt and active powers, a judgment of works of art already informed and exercised, Mr. Forsyth visited that enchanting country in 1801. [He went to France first, left Nice in December 1801 and actually entered Leghorn in January 1802.]"[71] These are the terms of Samuel Johnson's praise of the best travel writer. The reviewer engages in a courteous exchange of views. For example, he noticed, as no other did, that the route Forsyth took into Italy was unusual but "stands greatly recommended by the beauty of the scenery, in which it is seldom equalled by any part of Italy, and scarcely surpassed by that of the Bay of Naples itself." Nevertheless, he warns the readers, the feluccas Forsyth used were unreliable in turning up and were not for travelers on limited time. He politely demurs at Forsyth's denial that the duomo and baptistery at Pisa are Gothic: "To an architect they may not be such, yet to an ordinary spectator they do certainly convey the general sentiment of the Gothic of the north." (The modern opinion is that they are "Romanesque," a term first used by William Gunn in 1819 to describe medieval architecture that preceded the Gothic and retained Roman features.) All large quotations are deployed to display Forsyth's merits. They take up seven pages of the fifteen-page review. Forsyth, for the *British Critic* reviewer, is a writer for the discerning, who admire his "happy faculty of conveying his impressions to the mind of his reader, in few and forcible words." Eustace was not called into the argument. Forsyth's anticlerical comments, perhaps interpreted by the reviewer as anti-Catholic, were not remarked on. He was warmly recommended on his own terms: "We have no hesitation in expressing an opinion, that Mr. Forsyth's is the very best book for a *student* on the spot, a guide equally faithful, enlightened, and eloquent; and with the additional aid of Venuti [whose guide to Rome Forsyth commended], lately republished, the traveller will have only to blame his own want of diligence, if he fail to profit greatly by his residence in a city which in many senses is still a metropolis of the world."[72]

Coming out at the same time, February and March 1817, the *Anti-Jacobin Review* devoted thirty-eight pages in two issues to an approving account of *Forsyth's Italy*. Halfway through, it declares, "Our readers will have perceived, ere this, that Mr. Forsyth is a critic of no common cast; and that, besides a very large share of knowledge and information, he possesses a sound wit, and that sarcastic humour, which gives poignancy to his remarks, and effect to his animadversions," and it takes its leave "of the author, in whom we have found an agreeable, instructive, judicious and scientific, travelling-companion."[73] Substantial and well-chosen quotations give a good sense of the book, and particularly, it is strong on Forsyth's capacity to be a critic of architecture. However, the uses to which it puts quotations from *Italy* display a deeply politicized and willed interpretation in support of High Church conservative values. The *Anti-Jacobin* applies Forsyth's comments on Italian matters to English affairs. For example, Forsyth approved of the Grand Duke of Tuscany's breaking up estates to give a livelihood to the overtaxed poor, as it was a social leveling. The *Anti-Jacobin* thinks it would be a good measure in England, where larger farms are being made. This has "diminished a useful body of men—the yeomen" (their usefulness being to serve those higher up the social scale, it is implied). Increasing smaller farms could strengthen the hierarchy, and there is an economic benefit to those who are more wealthy. Large farmers can afford to wait on the market while "a little farmer is obliged" to sell cheap in order to pay his rent.

So having small farms cuts down the "dearness of poultry and eggs," benefitting the class of readers of the review but not the producers. The review misses no opportunity to gloss for its own agenda. Forsyth deprecates the rivalry leading to many wars between the Italian states, as it impedes progress to nationhood. He particularly criticizes Genoa's humiliation of Pisa. The *Anti-Jacobin* adds, as Forsyth does not, that it is to be expected for "such is the magnanimity . . . of Republicans," reminding the reader still to beware of the English Jacobins after the fall of Napoleon.[74]

When the review takes issue with Forsyth, we glimpse a radical incompatibility where we sense it would take little to bring him out of favor. According to the *Anti-Jacobin*, Forsyth had not been severe enough on Count Alfieri, who mocked King Charles I in a prologue of his play *Agis*. Forsyth had called it unmanly to insult "a prince fully unfortunate as he was criminal" (62). The *Anti-Jacobin* goes further: "We enter our protest against Count and commentator . . . the first Charles was mistaken in some respects, yet he was criminal in none."[75] It is surprised by Forsyth's account. Forsyth liberally favored the abolition of the death penalty and told of how when capital punishment was restored in Tuscany, crimes had doubled. The *Anti-Jacobin* comments that "no certain conclusion can be deduced from it." Diverting attention, it stresses the need to be more zealous in England where "our laws, to judge by the administration of them, were made less for the security of innocence, than for the protection of guilt." When Forsyth criticizes the supineness of the Florentines whose virtues were all the "timid, passive, Christian, Kind . . . every quality that can adorn a slave" (367), it replies, "We were inclined to suspect that the author had made a mistake here, and written slave where he meant to write christian."[76] Just how precarious was the conservative favor of Forsyth would be tested by the next turn in political events.

In 1818 came the publication of Byron's *Childe Harold's Pilgrimage, Canto the Fourth*, with Hobhouse's notes pitting Forsyth against Eustace. It was followed in April 1818 by the publication of Hobhouse's *Historical Illustrations*. In 1818, Byron was a divisive and controversial figure. The scandal of his separation from his wife, his self-imposed exile to the Continent, rumors of his promoting a nest of promiscuous incest at Geneva with Percy Shelley and Mary Godwin at Geneva in 1816, and the barely disguised infidelity of *Manfred* (1817) had drawn the fire of the editors of ultra-Tory periodicals, such as John Stoddart of the *Day and New Times*.[77] Nevertheless, Byron's title, celebrity, popular success (he was one of John Murray's best-selling authors), to say nothing of his genius, fended off attacks that might have sunk another writer. Murray, of course, protected his investment by ensuring that *Canto the Fourth* was favorably reviewed in the *Quarterly*; in fact, this conclusion to his "Romaunt" was widely noticed and generally acknowledged as the product of a brilliant poet writing at the height of his powers, however much the reviewers might deplore its tendency or the character of Byron himself.

But such favor did not extend so widely to Hobhouse, despite his being published by Murray also; he was altogether less important and regarded by many as a dangerous radical. This applies even to the *Quarterly*'s own reviewer of *Canto the Fourth* in April 1818, Walter Scott. His review was first in the field, praising Byron's "glowing imagination" and likening the experience of exhilaration and diversity in the poem to the "majesty and interest of a woodland chase." It saluted the poet and berated Hobhouse; the notes of Hobhouse, "the author of that facetious account of Buonaparte's reign of an hundred days . . . contain of course many political sentiments of a class which have ceased to excite anger, or any stronger feeling than pity, and a sense of the weakness of humanity which in all ages, has inclined men of talents and cultivation to disgrace themselves." If both Hobhouse and Byron "will needs identify their own cause with that of their country's enemies, we can forgive them as losers, who have proverbial leave to pout." They would *now* enjoy a liberty to travel won by the opponents of France and a respect for the "title of Englishman."[78] The rest of Hobhouse's notes required no further attention.

The *British Critic*, in May 1818, was less enthusiastic about Byron. Its views on Hobhouse were reserved until July 1819, when it produced a belated review of his *Historical Illustrations*. The review was colored by distaste for Byron and was further upset, one suspects, by Hobhouse's cutting remark in *Historical Illustrations* that "the unction of the divine" (Eustace was an ordained Catholic priest) might have made Eustace's *Tour* "something more and better than a book of travels but they have not made it a book of travels."[79] Its attitude to Forsyth had soured. Addressing Hobhouse's repeated preference for Forsyth over Eustace, the *British Critic* turned nasty: "The allusion near the end of this extract is intended, as we suppose, for Mr. Eustace, whose generous feelings and cheerful temper, do not suit Mr H. so well as the grumbling tone of Mr. Forsyth. If the first has too frequently invested the objects, which he describes, with a warmth of colouring which existed only in his own imagination; the second saw Italy with the jaundiced eye of a peevish valetudinarian." So much for its earlier opinion of Forsyth's "happy faculty of conveying his impressions." The *British Critic* then compared how both authors consider the entitlement of a descendant of the House of Stuart to be addressed as "His Royal Highness": "With Mr. Eustace, this is the height of delicacy [quotes Eustace]. Mr. Forsyth, though no unrelenting revolutionist, says surlily [quotes Forsyth]. The one gives a gloss, where the other throws a shade, and the true colour is changed by each; but the feelings of Mr. Eustace are enviable; whilst the latter must be pitied, as evincing a tone of uniform depreciation, a mind but ill at ease."[80] To consolidate the point, the *British Critic* ran in September 1819 a "panegyric" on

Mr. Eustace who "will be our closet companion, and one in whom we shall most and longest delight."[81]

The *Edinburgh*, despite its opposition to the *Quarterly*, welcomed *Childe Harold's Pilgrimage, Canto the Fourth*.[82] The other Whig organ, the *Monthly Review*, in November 1818, showed that the matter of Italy was a live issue, praising the Italian episodes of *Childe Harold* but regretting that Byron had been unfortunate in his companion, "who can dilute and reduce his poetry to the humblest prose." Hobhouse wrote with "ludicrous affectation," mistook his Horace in his notes to the poem, and in the *Illustrations* indulged himself in some "innoxious" [harmless, i.e., ineffective] republicanism. Only his criticisms of Giuseppe Parini and Ugo Foscolo received the reviewer's endorsement. (Ironically, these were not actually by Hobhouse.)[83] It is likely, however, that Hobhouse's remarks on Forsyth (unmentioned by the review) brought *Italy* to the *Monthly*'s attention. For, in May 1819, three years after the republication of *Forsyth's Italy*, the *Monthly* produced the review it had neglected to give, under the pretext of a comparison with Henry Sass's *A Journey to Rome and Naples* (1818). Perhaps strategically, it neither acknowledged Hobhouse nor repudiated its own earlier view of Eustace. Forsyth was recommended "as a very agreeable and fit accompaniment to the more extended tomes of Mr. Eustace."[84] However, the language of praise echoes that of Hobhouse. The reviewer even preferred a thinner volume to extended tomes: "It requires no great degree of penetration, and indeed a perusal of a few pages of his work is amply sufficient, to discover that Mr. Forsyth is a man of an enlarged and comprehensive mind; his observations are for the most part shrewd and original; his ideas, with but few exceptions are just and sagacious; and the language, in which they are embodied, is usually classical and chaste. We observe indeed a terseness in his mode of expression which has struck us as peculiarly happy, and, considering the taste of modern times, peculiarly rare."[85] As already noted, it added that the writer was personally self-effacing, leaving us "only with the more interesting observations of the antiquary, the scholar, and the man of the world." So rich was the material that quotation was difficult: "Amid the variety of interesting matter which is laid open to us in this spacious field of inquiry, we are almost at a loss to know what to select and what to admit."[86]

Despite the fact that Hobhouse's praise of Forsyth at the expense of Eustace had shifted the pattern of response to his *Italy*, his book came out of the battle of reviews relatively unscathed. For this one can see several reasons: he was a victim of Napoleon, not a supporter; he was out of the political melee from 1803 onward; his anticlerical comments could be glossed as anti-Catholic; and he was one of the conservative John Murray's authors (though that, as we can see, did not protect Hobhouse). In addition, his comments on landowning and its proper management (particularly in relation to the Campagna and Maremma) were acceptable to the Whigs, being very similar to those of Chateauvieux's agricultural and statistical commentary, favorably reviewed in the rival *Edinburgh Review* for March 1817.[87] Chateauvieux, who was a Murray author also (he produced the forgery of Napoleon's biography[88]), was an early recipient of *Forsyth's Italy*. He was named in Murray's ledger, along with Sismondi, who was to be sent a copy on March 10, 1817.

Eustace's editor, probably Joseph Mawman himself, hit back in the sixth edition (1821) with a preface attacking Hobhouse. It gave instances of Forsyth's errors and indirectly sneered at him by alluding to him as "another journalist."[89] Taking the longer view here, we should note that Hobhouse and Mawman were waging war as proxies, since both of the authors in question were dead. The issues that concerned them skew the contemporary appreciation of Forsyth and draw attention away from what was happening generally to the literature of travel on the Continent.

In all the weighing up of the merits of Eustace and Forsyth and in the polemics surrounding Byron and Hobhouse and Whig versus Tory journals, there is very little attention paid to the context in which Forsyth had worked. The *Edinburgh*'s handling of Forsyth's imprisonment in its 1814 review is a curious mixture of the sympathetic and the sanguine. It misses how imprisonment colors much of Forsyth's view of occupied Italy. It recognizes the emotional duress under which Forsyth labored in saying that the author "lingered out the interval in tedious, and till very lately, almost hopeless captivity. He dates his work from Valenciennes, June 1812." Although Brougham does recognize that he was "almost hopeless," a prisoner would not think ten years "an interval," not knowing when the end was in sight. Cheerfully for his own readership, the article concludes, "we have no doubt that the approaching peace will again let loose half the upper ranks in our country." When the review appeared, Forsyth still had fifteen weeks to go before his release. The *Monthly Review* in 1819, trying not to sound callous about Forsyth's plight, nevertheless noted his imprisonment principally as a way of paying a tortuous compliment: "[We] congratulate ourselves he altered his original plan [not to write] . . . nay, even if one of the prevailing causes may be found in the author's ultimate and disastrous captivity in France, we are almost afraid (such is our selfishness on this point) that our compassion for the exile might materially suffer from the recollection of the effect attributable to his misfortune."[90] Reviewers cannot be blamed for this. They were partly responding to and honoring Forsyth's own tight-lipped refusal to stir up readers' feelings of pity and indignation. As readers today, however, we are not bound to respect this reticence on his, or their, part.

2
FORSYTH'S PRISONS

SET FREE AND BACK IN ENGLAND, Forsyth spent time in November 1814 revising the book that he had published with Cadell in the tranquil and studious rooms of Montagu House. In 1754, it had become the British Museum; it had been refurbished, with the addition of a new gallery, the Townley, in 1808 (figure 2.1). There were many proofing errors that Forsyth needed to correct, and he made quite a number of stylistic changes. He never finished the revision, for he died in 1815, eight months before it was published, leaving his brother Isaac to complete it and to find a publisher. As we have seen, Isaac succeeded in placing it with John Murray. Among the surviving interchanges between Murray and Isaac is a letter saying that he had enlarged the book by about a quarter. He had found "new matter" in Forsyth's handwritten notes.

This new matter printed in the 1816 (Murray) edition consists of forty-four passages, varying in length. They seem to have been arranged in three groups, each in chronological order and each going over the same space of time. This curious order we will return to. No original manuscript survives, but the passages betray signs that they were not newly written in 1814–1815. Three of them—on Florence, Arezzo, and Verona—are clearly early drafts replaced by rewrites.[1] But the majority had been originally intended for inclusion in the Cadell edition, as part of a continuous narrative. Before Forsyth submitted his manuscript, he excised them. Like torn pieces of fabric, they left telltale edges, such as references in the retained text to the missing text. My 2001 edition of *Forsyth's Italy* presents evidence that shows how each passage may be slotted into a particular place in the Cadell edition of 1813. For example, Forsyth's footnote references in one chapter refer back to a discussion of Grand Duke Pietro Leopoldo, which he had cut. A discussion of unidentified royalty in another excised passage clearly belongs with a description of the visit of the king and queen of Naples at Caserta. Forsyth had made no attempt to revise the text for the first edition to smooth these "torn edges" for

FIGURE 2.1 British Museum at Montagu House, 1813

Cadell, probably because he needed to publish the book as soon as possible. He certainly did not intend the omitted passages to be seen by the French, although he kept all of them and had arranged them as though some would be incorporated in the new edition. When all the omitted passages are read in their original places (according to my reconstruction), they form an important strand of the evidence for what Forsyth was really thinking during his long imprisonment. A sequential list of the canceled passages showing the order in which they might have been composed is given in appendix B.

The second strand of this evidence comes from his letters (printed for the first time here, following chapter 6).[2] Although the French called civilian prisoners *détenus* [detainees], Forsyth told Isaac to address his letters to "M. Forsyth, Prisonnier Anglais [English prisoner]," insisting on the grim term and aligning himself, although a Scot, with the English. Few letters from civilian prisoners in France covering the period of the war have survived. In November 1806, Napoleon issued the *Décret de Berlin* [Berlin decree], forbidding all postal communication with Britain, and from then on, letters had to be smuggled out. Even before that date, they might just get lost or be thrown away by the censor. James Forbes, who had served in the East India Company and was almost sixty, did get his letters out and published them in 1806 as *Letters from France*, particularly mentioning his imprisonment in Verdun up to the year 1804. But those early years were less harsh times. Forbes was rich and distinguished, had the support of the celebrated naturalist Sir Joseph Banks, and was known as a *savant Anglais* [learned Englishman]. He made his case to the distinguished scientist and politician Lazare Carnot, whom he addresses as "President of the National Institute, at Paris"[3] in these terms: "My drawings and the descriptions of them, which were made during these travels, fill upwards of fifty-two thousand pages, and are contained in one hundred and fifty folio volumes, all the work of my own hands; and these labours obtained me the honour of being elected a member of the Royal and Antiquarian Societies of London." Forbes was not alone in making such a case. John Goldworth Alger, the historian who investigated the police records in the Bibliothèque nationale [National Library], listed in 1904 other "scientists, scholars, and physicians" who obtained release, supported by eminent scholars. He mentions particularly the successful representations of Sir Joseph Banks and Edward Jenner, and the personal involvement of Napoleon, who said of Jenner, "I can refuse nothing to so great a man."[4]

Maybe Forbes was in Forsyth's mind when he set to write his *Italy* to prove that he too was a scholarly Englishman. And in addition, there was another case at Verdun where a "savant" was released on the grounds of having written a book in prison, showing his learning. According to another prisoner, James Lawrence, on the eighth of February 1806, a Dr. Burrell Davis sent copies of two pamphlets he had written in French to be approved by the commandant of Verdun. One was on how to recover a seemingly drowned individual and the other on the dangers of too early interment of a seemingly dead person. They were approved by return with the words complimenting him on "*un si bel emploi de son tems, de sces facultés intellectuelles et de son experience*" (such a fine use of his time, his intellectual powers and his experience). This letter together with Davis's first, requesting approval, was printed with the second pamphlet, and he was released from prison soon after.[5] Alger's account may be more accurate, as he had access to police records, for he says Davis forwarded his work "to Corsivart, along with a petition to Napoleon."[6] So it is possible that the commandant acted after permission was granted at the highest level. Whatever the process, the testimony of Lawrence, as a prisoner of Verdun, shows that Forsyth had local examples, early on, to encourage him to write his book. Unlike the combatant prisoners of war, the noncombatant civilians, the "*détenus*," had no system of exchange of prisoners. The British government refused to exchange combatants for civilians "as this would have been a recognition of the validity of the detention."[7]

Isaac wrote that while Forsyth was in prison at Valenciennes (i.e., after 1811), he "was persuaded by some of his intimate friends to prepare the notes he had made while on his tour of Italy, and publish them in England" to obtain his release.

Murray's editor cut this down to read "was induced to prepare the notes he had made," leaving out the mention of friends and introducing a note of unwillingness on Forsyth's part. Neither of these accounts is wholly reliable. The editor had no evidence other than what Isaac gave. Isaac was asked late in the publishing process to write a life of his brother, for which he opted to provide an encomium in which he seems to have papered over cracks in his knowledge. We shall discuss the disparities between his account and those of others as they arise in my account that follows. What is true is that Forsyth did write the book in order to be released and that it was prepared from the notes he had made. The book was also published when he was at Valenciennes, and he may have been urged to finish it then. But the writing up and the study for *Italy* appears to have begun long before, probably in Verdun.

Forsyth wrote to Isaac knowing the censor would read his letters. After seven years in prison, he writes, "I have always abstained from writing on some public subject deeming it prudent" (*L* 18). He is stoical in order not to distress his family. He gets consolation by asking Isaac to tell him about his domestic affairs, which Isaac does in copious detail but no doubt their normality and sometimes banality were reassuring in the loneliness, terrors, and despair of prison. When the letters are read as a whole, the alert reader will catch the inflections that betray strong emotion and pressure of circumstances. They also give an idea of Forsyth's psychological state and his prison conditions. Used in conjunction with the papers that he rejected in the course of writing, we can get a good idea of what it was like for him to write a book that might save him from an unfair fate and chart the times of the different places of his imprisonment, which Isaac gets wrong.

The hints dropped by Forsyth's letters about the conditions that he suffered in his several prisons need to be amplified by firsthand accounts given by other civilians captured during the Napoleonic Wars about their experiences. Although there was a public taste for the heroics of captured soldiers and sailors,[8] such histories with respect to civilians are, like surviving letters, very few. The fullest and most relevant for our purposes is to be found in *A Picture of Verdun* by the previously mentioned prisoner James Lawrence (1773–1840), a "neat and fanciful minor poet" from Jamaica, according to his obituary.[9] He is better known as the "Chevalier Lawrence" who wrote *The Empire of the Nairs; or, The Rights of Women: An Utopian Romance* (1811), an acknowledged influence upon Shelley's *Queen Mab* and *Alastor*, and also, briefly, a correspondent of Shelley, whom he met in 1813 and with whom he shared antimatrimonial views. Lawrence's period at Verdun (1803–1809[10]) coincide with most of Forsyth's there, and he mentions Forsyth in his account. Useful background material also comes from James Forbes's *Letters from France* (1806), Joshua Done's "Narrative" (1826), and Seacome Ellison's *Prison Scenes* (1838). Only Lawrence and Forbes were noncombatants. Their memoirs are further supplemented by the valuable research of John Alger. According to Alger, a number of towns—such as Fontainebleau, Nîmes, and Valenciennes—were initially chosen for the detention of prisoners; subsequently, "on the 23rd November 1803 [Napoleon] ordered that officers, old men, and men with wives and children should be interned at Verdun" where numbers of prisoners ranged from 600 to 1,100, while "persons giving cause of complaint were to be confined at Bitche." The town claimed compensation in 1839 from the British government, saying the "number of prisoners always exceeded 1200, and frequently amounted to 2000." Alger insists in his footnote that it "never exceeded 1100."[11] Lawrence gives the number of noncombatant *détenus* as 300 initially, reducing to 200 in 1809 He noted Napoleon decreed that "all the *détenus* in France should be transported thither at their own expense."[12]

After his arrest at Turin, Forsyth was taken to Nîmes. This was a depot where the arrangements for captives were relatively lax. Sometime in the months of June to November, Forsyth slipped away to Marseille to take a Neapolitan boat to Italy. According to Lawrence, the master of the vessel, an Italian to whom he unwisely paid his passage in advance, denounced him: "He was arrested and sent off to Bitsche [*sic*]. The sum of money which he paid to the gendarmes for guarding him on a journey of five hundred miles must have been enormous."[13] Isaac's account diverges from that of Lawrence in a few particulars. His brother "withdrew to Marseilles with the intention of passing, in an American ship, to Malta, and thence back to England"; the broker who had arranged the passage (not the master of the vessel) "sold him to the police, by whom he was arrested when stepping on board." After being conveyed back to Nîmes under guard, "in the depths of a most severe winter he was marched from one end of France to the other, (a distance of 600 miles) to that most execrable dungeon, Fort de Bitché" (2). (The distance is 542 miles by modern highways.) By the word "marched," Isaac suggests that Forsyth went all the way on foot. This is possible. Some *détenus* were so marched from one detention place to another if they could not or would not pay for an escort and a carriage or if they were being punished.[14] Typically, however, pressure was put on the better-off victims to pay up and be fleeced in order to avoid a foot march. Since, according to Lawrence's testimony, Forsyth was escorted at great expense, this is likely to have happened in his case. Lawrence graphically describes "the manner in which a *détenu* is carried to Bitche":

> He was generally roused up about four o'clock in the morning, for the fate that awaked him had been kept a profound secret, lest he endeavour to avoid it by escaping the night before. He was ordered to march off immediately on foot, and was told that he should sleep every night

> among malefactors in the common jails of the town upon the road. Upon his expostulating against the harshness of this treatment, he was told that as an indulgence he might travel between two gendarmes in a carriage at his own expence, and lodge every night at an inn. The gendarmes intimated to him that they knew a man who let out horses and carriages, and who would convey him the whole of the way, and that they would go immediately and make the bargain with him. The liveryman, accustomed to these expenditures, agrees to convey them at an extravagant price, which he shares with the gendarmes.[15]

The gendarmes, whose food and lodging were also, perforce, paid for by the *détenu*, would lord it over him, stopping at expensive inns (from whose landlords they also received a cut), requiring "whatever the larder and cellar could produce for dinner and supper," laughing, singing, carousing, and becoming insolent, often while "the poor dejected prisoner was sitting in the corner ruminating on his lamentable situation."[16]

Lawrence is ostensibly drawing a composite picture, collected from several witness accounts. It seems likely that it incorporates at least some elements of Forsyth's experience. The detail about the gendarmes' custom to rouse *détenus* at four o'clock in the morning in order to take them by surprise coincides with Isaac's account of Forsyth's arousal at that same hour by gendarmes to inform him that he must leave Paris immediately (*1816*, 6). The detail supplied by Lawrence that Forsyth paid for the gendarmes alerts us to the fact he was a man of some means. From the letters, we know he insisted to his brother that he himself should pay all the legacies, debts, and funeral expenses of his mother (*L* 16). The fact that Lawrence estimated that he must have paid an enormous sum suggests that if his detention left him far from destitute, his savings must have been much depleted over his years in confinement.

He was then moved from one prison to another, as the following chronology, derived from the letters, shows.

1803–1806	Citadel of Bitche	29 months
1806–1810	Fortress of Verdun	48 months
1810–1811	Paris	15 months
1811–1813	Valenciennes	26 months, 14 days
1813–1814	Orleans, Blois	6 months
		Total: ca. 11 years (figures rounded)[17]

BITCHE, VERDUN, PARIS, AND VALENCIENNES

Bitche and Verdun were far from the sea, which—combined with their secure walls, ramparts, and moats—made them ideal for securing large numbers of prisoners of war. They owed their formidable defenses to the military engineering genius of Vauban, marshall of France for Louis XIV. Verdun was the fortress city of the general depot for prisoners, while Bitche, about eighty miles east, was the massive, grim, impregnable citadel to the northeast of Lorraine in the Vosges Mountains (see figure 2.2; other places where Forsyth was later imprisoned are also shown on this map of 1812). Bitche was a place of punishment. Accounts agree that it was "held up as an object of terror" to prisoners.[18] As Isaac says, Forsyth was probably put there to punish him for his attempted escape in Marseille. Maybe he was being made an example to frighten others, for Lawrence says that at the beginning of the rounding up of *détenus*, escape "quite grew the fashion at last; and those who proposed to follow their example made no secret of their intention."[19] Nowadays, Bitche is a destination for tourists. Images do not give a sense of the towering horror it was to someone about to be imprisoned in the depths of its lower rooms, carved out of the sandstone rock, away from daylight, and reached by tunnels and lit by lanterns.

From the air, you can see the zigzag walls designed by Vauban on a very high outcrop of sandstone rock, which has had its slopes steeply contoured, making an attack difficult. From a distance, it looms over a town that in Forsyth's day was much smaller and felt more remote. Nowadays the tunnels in the sandstone of the citadel are lit with electric light, but they still seem massy and claustrophobic. An approach to the citadel's entrance reveals how inhospitable it is. The ditch of its moat is cut from the actual rock, and on the far side is the rock face and going much lower behind that are the prisons. Much of the citadel is underground. Figure 2.3 shows a contemporary illustration from an account by Seacome Ellison, master of the Liverpool brig *Rachel*, who was also imprisoned there. He writes that the citadel of Bitche

> ascended on one side by a zig-zag foot-path, and on the other by a carriage-road, winding round, and ascending gradually till both meet at a draw-bridge, that communicates with an inclined plane raised upon arches, leading to the gate at the entrance of the fort, the approaches to which are exposed to a battery of ten pieces of heavy artillery. The entrance is by a tunnel, cut through the rock, 120 feet long, having a massy gate at each end, and one in the center. The rock has been cut through in two places, as low as the ditch; one extremity called the *grosse tête* [big headland], the other the *petite tête* [little headland]; both connected to the body of the fort by draw-bridges.[20]

FIGURE 2.2 Prison locations in France, 1812

FIGURE 2.3 Seacome Ellison, 1838: Prisoners marched to Fort de Bitche. Reproduced by kind permission of the Syndics of Cambridge University Library. PR-S-00018-00037-000-00002.

Another engraving (figure 2.4) from Ellison's book shows the "souterrain" [underground] dormitory and explains the conditions of the prisoners:

> It was no uncommon sight to see thirty or forty of them chained together in a line, like so many horses going to a fair, but not quite in so comfortable a manner. He who has not been an inmate of a French prison, can form no adequate idea of what these poor creatures suffered, particularly in the winter season—in cold damp places, often without fire, and nothing to keep the cold out but the iron bars across the windows, and no covering except a very short allowance of straw. Numbers died under the hard treatment, which was no more regarded than if they had been dogs.[21]

He continues, "We were regularly mustered three times a-day, and counted down at night. In summer, locked up at eight o'clock in the evening, and unlocked at six in the morning; in winter, at four in the afternoon, and eight in the morning."[22] Ellison contracted a high fever and had to put up with the riotous noise of his fellow prisoners "dancing upon the benches, singing, carousing."[23] Some recaptured escapees were executed and mutilated, and prisoners were forced to witness their mangled bodies and assist in their burial.

FIGURE 2.4 Seacome Ellison, 1838: Souterrain of Fort de Bitche. Reproduced by kind permission of the Syndics of Cambridge University Library. PR-S-00018-00037-000-00001.

The commandant was Colonel Clement. Reports are split as to the degree of his harshness or humanity. Joshua Done, a civilian studying music in Paris, was arrested at the age of seventeen and sent to Bitche. He said there never was "a more unfeeling and sanguinary disposition concealed" under a prepossessing countenance such as Clement's. Done had been angered by seeing two friends cut to pieces when they tried to escape; as a result, he himself had been violent and had been restrained.[24] Ellison, on the other hand, saw Clement as tolerant and fair.[25] According to Lawrence, he was "beloved for his humanity."[26] He did release some prisoners for good behavior from the underground cells (shown as *C* on the plan in figure 2.5) and allowed them to live in the barracks (at *H*). The garrison was small, numbering just over one hundred, and the prisoners outnumbered guards, so it would not have been possible to grant this to more than a few. Ellison describes the underground area as having "the dampness of the dungeon, the descent to which numbered upwards of thirty steps, having little light, or circulation of air therein, and never free from water."[27] This was the general living area, two underground spaces, a small and a large souterrain, with another cell for solitary confinement known as the *cachot*.

Probably Forsyth was put in the *cachot* and then the souterrain. Later he may have been transferred to the barracks. According to Isaac, Forsyth's "confinement at

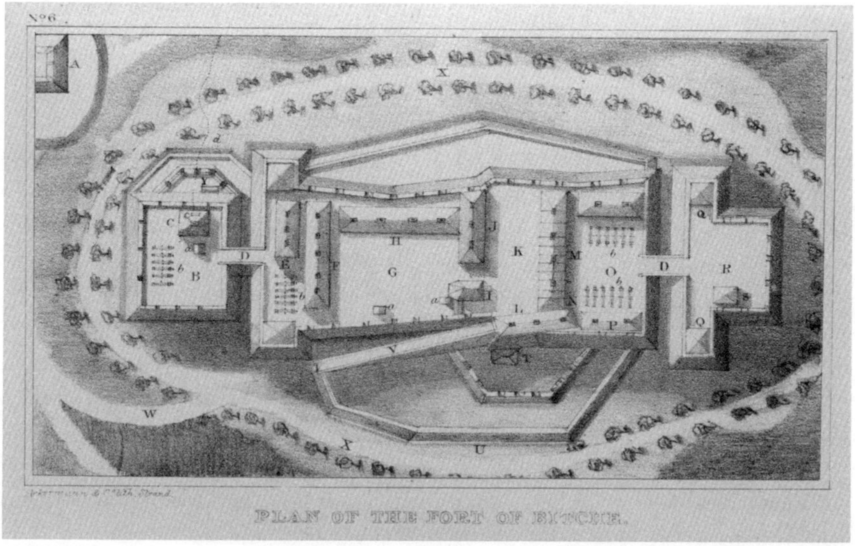

FIGURE 2.5 Seacome Ellison, 1838: Plan of Fort de Bitche. Reproduced by kind permission of the Syndics of Cambridge University Library. PR-S-00018-00037-000-00003.

first was intolerably strict" but his knowledge and facility in French "procured him the notice and the esteem of the commandant, who afterwards paid him particular attention" (5–6). Writing from Verdun in April 1806, after his transfer, Forsyth said, "Of Bitche I have nothing to complain. I enjoyed every indulgence which the situation would admit" (*L* 12). In retrospect, we can see an ironic humor in the idea of enjoyment and indulgence but Forsyth's natural stoicism, his wish to reduce the worry for his family, and the dangers of the new state of affairs made him cryptic. Most of the time Forsyth gives the impression that he is coping well; it takes some searching to see what trouble he was in. The letters show that he did have contact with a solicitor in Queen's Square, London, called Thomas Dax[28] since prisoners were expected to use their own funds to buy privileges. But he received none of the frequent letters that Isaac sent, even before Napoleon's decree of November 1806 forbidding the post, and Mr. Dax let Isaac know that Forsyth told him he felt forgotten. When he did get a letter, in 1805, two years or more had passed without direct contact. In 1807, he wrote that he felt he had lost his identity and become "a thing detached and exiled from his own country." By 1810, his health had deteriorated. In April, he let slip that he had agues at Bitche but "even at Bitche," he was better than now. The words "even at Bitche" hint at the arduous nature of that experience, which he had treated so lightly as a place where he "enjoyed every indulgence it could afford." In truth, it afforded very little, and according to Lawrence, when Forsyth was at Bitche, he was "in a bad state of health."[29] How much he had deteriorated Forsyth was compelled to admit in the April letter. A false promise of release made him prepare Isaac to find that "seven years of captivity has so completely altered my features that you will hardly recognise your brother" (*L* 28).

This deterioration was not wholly due to his imprisonment. When the opportunity for European travel came up in 1801, he had been recuperating from a chronic condition, which in letters he calls his "old complaint." Isaac's biographical notice gives more details: "Having a tendency to pulmonary complaints he was, during this period [1788–1801], twice reduced by them to the brink of the grave. Seeing the impossibility of struggling longer with such incongruous duties as the care of his health and the conscientious superintendance of the education of nearly an hundred boarders, he resigned the charge, and retired to Devonshire in the spring of 1801" (2).[30] In one of his letters to Forsyth, Isaac also speaks of "dreadful" episodes of ill health that "are so oppressive to you" (*L* 21). Forsyth rarely mentions his illness, it not being appropriate in his book and wishing to spare his family in his letters. But he does admit to having agues and that his asthma hurts his chest. Before transferring to Paris, he says, "I was free from any complaint in my breast; but here I feel some return of my old asthma and find the mounting of their immense staircases very laborious—no colds however—my lungs are much sounder than when I left you" (*L* 18).

On April 20, 1806, Forsyth was transferred to the general depot of Verdun. World War I altered the eighteenth-century town immensely, but we can get an idea of what it used to look like. The town was far less daunting than the citadel of Bitche. Vauban's plan of 1695 (figure 2.6) shows it to be protected within a bend of the river Meuse and as having Vauban's characteristic fortifications: zigzag walls, the river canalized in part to make a barrier to invasion, and also deep canals, like the moats of Bitche, ready to be filled by opening sluices in the river, running behind the zigzag walls, making a route for boats inside the town and another barrier to advancing enemy troops, unaware of a network of bridges in no obvious pattern. This is how Vauban intended it to be, but the work was interrupted by the War of the League of Augsburg (1688–1697), and changes occurred later. The interior waterway is colored blue in the illustration. The map is upside down in relation to modern convention; south is at the top.

Two engravings of Verdun (figures 2.7 and 2.8), dated 1837, give an idea of its appearance in 1803. These were made from drawings by William Light, an Australian who had become a civilian after service in the army and the navy who was imprisoned in Verdun in 1803. With its walls, the town was easily garrisoned, and the entry and exit of prisoners was easily policed. The river was an impressive deterrent to would-be escapees. Nevertheless, it was not entirely proof against

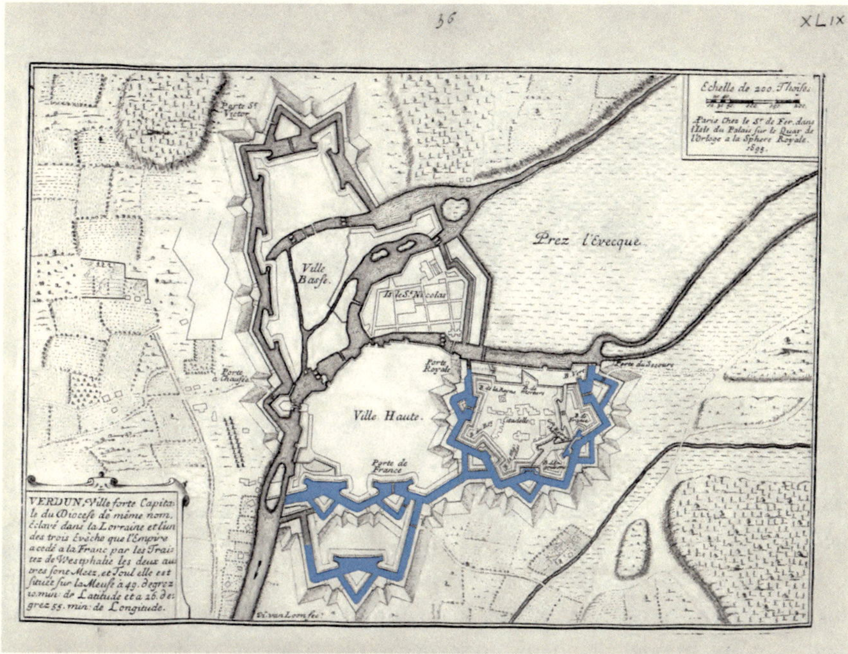

FIGURE 2.6 Vauban's plan for Verdun, 1695

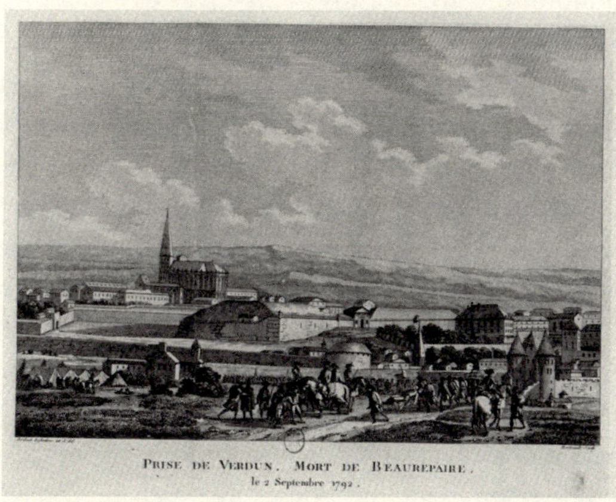

FIGURE 2.7 William Light, 1837: Verdun's walls and citadel. By permission of State Library of South Australia B+15867.

FIGURE 2.8 William Light, 1837: Verdun with the River Meuse. By permission of State Library of South Australia B+15866.

determined attempts to break free.[31] The rich could live outside on parole, where they became the prey of the avaricious, unpredictable, and capricious commandant, General Wirion. Forbes, in his relief at having an early release, wrote gratefully in his book of his "respect and gratitude" to Wirion, but Lawrence commented that Forbes "unintentionally rendered no service to his countrymen there, by representing [the conditions in Verdun] equally mild as it was in the beginning, as it rendered our government less interested about their fate; and when the work appeared at Verdun, the surprise and indignation of the *détenus*, who were every day suffering from the unfeeling caprice, insolence, and rapacity of an upstart, may be imagined at reading such passages."[32] Lawrence himself wrote with some vehemence against the General and his wife, "Madame la Generale," for reasons that he explains: "I am almost afraid of reporting some of her *bon mots* [witticisms], least they should offend any of my readers, but as the intention of this publication is to deter our countrymen, and particularly our countrywomen from visiting France, it is better that they should read them *here* than be obliged to applaud them *there*." Lawrence gives a string of examples of Madame Wirion's coarseness, venality, and abuse of power. As a specimen of her wit, he recounts her advice to one gentleman who had been insulted by another: "He has a pretty wife, you must cuckold him."[33] Wirion imposed himself on aristocratic dinner parties, extorted money from rich people on trumped up charges, and set up gambling houses in which he reaped the benefits. In fits of pique, he would send prisoners off to Bitche at a nod. When he was summoned in 1809 to answer before Napoleon, he shot himself in the Bois de Boulogne.

The surrounding countryside was bleak and remote from escape routes. Forbes painted a picture (figure 2.9) of a semaphore telegraph station outside the walls. This was the system of communication adopted by the French in 1793 and shows that despite its remoteness, Verdun was connected to the wartime alert system. He said you had to be careful to whom you spoke for "spies were everywhere, even among ourselves," and in the woods, there were "wolves, who frequently molest the villages." In August 1803, four miles from Verdun, they savaged a dozen inhabitants; the wolves appear to have been rabid, for "seven of [those bitten] died shortly after of the hydrophobia."[34] In winter, townspeople slaughtered squealing pigs by cutting their throats in the street, where their blood froze in the snow. It brought to mind vividly the terrors of the guillotine. Forbes had met a woman prisoner who had been "compelled to stand upon the scaffold and behold her mother and two sisters beheaded . . . remanded to prison until her next birth-day, when she was to suffer the same fate."[35] Before he was released, he himself feared death. Lawrence observed that the civilian prisoners had a poorer deal than regular combatants. "The officers, who were taken with arms in their hands, who landed as enemies, were treated with greater lenity and indulgence than we, who arrived as friends. In short, the government shewed a rancor against the English"; nevertheless, at Verdun, the "physical situation was not disagreeable."[36]

FIGURE 2.9 James Forbes, 1806: Verdun from the signal station

For some people, Verdun, despite the dangers, had some charms. At the beginning of the establishment of the prison, soon after the English arrival, "the whole town was alive." While Forsyth was enduring his twenty-nine months in Bitche, shops in Verdun were filled with crystal glass from Paris, and silks and muslins. A circulating library was revived: "One street from its noise and bustle, received the name of Bond-street, and became the morning lounge."[37] During Forsyth's time at Verdun, inmates had their own theater: "Mr Concannon, who was the life and soul of all gaiety and fun that reigned at Verdun, was the chief promoter of this branch of amusement. His house was the green-room, where the parts were distributed, the wardrobe arranged, the rehearsals performed, and the prologues recited."[38]

Not all the French were unsympathetic. When Wirion gate-crashed a subscription ball and threatened prison for those who had not invited him, "the French families were so disgusted, that they made a point, each in its turn, to give a ball to the *détenus*. This the general could not prevent, and to these entertainments *Madame Angot*, as the French used to call Madame Wirion, from the character of a vulgar woman in a French comedy, was pointedly not invited."[39] (The character of Madame Angot first appeared in 1767 but became popular under the Directoire. The part was originally played by a man. At least twelve Madame Angot theater-pieces were staged between 1796 and 1803.) Lawrence credits the ordinary French people with points in common with the British. Some were nostalgic for the pre-Revolutionary ancien régime and found the Napoleonic rule irksome. In particular, according to Lawrence, they chafed at the censorship that clamped down on any gaiety that might be construed as criticism of Napoleon: "The old government was good natured, and a Frenchman was half reconciled to every imposition that offered him an opportunity for a *chanson*, or *bon mot*, but the Corsican is too jealous of his authority to allow the French to laugh at their own misfortunes." As an instance of this, he recounts how locals distrusted the propaganda sheets that proclaimed a great French victory at Trafalgar by saying, "*Il ment comme un bulletin*" [He lies like an official report]. A lie was called a *fagot* [*also*: bundle of firewood]. In Paris, the bellman announcing the destruction of the British fleet was followed by another calling "*fagots* for sale."[40]

Forsyth came to Verdun with hopes of an improvement and initially found it. On arrival from Bitche in 1806, he wrote to Isaac, "You may easily imagine the advantages . . . the society of respectable men, and the renewal of former acquaintances. . . . I mess with some gentlemen whom I have long known, and for an excellent dinner and a bottle of good burgundy, pay about 3/9 . . . the English fashions prevail here" (*L* 12). He mentions going to chapel where a friend, Mr. Gorden, officiates, and the presence of English taverns and schools. However, this period of relative optimism did not last. Forsyth found that desperate gambling and drinking dominated much of the social life. General Wirion played on hopes and fears to fleece his "English sheep," and many townspeople spoke of *mon Anglais* whose feathers they hoped to pluck. In addition, as Forbes had said, spies were everywhere and others ready to turn informant, as Forsyth knew to his cost. Lawrence recounts a tale of an informer also spying on Wirion and two policemen spying on each other. The prisoners had to find strategies to avoid being caught out, such as ticketed social meetings: "It was a great comfort to be able to meet, in a convenient room, one's friends and acquaintance, and a society, which being chosen by ballot, a spy or informer could not easily enter, and where there were all the gazettes and pamphlets of the day, a good library, and for those who understood not French, a number of English books."[41] But Forsyth cut himself off from these meetings, despite the fact that he was a sociable man.[42] In cutting himself off, he may have deprived himself of contact with groups that might have benefited him and kept up his spirits, but it is not hard to understand why he would have withdrawn into self-imposed seclusion. He had been made cautious in his contacts as a result of his betrayal at Marseille. He was unwilling to suffer confinement in Bitche again after it had made him so ill. He was now a marked man and likely to be less believed and given more condign punishment for overstepping some capricious rule. If he had belonged to the society, it was likely that he might have been involved in some group misdemeanor as a result of their license and unruliness, and in any case, he objected to them on the grounds of morality and taste. In October 1807, he wrote that few prisoners had escaped ruin "since their captivity by a society of Englishmen the most vicious and prodigal I ever witnessed on earth," and as a consequence, "I mess with one companion and see very little of the world or desire to see." His spirits were at a very low ebb: "My prospect of returning home being now more remote and unreal than ever." A wish to see his brother prompted his remark that "sometimes, indeed, ladies venture over hither with their husbands; but your situation precludes you from catching such an occasion" (*L* 16).

As a Scot, Forsyth may also have felt the injustice of his imprisonment even more keenly than an Englishman might have done. He had been brought up in the Scottish tradition, where one of the most liberal systems of legal penalties existed. Historian David Walker argues that imprisonment was used "as a means of holding the accused persons pending trial, rather than as a form of punishment."[43] In 1800, this had not been prolonged beyond a year, compared with "those long terms of four or five years which had happened in England." Fines, hard labor, corporal punishment, and transportation for fixed terms were the usual sanctions. Capital punishment was far less used than in England. One account argues, "On an average of 30 years preceding the year 1797 the executions for Scotland have not exceeded six in a year," and Manchester, in one-quarter sessions, "sent more felons to the plantations, than all the Scots judges do for ordinary in a twelvemonth." Sedition was the one crime in which the law showed more ferocity.[44] Forsyth, who approved of Leopoldo's legal reforms (see chapter 4), would have had additional reason for feeling that his eleven-year imprisonment was a monstrous outrage.

By 1807, letters were few and far between. Lawrence maybe overstates the case when he says, "Since December, 1806, no letters directed to England were received, as the post-office, and all communications between the two countries, was prohibited by an imperial edict,"[45] but his words convey a general feeling of being cut off. Judging from the letters exchanged between the Forsyth brothers, it took about fifty-two days on average for one to be delivered after sending, and many did not get through. From September 1806 to September 1807, neither heard from the other, despite writing frequently. There was a postal route via Holland that sometimes worked, as the letter was not franked with a British origin, and visitors sometimes were able to smuggle letters in. Isaac speaks of using "a friend" and Forsyth of using "the surest channel I can find." In a letter from June 29, 1809, when matters were more relaxed, Isaac describes an elaborate system of employing the good offices of Lady Grant of Monimusk and General Le Febre and, as a backup, "the medium of a conveyance to Rotterdam" known to a Mr. Baird (*L* 17).[46]

PARIS, VALENCIENNES, ORLEANS, AND LIBERATION

On March 11, 1810, Napoleon and Marie-Louise of Austria celebrated their civil marriage, followed by the religious ceremony in the Musée Napoléon, in Paris on April 1. Festivities and processions occupied Paris and the gardens of the Tuileries (see figure 2.10). Forsyth was transferred to Paris—probably on April 22, 1810—after making applications. He was helped by "a lady in the suite of the King of Holland, then a kind of state-prisoner in Paris," according to Isaac. This may relate to an upheaval that was imminent in Holland. The king of Holland was Louis Bonaparte. His brother Napoleon had installed him as a puppet monarch in 1806 and forced him to abdicate on July 1, 1810, reannexing Holland in the same month. Isaac wrongly says that Forsyth's transfer took place in the spring of 1811 (5). He arrived in Paris when the marriage celebrations were still continuing. They impeded him from going to libraries, where he planned to work seriously on the book that he had already conceived. "Unfortunately for me," he wrote his brother, "the library and the museum are in the most fashionable part of town," but he nevertheless looked forward to "the reflux of the present crowd" (*L* 18), when he would be able to enjoy these and, according to Isaac's memoir, "easy access to the society of learned Frenchmen." But in 1811, an order from Napoleon forbidding Englishmen to reside in Paris put an abrupt end to this welcome respite. Thanks to the intervention of two friends at the Institut, Forsyth, when told to leave Paris instantly, was able to secure a respite of two days and a choice of evils: to go either

FIGURE 2.10 Étienne-Barthélémy Garnier: Marie-Louise and Napoleon in the Tuileries, 1810

back to Verdun or to Valenciennes, a frontier town in the north of France near what is now the Belgian border, another Vauban fortification, but a town with a richer cultural history than Verdun. He chose Valenciennes. We have very few glimpses of his life there, but he did not, Isaac reported laconically, regret his choice.

While Isaac does get dates and circumstances wrong, there is no reason to disbelieve that efforts were made on Forsyth's behalf to secure his release when he was at Valenciennes: "His correspondence at this time shews unwearied applications to his friends at Paris, to the government, and even personally to the Emperor, but without any effect. Nor were his friends in Britain less anxious, or less zealous in the same good cause; yet, although persons of high rank and influence lent their earnest assistance, no beneficial effect resulted from it" (7). The only persons of "high rank and influence" who can be identified are Viscount Castlereagh and the Marquis of Huntly, to both of whom Isaac urges his brother to pay his respects in letters of 1814 (*L 26, 27*), when Forsyth had been moved to Orleans. Shortly afterward, a Mr. Kitchen received a letter from Forsyth at Orleans. This letter was written after the publication of the first edition of the literary work on which Forsyth pinned his hopes of release. That, too, had by then failed in its effect, though it had been sent to Napoleon from England with "solicitations in his favour by some of the most eminent literary characters in London" (7).

3

THE 1813 AND THE 1816 VERSIONS OF *FORSYTH'S ITALY*

ACCORDING TO ISAAC, it was in the Valenciennes period that Forsyth decided to work up the notes he made during his Italian tour into a book. He implies that his brother was unable to fasten his mind on purposeful study during the earlier part of his imprisonment: "Mr. Forsyth's favourite pursuits during his detention seem to have been the classics, Italian poetry, and architecture: but the anxiety which he incessantly felt to be delivered from restraint, absorbed every other consideration, and prevented the application of his mind to any fixed subject, or to composition of any kind" (7). Yet when he was still at Verdun, Forsyth *had* fixed his mind on a project. He wrote to Isaac on October 4, 1807, "I mess with one companio[n] and see very little of the world or desire to see—Some time ago I applied for leave to reside in Paris in order to continue a study which requires access to public libraries and museums. The interest used for me would have obtained for me that permission, had not my adventure at Marseilles been brought into the Minister's notice.[1] My friend at Paris has not given up the point and still encou[rages me]" (*L* 16). The word "continue" shows that Forsyth was already engaged in a learned study ("some time ago") requiring reading at a time when he had no friends in the prisons to speak of and little communication with the world outside. Nor could he have been totally disabled by anxiety, as he himself speaks of studying despite impediments. It may be that some other learned study than the travelogue of *Italy* was in Forsyth's mind, but there is nothing to corroborate that and no reference to works of art that were then in the Musée Napoléon. Initially, Forsyth could not get into the museums in Paris because of the celebrations for Napoleon's marriage to Marie-Louise in April. And then he was distracted by the possible exchange of prisoners and *détenus* through the efforts of Colin Alexander MacKenzie between April 24, 1810, and November 6, 1810.[2]

Colin MacKenzie was an agent of the transportation board, one of three boards responsible for running the Royal Navy. He was a friend of Lord Wellesley (the foreign secretary, Wellington's brother). In April 1810, he was appointed to negotiate an exchange of prisoners shortly after the wedding of Napoleon and Marie-Louise. The negotiations foundered on the fact that Napoleon had far fewer British prisoners to exchange than Britain had French prisoners. Napoleon demanded that all French prisoners should be repatriated, with the French deficit made up from the release of prisoners from other nations such as Portugal and Spain, whereas the British favored a straight numerical swap. Either proposal would have left the other side at a disadvantage. The French were also offended because their negotiator, Clément-Édouard, marquis de Moustier, was a nobleman and experienced plenipotentiary, while MacKenzie was a comparatively low-ranking official. The protracted negotiations had broken down by the end of 1810.

When Forsyth wrote his letter, hope was still in the air. By April 22, 1810, Forsyth had already been made aware of the negotiations: "I was preparing to settle here & pursue some studies, when the unexpected apparition of a commissary for the exchange of prisoners has agreeably deranged my plan and drawn my thoughts to objects far more pleasing than those of Paris. Were I not half ashamed to confess, after so many disappointments, that I can still hope, I should think myself now nearer home than ever." The emotional pressure of "so many disappointments" is clear, as is Forsyth's determination to stay in control. It almost breaks down in the continuation of this letter: "I had gazed & gaped my fill of Paris & was just settling to my book when the account of McKenzie ~~derang~~ unhinged me. Should his mission terminate favorably, we shall soon meet & I will not be long in Britain without seeing you.—" (*L* 18). The mention of "my book" confirms that "some studies" referenced earlier are to be published, although, writing guardedly in a letter to be seen by the censor, he does not say what they are.

Isaac suggests that it was only at Valenciennes—that is, after 1810—that Forsyth first conceived the idea of writing a book: "Having seen some of the *détenus* obtain their release in consequence of appearing before the public in the character of authors—(Buonaparte affecting to be considered the patron and protector of literature)—Mr. Forsyth was induced to prepare the notes he had made while he was on his tour in Italy, and publish them in England" (7). As we have noted, by 1807, James Forbes and Dr. Burrell Davies had become examples of such success stories in Verdun. It is likely that Forsyth would try that route at that time as well as any other. It seems reasonable to speculate that in Verdun, when transfer to Paris was not assured, he might have begun preparatory study for a more ambitiously planned work that eventually became *Forsyth's Italy*. If he was to be released as a result of the petitions sent by letter, he would need to have evidence to show off his learning. To reconcile this reconstruction with Isaac's account, it is only necessary to gloss his remark by saying that encouragement to publish the preparatory work (if such it was) was renewed in Valenciennes. While we may disagree with the timing that Isaac represents for the commencement of the book, it is valuable to know that Forsyth had difficulty coping with the anxiety of being in prison, which accords with his unusually self-revelatory letter about MacKenzie, his despair, and his feeling "unhinged." So I argue that the book was begun a year and a half after his release from Bitche to the fortress of Verdun, where he "lived almost in solitude," avoiding the drunken and gambling community of prisoners and presumably making use of the library (which, although described by Lawrence as a "good" one, would not have catered for the requirements of scholars). He finished *Italy* in Valenciennes after ten months there, on June 1, 1812 (the date he gives in what, in the 1813 version, is his final sentence).

Despite the absence of any surviving manuscript material, it is possible to make a conjectural reconstruction of what the manuscript at its penultimate stage must have been like. It would have been arranged in chronological order, as I argue below, and would have contained the many passages that Forsyth removed before submitting the final version to Cadell, most of them for prudential reasons of various sorts. When these passages are returned to their original locations, it becomes clear that at least one of them records an event after he was imprisoned in 1803. This occurs when he is describing his impressions of Naples in 1802, about two-thirds through in the 1813 edition. For a moment, Forsyth's historical narrative turns into a diary of the present, relating an incident seemingly prompted by seeing all the European aristocracy celebrating Napoleon's marriage in Paris to Marie-Louise in 1810. It seems that this episode (to which we shall return later) was written when he was in Paris from 1810 to 1811. Using evidence like this together with the letters and Isaac's memoir, we can work out a probable sequence of his writing. Then we can see that the text reflects the conditions he experienced. For clarity, I will split an account of these conditions into different periods relating to the prison he was in, beginning with October 1807, when Forsyth wrote that he wanted to "continue" research for his book in Paris.

When Forsyth began his work on a book on Italy at Verdun in 1807, he turned his mind from the misery of prison to the pleasure of Pisa and Florence. When writing of Florence, his mental image would have been something like the engraving of Florence (figure 3.1) made by James Hakewill for *A Picturesque Tour of Italy* in 1820. Hakewill had intentionally followed Forsyth's and Eustace's journeys, observing and drawing sights that had caught their attention. At this juncture of writing about his travels, Forsyth referred to the translator and poet Melchiorre Cesarotti, the physicist Felice Fontana, and the archaeologist Jörgen Zoega (*1813*, 23, 39, 261) as though they were alive. So they were when he visited in 1803, but they had died on November 4, 1808, March 10, 1805, and February 10, 1809,

FIGURE 3.1 William Hakewill, 1816: Florence

respectively. This confirms that the pages about Pisa and Florence were originally written at Verdun, out of contact with current affairs. It also indicates that he wrote the book in chronological order. He had the means to find out whether they were still alive while living in Paris, but he did not do so, even though material added during or subsequent to his Paris sojourn is up to date. A puzzle hangs over whether he updated his writing about Rome. He mentions Venuti's guide in the running text and then adds a footnote to say that there is a new edition: "This book, which was rather rare, has been re-published since I left Italy, by Philip Visconti, brother of the great antiquary" (*1813*, 141n). Filippo Aurelio Visconti was the papal *commissario delle antichità* [commissioner for antiquities], an office once held by Venuti, the great Johann Winkelmann, and Visconti's own brother. He was the immediate predecessor of the Abate Fea, whom we shall discuss later. As the republication was in 1803, Forsyth might have learned this piece of rather specialized news at Nîmes from an informant in Rome before his internment at Bitche.[3] A different puzzle is thrown up by another event that he recorded as happening "since [he] left Italy." He had learned that Bassano, evidently near Naples, had sunk into the crater of the Lago d'Agnano (*1813*, 303; *1816*, 276). But I have been unable to identify this Bassano or the event to which Forsyth refers.

In the John Murray Archive, there is a record of a play Forsyth wrote called *The Condottiero* (The mercenary captain).[4] Forsyth's brother Isaac had written two letters about it, also in the archive, and then sent the play in 1829, long after the publication of *Forsyth's Italy*, but as far as is known, it was never published. It is not known when he wrote it, but it may have been at Verdun during his earlier, more sociable phase. All we know of it comes from two letters that Isaac wrote to Murray. He described it as "a Tradgedy completely finished and written out in his correct elegant manner, on 104 pages Post 8vo.[5] It is founded on a portion of Italian History in the 14th Century." Isaac supplied a cast list: the Duke of Cremona; Catherine, Duchess of Cremona; the Princess Rosalba, their daughter; Ferrant, chamberlain to the duke; Fango, the condottiero; Count Julian, Fango's lieutenant; the *podestà*; the chancellor; the syndics; a knight; officers; a sentinel; and so on. It was set in Cremona "towards the end of the fourteenth century, when several of the Condottieri, or leaders of mercenary troops, rose from very low origins, some from mechanic trades, to be sovereign princes in Italy." Isaac observed, "It strikes me that he had Bonaparte in his eye when drawing The Condottiero. Some of the situations and many of the expressions carry a strong allusion to him." This play suggests that Forsyth had a need to set down his feelings about the man who was his jailer and a Corsican mercenary of the French army—a counterpart of the condottieri of the Italian Middle Ages, leaders of mercenary armies, some of whom gained power and ruled Italian states as despots. But what is conjectural with respect to *The Condottiero* is patent in *Forsyth's Italy*. Bonaparte was in Forsyth's eye, and many of the expressions carry a strong allusion to him.

When we turn to the 1813 Cadell version that was laid before the French authorities, one is struck first by their callousness in denying liberty to the cultivated and dignified author and then, perhaps even more, by surprise that Forsyth—and the eminent literary gentlemen who supported him—should have thought that the book as it stood could possibly have succeeded in its ostensible object. For while there is no ranting against Napoleon or tactless mention of British victories, the 1813 *Italy* is remarkable for what it does *not* say. There are no obsequious expressions of regard for Napoleon—no crooking the knee, no reminders of his magnanimity, his great victories, or the felicity of Italians under French domination. In places, we can even detect subtle but studied insolence, opportunities for a tribute to the emperor Napoleon deliberately sidestepped. What, for instance, has he to say of Lodi, the town in Lombardy where, in 1796, during Napoleon's first Italian campaign, Bonaparte's army won a stunning and legendary victory, putting to flight an Austrian army? Just this: "Lodi is not the only mart of Parmesan cheese. I saw large warehouses in the surrounding villages where it is sold wholesale" (*1813*, 350).

Covert and sometimes overt criticism enabled Forsyth to vent his indignation at his treatment by Napoleon, to write an indictment of the crushing of Italy and, in particular, of the appropriation of its art treasures. This began during Napoleon's Egyptian campaign, before the peace of Amiens, and continued under

Napoleon's director general of museums, Dominique Vivant Denon. Antoine Quatremere de Quincy, Jacques-Louis David, and others had protested against this plundering during the French Revolution, so such opposition had respectability. It could just about be argued that Forsyth's criticism was not especially aimed at Napoleon. But it was one thing for Frenchmen to voice it and another for a British captive, suing for clemency, to do so. The 1813 *Italy* sailed more than close to the wind, as though such daring helped Forsyth preserve his sense of his own personal worth in circumstances that wasted away the prime of his life, felt monstrously unjust, and denied him the liberty that he treasured as a man of the Enlightenment.

The impact of looting was devastating to Italians. They were proud of their heritage, which they saw in the normal course of their lives and felt it to be part of the identity of the place to which they belonged. Intellectual honesty and sympathy for the Italians compelled Forsyth to keep the idea of the lost treasures before his reader, as in the following: "The Florentines seem now to desert a place where vacant frames and idle pedestals only remind them of treasures that are gone, and lessen their esteem for those which remain" (*1813*, 39). For persuading the pope to resist the French, Cardinal Albani was punished by having his collection raided: "Two hundred and ninety-four pieces of ancient sculpture were sent hence to Paris, or lay in cases at Ripagrande ready to be shipped. Some have been fortunately ransomed; and the Prince, though reduced in means, is now courageously beginning to re-combine the wrecks of this celebrated collection. It was affecting to see the statues on their return to the villa. Some lay on the ground shattered by their passage to the river, others remained in their tremendous coffins, and a few were restored to their former pedestals" (*1813*, 222). Criticism of Napoleon is encoded in the Latin epigraph to Forsyth's chapter on the Vatican Museum, Rome, an adaptation of a quotation from Cicero's courtroom attack on the extortion, theft, and embezzlement by Verres, the governor of Sicily in 73–70 BC. When translated, it reveals a parallel situation of loss: "Hi qui hospites ad ea quae visenda sunt ducere solebant—ut ante demonstrabant quid ubique esset, ita nunc quid undique ablatum sit ostendunt" [*1813*, 217; As those who acted as visitors' guides to the various things worth seeing once used to show them what was everywhere, so now they point out everywhere what has been taken away].[6]

Napoleon, the creator of absences, is himself an absence within *Forsyth's Italy*, yet he is everywhere. He is never named but is pointed at silently. Another recondite allusion to his depredations occurs early in *Forsyth's Italy*. Some of the earliest encounters in his travel brought Forsyth closely into contact with Italian intellectuals, who were most conscious of their plight and also very articulate in their distress. Among these were a number of celebrated poets at the University of Pisa, writers of panegyrics, moral tales, and sometimes, epic verse and satire. In a section headed,

"Poets," Forsyth comments pointedly, "Satirists, perhaps the most useful of poets, write under other discouragements—the censure of the press, and the sacredness of public men and measures. Hence their brightest things are confined to private circles (where they come out with hesitation and fear) from the pocket-book." This is true of any period of satire, but the sacredness of Napoleon and his ever-present spies were also in Forsyth's mind. The "hesitation and fear" is a telling instance of how ordinary Italians were compelled into mutual suspicion and a continual feeling of vulnerability.

The theme of looting reappears in an apparently throwaway remark within "Poets," which begins with Lorenzo Pignotti (1739–1812), professor at Pisa. Forsyth describes his moral fables and his "refined satire," comparing them to Alexander Pope in elegance: "Some of his best novelle [short stories] are reserved for private circles. I heard him read one on 'the art of robbing,' which could not be safely published by a Tuscan placeman" (*1813*, 22). The ambiguous title of this work might suggest an innocuous poem on the standard quarrels of authors, a satire on plagiarizing poets, say, or a defense of the poetry of allusion. However, the fact that it "could not be published by a Tuscan placeman" strongly hints that the satire was political. Although many of Pignotti's poems are Aesopian moral tales or elegant celebrations, some, such as "Roberto Manners" and an "Imitation of Juvenal's Tenth Satire," reflect on or satirize contemporary events. And Pignotti *was* a Tuscan placeman. In 1801, he had been appointed Historiographer Royal to the "Kingdom of Etruria," a puppet state created by Napoleon under the nominal rule of the Grand Duke of Tuscany, King Louis I, and was not in a position to publish a critique on his paymaster's overlord.[7] As this poem was read covertly, the likely subject of "the art of robbing" was Napoleon's robbery of art. It appears never to have been published, despite its receiving acclaim in private circles, and may not have survived. Perhaps the death of Pignotti in 1812, before the end of the Napoleonic Wars, prevented its publication in his lifetime and subsequently its inclusion in the collected editions.[8]

If Forsyth was to get his freedom, it would be prudent in him to mute his criticism of the removal of the art treasures and his anger at the injustice and the loss of seeing them in an appropriate context. But in the 1813 edition, he did not suppress completely his personal disappointment and regret that some great paintings from artists such as Titian, Tintoretto, Correggio, Veronese, Guido, and Guercino were not there for him to see and comment on. At Herculaneum, he says, "Unfortunately for me, the more precious articles were then at Palermo" (*1813*, 286). A note on Cremona laments that "the admired Perruginos are gone." It may be no coincidence that, contemplating the tower of Cremona, the words spoken on the scaffold by the condottiero Cabrino Fondulo, tyrant of Cremona (and setting of Forsyth's play, *The Condottiero*), come into his mind: "I repent of nothing . . .

but this—that when I had the Emperor and the Pope together at the top of my great tower, I did not hurl them both over the parapet" (*1813*, 350). His sage observations on the Lodi area as a center for cheese-marketing follow immediately.

FROM THE 1813 EDITION TO THE 1816 EDITION

From 1814 to 1815, Forsyth revised and corrected his 1813 publication, sharpening his criticism of the conquerors' contemptuous disregard for Italians. Of the few actual additions that he made, the most important, substantial, and conspicuous was a new opening paragraph of great significance. The 1813 Cadell edition begins with his arrival at Nice. The 1816 Murray edition begins, "I travelled through France, and stopped some weeks in Paris, engaged by the great museum, and the revolutions that that capital had undergone since my former visit" (11). We learn from this (what is not mentioned in *1813*) that he had visited the Musée du Louvre in Paris, then called the Musée Napoléon, in which Napoleon's looted treasures of Italy were triumphantly displayed: figure 3.2 satirically shows Napoleon boasting that the Apollo Belvedere is worth two million gold francs (called "Napoleons"). So Forsyth's awareness of this act of rapine is announced, sotto voce, in the very first sentence and sets the agenda: the book is a critique. The looting is particularly on his mind, and he will recur to it throughout his narrative. To a comment on the Palazzo Belvedere, Rome, he gives an edge by adding in the 1816 version, "Who, *but a Frenchman*, can enter the present museum without some regret?" (199; emphasis mine).

Most of the differences between *1813* and *1816*, however, stem not from Forsyth's own additions of 1814–1815 but from the material written during his captivity as part of his narrative and dropped from *1813*. The decision to include them in *1816* was taken by Isaac. Almost three-quarters of that material relates to Pisa and Florence and was written when Forsyth's circumstances in prison were at their hardest and his memories were freshest.

Turning to these passages, we find (what does not emerge clearly from *1813*) that the University of Pisa was divided in its stance toward the French occupation of Italy. The university directors were opposed to it, a position that placed them in conflict with some members of staff: "Of the present professors the most eminent were lately suspended for their partiality to the French." The students approved the republican sentiments and were "all enthusiastic, armed and eloquent in the cause of revolution," but Forsyth, not believing in a "clean war," observed they did not "calculate the certain expense of crimes and misery that was to purchase an uncertain good." They "were swindled out of their innocence" and "betrayed friendship for the promise of liberty." Forsyth valued the more private virtues more highly

FIGURE 3.2 Anonymous: Napoleon valuing the Apollo Belvedere ("Eh bien, messieurs! deux millions!"). By permission of Library of Congress.

than fighting for large causes, writing, "I believe no man ever became a patriot after his fortieth year" (*1816*, 422–423). He was then forty-five years old.

Forsyth cut from the 1813 edition some of his other assessments concerning the readiness of Italians to resist or succumb to the French, including those reporting that poverty and discontent were everywhere: In Lucca, there was a sullen, negligent stateliness and a feeling of departed power. Romans were "sudden and quick in quarrel with strangers," but they were street fighters rather than soldiers and vented their feelings by leaving anonymous pasquinades on the statues. Ferrara and Mantua had fallen into disrepair; their inhabitants were greatly reduced in number and miserable under petty tyrannies. People spoke of "before the French came" and "after they came" and secretly abhorred them. A priest sardonically remarked (referring covertly to Napoleon), "It lately lay with one young man whether there should be a church or no in France and Italy. His political calculations determined there should" (*1816*, 330, 349, 450). Forsyth did not want to share any of this inside knowledge with his captors—it risked betraying his friendships and putting himself to searching interrogation—hence the probable omission of these portions.

Another set of passages that Isaac restored in *1816* are among those in which Forsyth shows himself at his most partisan. Many of them contain vigorous judgments of and information about living individuals. A number seem not to be drawn from firsthand impressions but from persons whose judgment he trusted, or are records of the common gossip about them. Some remarks verge on the libelous. They disrupt the image of the coolly objective and judicious student of art and man of cultivated taste that the 1813 version tried to project. They are among the most lively portions of his book and the most emotionally charged.

Some of the disgust at the situation Forsyth found himself in, in which miscreants prospered and men of integrity suffered, can be felt in his pen-portrait of the poet Vincenzo Monti (1754–1828), who had in 1801 recently emerged as a panegyrist of Napoleon, although, once again, Napoleon is not mentioned. This vignette was omitted in the 1813 section "Poets," but *1816* records the following of Monti: "This sanguinary drudge of revolution delights to mangle the murdered"; long after the guillotining of Louis XVI, Monti worked up his passion into "the acrimony of fresh rancour." He obsequiously dedicated poems to Pius VI while at Rome and then ferociously attacked him as a tyrant once out of the Vatican. He had been a pimp to the pope's niece. People hated Monti, and "he owed his safety to the charms of his wife." At Pavia, when they made him an official poet, they awarded him the "golden twig"—a disparaging remark belittling the "golden bough" awarded to the supreme poet—and "bound him by a pension of 8000 lires to write patriotic plays." However, "in justice even to the bad," Forsyth was obliged to acknowledge that Monti's *Caio Graccho* and *Aristodemo* were the best of Italian dramatic tragedies, always excepting those of Alfieri. "How beautifully does he describe his own patriotism!" he ends witheringly, citing lines from Monti's pro-Napoleonic poems relating to Lorenzo Mascheroni, *Mascheroniana* (1801): "L'amor di libertà, bello se stanza | Ha in cor gentile, e, se in cor basso e lordo, | Non virtù, ma *furore e sceleranza*" [*1816*, 421–422; Love of freedom is beautiful if it resides in a noble heart, and if it dwells in a foul, base heart, it engenders fury and wickedness, not valor].[9]

Another lengthy passage that Forsyth took out of the 1813 edition was an extended account of Pietro Leopoldo (1747–1792), Grand Duke of Tuscany until 1790, thereafter Holy Roman emperor (see figure 3.3). His chief sources were two remarkable men, Felice Fontana (1730–1805) and Giovanni Fabbroni (1752–1822; figures 3.4 and 3.5), whom he met in Florence. They had known Pietro Leopoldo intimately; he had appointed them, sent them abroad, and worked with them. From them, Forsyth had unrivaled information.

Fontana was the director of a spectacular anatomical museum, the Gabinetto Fisico (Museum of Physiology) in the Pitti Palace, that used waxworks to show

FIGURE 3.3 Anton Mengs, 1770: Archduke Pietro Leopoldo

FIGURE 3.4 Felice Fontana, 1813. By permission of Wellcome Trust.

FIGURE 3.5 Giovanni Fabbroni, 1828. By permission of Wellcome Trust.

dissections and states of disease, which were greatly useful to a medical school. They embraced the disciplines of physiology, anatomy, botany, toxicology, chemistry, and experimental pathology. Fontana had traveled to France and to England, where he gave a lecture on combustible air to the Royal Society in 1799. He held a chair at the University of Pisa. He was a man of considerable ability, but Forsyth, in a passage that he did not suppress in *1813*, saw through his showmanship and self-publicity: "Fontana seems to preside here in the scientific world, rather by the diffusion than the depth of his knowledge; by bringing into science the man-of-the-world faculty, by a well-managed talent of display and evasion, which gains him credit for much more than he knows, by the art of improving the inventions of others, and passing their joint work under his own name" (36). Forsyth had observed the excellent work of a young assistant called Clemente Susini who "has lately developed the whole lymphatic system" with "an accuracy which astonished the Pavians." He drily adds, "Fortunately for Fontana's pretensions, this young man is as modest as he is ingenious." His lifelike waxworks, which also attempt to be works of art, became celebrated and were sold to universities specializing in anatomy and medicine.

Under the directorship of Fontana, the Gabinetto Fisico in some respects was far from satisfactory. Forsyth was informed by Fabbroni, his deputy, that displays needed refurbishing; many were useless and fit only to be melted down. Fontana himself, instead of improving the existing displays, was directing the building of what was evidently to be the moving anatomical model of a man, made of wood, which when finished would have "three millions of distinct parts." Forsyth saw the half-made model; it was already warped by the heat of the climate. Fontana dismissed Forsyth's objection to wood as a suitable material: "Ivory is too dear; papier mâché has been tried, but it failed." The foredoomed project drew from Forsyth the witty comment "This active Prometheus is creating a decomposable statue" (37–38).

While Fontana was like a god creating what uncreates itself, his deputy, Giovanni Fabbroni, who accompanied him abroad, was the greater scholar, a polymath who corresponded with Humphrey Davy, Joseph Banks, Georges Cuvier, Alexander von Humboldt, Thomas Jefferson, Benjamin Franklin, Angelica Kaufmann, and the Marquis de Lafayette. (Jefferson had wanted him to live in America and had a country house, called "Monticello," built for him in Virginia.) His expertise in natural sciences showed in a multitude of essays and activities. His essays included writing on the state of agriculture (*Réflexions sur l'état actuel de l'agriculture* [Thoughts on the current state of agriculture], 1780) and on mining for anthracite (*Dell'Antracite*, 1790), and refining the ideas of Volta and Galvani (for example, in relation to animal locomotion). He was active in regularizing weight and measures in Paris (1798), in fixing lightning conductors (recently invented by Franklin) when storing gunpowder (1800), in identifying a contagious disease in Livorno (1805), in reestablishing financial stability in Italy, and in introducing the metric system (1806).[10] In 1802, Forsyth recognized his superior genius as a "singular man" before whom "language, literature, science broke down . . . and left him nothing to conquer but invidious, academic cabals" (39).

In 1799, Fabbroni had secured from the French an agreement that Tuscany's treasures would remain, except for the Venus de Medici. General Pierre-Antoine, comte Dupont de l'Étang (1765–1840), had entered Tuscany ready to visit the *courroux du vainqueur* [wrath of the conqueror] on the duchy but was prevented from doing this by Fabbroni's eminence and skill. The French felt they could work with Fabbroni and, in time, honored him. In 1811, he was awarded the Légion d'honneur and title of Baron of the Empire; in 1821, he was created Chevalier de l'ordre de St.-Joseph. Not everything turned out favorably; the Venus did eventually go to France. Tommaso Puccini (1749–1811), the director at the Uffizi, shipped off the Venus de Medici to Palermo in 1800, having heard Napoleon say, when he saw the sculpture in 1796, that if ever "Tuscany should declare war on France, he would have her taken to Paris."[11] Puccini's foresight was in vain, for in 1803, King Ferdinand IV of Naples gave up the statue to the French. Fabbroni himself suffered reverses. When Fontana died in 1805, Fabbroni was dismissed from the Gabinetto by Queen Maria Luisa, widow of King Louis of Etruria (d. 1803).[12] His dismissal was surrounded by devious plots and counterplots, providing an example of the behavior that Forsyth had identified as "invidious, academic cabals."[13] When reinstatement was offered, he refused and preferred to remain an honorary professor of Pisa and, in 1808, became its director. He was also the director of public works on highways and bridges from 1810 and overlooked mines and factories from 1816. He was "une sorte d'encyclopédie vivante" (a kind of living encyclopedia).

Forsyth devoted seven pages to an admiring account of Pietro Leopoldo and referred to him at other times in the course of his narrative.[14] His reflections had impelled him to contrast Leopoldo with the self-aggrandizing and undemocratic qualities of Napoleon. Although both were despots, Leopoldo represented much that the self-aggrandizing Napoleon was not. Leopoldo cut down the army and abolished the navy. He democratized the court and simplified the law. He abolished capital punishment and reduced the legal penalties. He reduced taxes levied on goods transported from one part of the country to the other. He drained marshes and improved roads. He promoted the arts and sciences and took a lively interest in them as an amateur.

At no point does Forsyth *explicitly* mention Leopoldo in relation to Napoleon but instead, in a passage that appears only in *1816*, offers a sustained comparison between Leopoldo and the Medici family, the subtext of which is that the Medici are a composite stand-in for Napoleon:

> [Leopoldo's] establishments in the fine arts, though less splendid than those of the Medici, were perhaps more directly useful; not galleries, but schools of painting. The Medici revived and protected literature. Leopold created for science the first cabinet in Europe. The Medici were fond of raising statues to themselves; Leopold refused one which was offered by

> his grateful people. The Medici turned all the treasures of their little state into such a mausoleum for their ambitious dust as beggars every monarch's in Europe, a mausoleum lined with the rarest marbles and incrusted with precious stones; Leopold designed for his family the same common grave that receives the meanest of his subjects. Those upstarts, risen from the counting-house to the throne, arrogated all the attributes of majesty; Leopold, the son, the brother, and the heir of emperors, freed his subjects from the debasement of kneeling. (*1816*, 379–380)

More complex reasons underlie the suppression of a passage that belongs to Forsyth's period of imprisonment in Paris. It concerns the episode referred to earlier, when all the nobility of Europe flocked to Napoleon's wedding in 1810. Once again, Napoleon is not mentioned. A heading, "Naples," is followed by an abrupt switch to a walk in the gardens of the Tuileries in Paris: "A friend pointed out to me at the Tuillerie, one Sunday morning, so many wild sprigs of the nobility, that he proposed to prune and even to replant the old tree." This introduction is followed by two pages of an amusing account of his friend's bravura speech, in which he explains how he would redistribute wealth and land if he were king. He would prevent "such accumulations of property as the Monteleone, the Mondragone &c. . . . Then (cried the exultant lawgiver) those titled vagabonds who are now concerting in these alleys fresh plots for their subsistence, would be reduced to plain dons; but those dons would have homes and acres of their own." His reforms would improve the happiness and morality of every home; then, in a teasing remark—no doubt aimed at Forsyth, a bachelor—the friend declares, "No bachelor should govern a province, nor bear an embassy, nor command a regiment, nor wear a ribband." He foresees a future paradise in which he, the king, would "resign his unjust prerogative." At this point, Forsyth comments, "He was going on, building his castle very liberally on the rights and property of others, when some friends broke in upon the scaffolding" (*1816*, 457–458). Of course, Forsyth did not put this description in his book, and probably much of it was never intended for inclusion. The papers on which he wrote were sometimes a place to pool his thoughts, and here they were partly a diary. Thirteen pages of his writing on Naples were omitted from the 1813 version.

In these omitted pages, we can see how intertwined the events of which he writes are with those of the time he was writing. His anecdotal recollection of his friend in the Tuileries is matched by his anecdotes of Sir John Acton and the Earl-Bishop Frederick Hervey in Naples (see chapter 4 below). The discussion of nobles in Paris is matched by descriptions of the nobility surrounding the king of Naples. We shall return in the next chapter to this variability in the canceled passages. For our present purposes, in order to follow the emotional drive behind the composition of *Italy*, we should notice the happiness it arouses. Forsyth has a friend to talk to and others to join him. The Italian examples (Monteleone, Mondragone) suggest an Italian friend or at the least a fellow Italianist like himself. He is walking at some liberty; he has access to books. Forsyth was writing at a time when, according to a letter written during this period, his hopes had been raised of "being free very soon," after which "we shall soon meet & I will not be long in Britain without seeing you" (*L* 18). Happiness energizes his writing here and what follows on Naples.

The remarks on Naples (also absent from *1813*) were singled out by the reviews for the way they communicated the lively spirit of that city:

> If Naples be "a paradise inhabited by devils," I am sure it is by merry devils. Even the lowest class enjoy every blessing that can make the animal happy—a delicious climate, high spirits, a facility of satisfying every appetite, a conscience which gives no pain, a convenient ignorance of their duty, and a church which ensures heaven to every ruffian that has faith. Here tatters are not misery, for the climate requires little covering; filth is not misery to them who are born to it; and a few fingerings of maccaroni can wind up the rattling machine for the day. (412)

However, in a part of his panegyric to Naples that he did not drop from *1813*, he compared the city with London:

> Naples, in its interior, has no parallel on earth. The crowd of London is uniform and intelligible: it is a double line in quick motion; it is the crowd of business. The crowd of Naples consists in a general tide rolling up and down, and in the middle of this tide a hundred eddies of men. Here you are swept on by the current, there you are wheeled round by the vortex. A diversity of trades dispute with you the streets. You are stopped by a carpenter's bench, you are lost among shoe-makers' stools, you dash among the pots of a *maccaroni*-stall, and you escape behind a *lazarone's* [dirty rogue's] night-basket. In this region of caricature every bargain sounds like a battle: the popular exhibitions are full of the grotesque; some of their church-processions would frighten a war-horse. (266)

A prospect of his own adopted city of London becomes alive in cheerful contrast to the exotic whirl of a city abroad. It is animated by the freedom of Paris and the hope of liberty. Both proved to be short-lived. His transfer to Valenciennes quenched both of these joys.

The passage that he did cut (of "a paradise inhabited by devils") had to go, perhaps because it revealed too much of his own emotion (a characteristic discussed further in chapter 4) and what followed may have been too close to the Napoleonic narrative, for the context is the siege of Naples, when the French deposed Ferdinand. It is followed by an anecdote from a gentleman whom Forsyth met, who was forced by others to eat the flesh of a Jacobin. Forsyth draws a parallel with a cannibalistic incident in Juvenal (*1816*, 413). His note seeks "to draw a veil" over the matter and says the Juvenal is "too horrible for modern language." Incidentally, if this had been just a transcript from Forsyth's journal that Isaac had found and it had never been intended for inclusion, there would be no need for him to consider the delicacy of another reader. It is more likely that he drafted this to go in and then decided not to include it. The indexer to the second edition skips the passage altogether, probably on the grounds of decency.

At the Capodimonte museum in Naples (kept in *1813*), Forsyth gives a cameo of a curator made wretched by the events: "Here are still some remains of the Parma gallery, though most of the pictures serve as mere upholstery. Indeed, the keeper himself felt shame for his stores, and condemned by a '*non guardi*' ['don't look'] whole rooms to neglect" (269). The tussle between France and Naples over possession had meant that some sculptures went back and forward; the result was to deprive them of appropriate respect. Forsyth says that in the Palazzo degli Studi, "I found the Farnese statues rather warehoused than arranged. There lay the *Urania* returned, for the second time, from Rome, in a tremendous case which had been prepared for this colossal captive. The great *Hercules* stood daubed with plaster amidst the rubbish of a workshop" (270). Together, these remarks make an emotional case against the removal of works of art. But a more unguarded passage, omitted from *1813*, expands on how Puccini tried to save the works and the petty state of affairs that ensued between greedy heads of state, when all the time the treasures were not theirs:

> All the treasures of the Tribuna, the Venus, the dancing faun, the wrestlers, the grinder; all the Raphaels, Titians, Correggios, lay then at Palermo, in the custody of the director Puccini. The Florentines murmured at the detention of objects so dear to them. Ferdinand claimed them in right of his family; Lewis [king of Etruria], in right of his Florentines murmured at the detention of objects so dear to them. Ferdinand [king of Naples] claimed them in right of his family; Lewis, in right of his crown; and the King of Naples detained them till the stronger claim should prevail. Thus was this precious deposite disputed by two princes, in the hands of a third [Puccini], and at the disposal of a fourth power [France], though it rightfully belonged to none of them; for Leopold [i.e., Pietro Leopoldo], as if presaging some contention of the kind, had solemnly declared the gallery to be the property of the nation. (*1816*, 426)

When Forsyth wrote the closing chapters at Valenciennes, the pressure of ten years of imprisonment urged him to complete his appeal for release. There were not the same opportunities of Paris for continuing his research. The latter part of his journey in Italy had been carried out in haste, and his journal would necessarily have contained less material to process. The cities he visited received less attention; reviews regretted that he had not written more. Although Bologna does not come right at the end, it is memorable for how it returns to the issue of looting and the city's glorious history now reduced by the French invasion. It makes an elegiac end and farewell to a culture before his hurried escape. Bologna, Forsyth wrote, "excelled in painting . . . but the late revolution has shut up or desecrated half the churches, and has robbed the rest of all their principal oil-paintings" (*1816*, 328). But there was one painting that remained and stood out in his mind.

This was Guido Reni's *St. Peter and St. Paul* (figure 3.6). The Sampieri family, whose palazzo was in the Strada Maggiore, held the painting until 1811. Forsyth commented, "Here are Guido's two apostles, a picture considered as the finest left in Italy. I can conceive no excellence beyond the figure of Peter. Indeed, so excellent is art here that it disappears, and gives up the work to sentiment. I might heap technical praises on this divine picture; but I could not convey my own impressions" (*1816*, 328).

Forsyth is typically reticent about his own emotions, so we must surmise them from our own viewing of the painting. St. Peter is in tears before St. Paul in the sacramental act of penitence for a sin. He explains this with his left hand extended toward the past and with his bald, elderly head supported by a hand, puffy with age and clawing into feathery curled hair above his ear. Some of his former vigor shows in the stretched forearm, the strong nose and brow and the honest and direct look into Paul's eyes. But a vein throbs at his temple and many loose wrinkles run across his brow. He projects weariness, aging, and regret for the past. Forsyth, who knew he, too, had altered almost beyond recognition physically and had lost ten years of freedom, could well relate to this fine image from Bologna. ("Seven years of captivity has so completely altered my features that you will hardly recognise your brother" [*L* 28].)

Setting aside the question of lengthy passages intended or not for eventual insertion, Forsyth made many revisions to the second edition.[15] He corrected many errors, probably introduced by Cadell's printer, especially the transcription of Greek quotations. Many changes were directed toward phrasing ideas more elegantly; he lowered the temperature of his criticisms of various issues. He had noted that painters introduced their "strumpets" into religious groups but now calls them "mistresses." He cuts out a criticism of "the fury of ancient mobs" as the cause of the broken noses of statues. The suppression of the actors "in the pope's dominions" loses the personal attack on the pope by the substitution of "at Rome." The venerated Madonna of Arezzo, originally "a puppet scarcely a foot high, a squat, ugly figure of painted chalk" becomes "a little, ugly figure of chalk." These are all changes

FIGURE 3.6 Guido Reni: *St. Peter and St. Paul*

to passages within the section written at Verdun. They are traces in the published text of the anger he felt and now wishes not to exhibit. In 1814, free and much older, he can allow himself to be more urbane.

However, he had not finished the new edition when he died. He may have intended to expand the text he improved; it is almost certain he supplied the titles to the passages he cut out. An obvious case is the heading of "Naples" (*1816*, 457) for the section beginning with a long digression on the Tuileries. Forsyth knew that most of that section related to what he was writing about Naples. Another section is headed "Pavia" (*1816*, 439) and has no counterpart within the published text. Isaac did not add these titles, for he had little understanding of the geography of Italy or the language and didn't even see there was a jumble in the pieces he added. But Forsyth may have been putting into order these rejected passages so that some of them might return to the text for what I have called his critique. That would account for his not removing what I have called the "torn edges" until he had made these repairs. Passages that are candidates for a return would be the account of Leopoldo and, suitably rewritten, the remarks on the state of the populations in Florence, Siena, Rome, Naples, and Pavia. These are all in the first of the three groups of the passages Isaac added. Maybe they represent already Forsyth's order of selection of the passages he wanted to restore. In the second and third group are two pieces on Cardinal York, the remaining survivor of the Stuart monarchical line. These are firsthand accounts of the man and for that reason alone are interesting, but already the first edition had given cause for the *Edinburgh Review* in January 1814 to criticize Forsyth for whining "in favour of the Stuarts," so they could be in the doubtful category. But more should be said about what Forsyth might have done, after looking at his experience of meeting Italians and a closer inspection of his remarks on fine arts.

4

TALKING TO ITALIANS

IN 1802, WHEN FORSYTH WENT TO ITALY, the phenomenon known as the Grand Tour, the ritual visit to France and Italy undertaken by young men of the upper class to complete their education, was in a period of transition that eventually morphed into mass tourism. Italians had been highly participative in shaping the experience of the tour during the latter part of the eighteenth century, as Ilaria Bignamini points out. The popes Clement XIII and Pius VI had established the Museo Pio-Clementino as one of the Grand Tour's greatest attractions. It offered the sight of spectacular works of art to "visitors who were wealthy enough to travel to Italy but not sufficiently so to buy ancient marbles."[1] Paintings and statuary were available to see in the churches. In addition, as Forsyth noticed, grand villas in Rome, such as the Borghese, displayed their treasures, making them accessible to all, in contrast with the English custom of excluding all but the gentlemanly class from aristocratic collections: "What English villa is open, like the Borghese, as a common drive to the whole metropolis? and how finely is this liberality announced in the inscription which I have copied above from the pedestal of an ancient statue in that park!" (215). Some of the Latin words Forsyth copied seem to be a prescient reference to his own imprisonment; retrospectively, they evoke the comfort of a liberal society that he had once enjoyed. Their sense, when translated, is "Whoever you are, if you are free, do not fear the shackles of the law here. Go where you wish, seek what you desire, depart when you wish. These buildings are provided more for outsiders than for their owner, in a golden age when everything is golden, ensured by the safety of these times" (215).

The present times, of course, were far from safe. Many of the British already resident in Italy before the Napoleonic conquest had had bad experiences. When the looting of Italy began, the British in Florence were advised to move to the countryside. Frederick Hervey, the disgraceful fourth Earl of Bristol, whom Forsyth heard talk of, was arrested and released but remained in Rome. His collection of artworks in Rome were taken by the French in 1798 and his huge collection from Naples was lost in a shipwreck on its way back to England. Nevertheless, there was a stream of British tourists to Italy in 1802, though not in the swarms that later were to infest Rome and Florence after the Napoleonic Wars.[2]

In the process of writing a book designed to extricate himself from prison, Forsyth could not hold back his sympathies for the Italian people. Contempt had been shown to an Italian heritage that Forsyth had come to understand not only from extensive study of the cultural history of Italy but by meeting and talking at length to about seventy contemporary Italians. Forsyth's references to the British he encountered over the course of his travels are not numerous. He evidently preferred the company of Italians. He thought it likely that being with travelers of his own nationality would dilute the purposefulness of his inquiries into antiquities, arts, and letters and reduce his observation of manners and politics; he was too advanced an Italianist for the generality of British travelers. In a passage where, barely disguised under the impersonal "you," he is obviously speaking of his own preferences, he writes,

> Whoever goes abroad merely for observation should avoid his own countrymen. If you travel in a party, your curiosity must adopt their paces: you must sometimes post through towns rich in art or antiquity, and stop where the only attraction is good cheer. While you linger with fond delay among the select beauties of a gallery, your friends are advancing into other rooms, and the keeper complains when you separate; you thus lose the freedom of inspection, your ears ring with impatience, and often with absurdity. If you travel with one who is more ignorant of the language than yourself, you must stand interpreter in all his bickerings with the natives; and will seldom content him, for a man is usually harsher, when his spleen is to pass through the mouth of another than when he speaks for himself. (342)

So Forsyth sought out Italians for serious conversation. As argued in the last chapter, it is clear that much of this would have been political. In this, as in other respects, he appears to have been atypical. British travelers were, of course, encouraged to make contact with Italians, but conversation leading to "useful information" was most often sought. According to J. R. Hale, the majority of British travelers had little regard for the political opinions of Italians during the long eighteenth century.[3]

Forsyth's very different approach emerges strongly when we compare *Forsyth's Italy* to Eustace's *Classical Tour*. In his "Preliminary Discourse" to the *Tour*, Eustace impresses upon his readers how desirable it is for an educated person to meet Italians of the "best company" with a view to gaining a general cultural impression.

Disappointingly, however, he provides nothing more than a cursory reference to individual Italians he met. Fabbroni, along with other museum directors, is given a nod. A promised discussion with the literati of Cortona is dangled and withheld because it was too late to visit them. Eustace appears to find it more pleasant and of more lasting value to meet the British naval officer, Captain Gore, in Naples, Florence, and Leghorn (where he will convey Eustace by the frigate *Medusa* to Genoa). Indeed, for Eustace, the lasting friendships that might be made with English gentlemen met abroad were among the benefits of travel in Italy:

> We do not, doubtless, travel to France or to Italy *to see Englishmen*, but yet we travel for improvement and for amusement: and whatever society contributes to either, ought to be cultivated with an assiduity proportioned to its advantages. The traveller, therefore, ought by all means to procure an introduction to the best company of the great towns through which he may pass; and at the same time he may become acquainted with such English gentlemen as may chance to be in the same place. . . . That casual acquaintance not unfrequently ripens into settled and permanent friendship. Continental connexions in general are of a very different nature; however agreeable, they are contracted only for the occasion, and cannot be supposed, in general, strong enough to resist the influence of absence.[4]

Fifteen years later, in post-Napoleonic Italy, the English "as may chance to be in the same place" had multiplied. As Byron complained, they were blotting Italians and art from view.[5] Henry Matthews, author of the travelogue *Diary of an Invalid* (1820), attended a party on New Year's Day, 1818, where the English outnumbered the Italians: "In the evening, we went to a party at Torlonia's the banker;—or as he now is,—the Duke of Bracciano. A suite of rooms was thrown open, in which a mob of people wandered about, without object or amusement. Such a scene could afford little insight into Italian manners, even if the mob were composed exclusively of Italians—but, at present, two-thirds at least of the company at every party, are English."[6] Although Eustace advised a journey of at least a year and "even two years might be devoted to this useful and amusing part of our travels,"[7] he spent only eight months in Italy, including traveling in July and August, which he advised against as dangerous to health. His stays were correspondingly short in the major cities: seven weeks at Rome (including two weeks of excursions), four weeks in Naples (including excursions to Pompeii, Vesuvius, etc.), three weeks in Rome on his return, just under four weeks in Florence, and eleven days in Pisa. He missed out Siena where, chronologically, he and Forsyth might otherwise have crossed paths. Forsyth's plans were on a much more generous scale: Pisa for three months, Florence for three and a half months, Siena for five weeks, and Rome and Naples for seven months. His visit would have lasted more than eighteen months had he not had to hurry back at the "dread of an impending war" between Britain and France (342).

In the previous century, travel and accommodation could be extremely expensive. Giuseppe Baretti (1719–1789), who may be seen as someone with insider knowledge, planned in 1776 a visit to Italy for the rich brewer Henry Thrale; his wife, Hesther; their daughter; Dr. Johnson; and himself. He wrote to friends and relations inquiring about the best hotels; his brothers had to be persuaded that it was not degrading for him to act as a cicerone. There would be three four-wheeled chaises, a German courier preceding them, a maid, and two grooms (one on horseback). When they stayed at his brothers' estate, they were to hire silver and majolica plates and borrow old Greek and Latin books so that the house did not look illiterate.[8] Others not so wealthy as the Thrales could cut their cloth a bit finer, but as Jörg Garms noted, however it was done, "the Grand Tour was an expensive undertaking." Traveling with cash was risky and "besides letters of introduction and letters of credit, one needed exit permits, *laissez-passer* [a travel permit] and health certificates." For the income group that did make the Grand Tour, "there was accommodation to suit every pocket in all the main stopping-points along the way: hotels and guest houses (often run by fellow countrymen), *pensions* [boarding houses] or *locande* [lodgings], or private accommodation. Finding somewhere to sleep away from these places was more of a problem; even aristocrats sometimes had to make do with not very fresh straw, though even this was often preferable to the *letto abitato* [shared bed], used by more than one person and infested by bed-bugs."[9] Travelers going south of Naples "had to be armed with sheaves of letters of introduction if they were to have any hope of staying in a convent, with the local mayor or in private houses."[10]

Eustace went from inn to inn and complained of the low order of comfort. He said it was the result of their not being used by the wealthier Italians: "[Italian] travellers of rank instead of frequenting inns, went from villa to villa, and abandoned such receptacles to the lower orders."[11] Forsyth, when he had to, stayed in public accommodation with other tourists and took his due share of the *letto abitato* and the Bad Italian Inn experience. There was only one inn at Noli, where "four of us passed a sleepless night on two filthy beds" (1). At Vallombrosa, a guide lost the way; Forsyth and others were forced to stay in the solitary inn called the Uomo Morto (Dead Man; 85). There was no inn at Colle so he "retired to Borgo" (114). At San Quirico, Forsyth learned that the Devil—or at any rate, an alarming specter—had recently appeared in the sky. The Devil had turned out to be an eagle preying on lambs; it had been shot and roasted for supper at the inn where he was staying (118). The inn at Baccano was the "worst I ever entered" and had carriages outside as a "decoy" to deceive travelers into supposing that it was patronized by prosperous guests (121). Two Pisans of his acquaintance stayed at the Locanda Pietra Mala on the road between Florence and Bologna and recounted a frightful tale of its having once been the resort of a gang that murdered and robbed the guests.[12]

More often, however, Forsyth lodged with Italians who became his friends and introduced him to others. In this, he was adopting an Italian manner of travel, in contrast to that of Eustace. His ability to travel in this way is evidence of a network of hospitable Italians ready to receive guests known or recommended to them. Through these contacts, he was able to talk to artists, writers, and savants, and to gain information, or gossip, about the illustrious or the notorious. As a sample of this networking, we might begin with Giuseppe and Rosa Baldi, who looked after him at 116 via della Crocetta, Florence, and introduced him to the prior of the Certosa, two miles away, where a young artist, Benvenuti, "had lately painted . . . two fine St. John Baptists" (447). Pietro Benvenuti (1769–1844) had just executed *Il martiro del B. Signoretto Alliata* (The martyrdom of the blessed Signoretto Alliata) for the duomo at Pisa (1802), which Forsyth might also have seen; Benvenuti would become, in 1803, on the recommendation of Canova, director of the Accademia di Belle Arti (Academy of the Fine Arts) at Florence. He was already an academician of Lucca. Forsyth eventually caught up with Benvenuti in Rome, where Benvenuti told him personal anecdotes about the eccentric behavior of Lord Frederick Hervey (discussed below).

Count Vargas, president of the Accademia Italiana (established with forty members in about 1797), gave lodgings to Forsyth in Siena and, later, showed him his military museum at "Castel Nuovo" (possibly Castelnuovo Beradenga, five miles east of Siena). The *accademia* was "diffused over Italy" as Forsyth wrote (451). Vargas (whose permanent residence was Naples) was probably the person who gave Forsyth entrée to another set of distinguished contacts. It was, for example, Count Vargas's secretary, Sacchetti, who told Forsyth about Vittorio Alfieri's proud refusal to join the Accademia Italiana. Alfieri (1749–1803), who spent the last decade of his life in Florence, was particularly admired by Forsyth for his plays. When the narrative of *Forsyth's Italy* reaches Florence, he includes a critical examination of Alfieri, whose tragedies he regarded as rivaling Schiller's. The topic was a natural one to raise in the context of Florence, because Alfieri was then Florence's most famous inhabitant, and people would naturally be talking about him there. Forsyth was clearly conversant with Alfieri's tragedies, thanks to his reading before traveling to Italy. He might have chosen to place this examination at the section where he tells of his visit to Turin, where Alfieri was educated, but his preference is for discussing the works of individuals in their contemporary location.

In Siena, Forsyth met Anna Rinieri, the governor's daughter (450); it is likely that he also met the red-haired Elizabeth Steuart, Countess Cicciaporci (d. 1816;

456) at Rinieri's conversazione. The countess was one of the few British expatriates whom he is known to have interacted with. She showed him private correspondence of her brother-in-law, Sir John Coxe Hippisley (1747–1825), an unofficial diplomat. He was writing to Gilbert Elliot, first Lord Baron Minto, Viceroy of Corsica (1751–1814), and to Henry Clementi, Cardinal Duke of York, the last surviving claimant to the British throne of the House of Stuart (1725–1807). Forsyth later met Cardinal York at the Palazzo La Rocca, at Frascati, outside Rome.[13]

Forsyth has much else to say about the social change in Tuscany brought about by the Grand Duke Leopoldo. His account is the more valuable, as later writers lose touch with the kind of firsthand oral reports he obtained and depreciate the contribution of this remarkable, enlightened prince. Sismondi in 1816 noted that Tuscans were forgetting what they owed him and was inclined to the view that perhaps Leopold had been too hasty in his reforms: "The prejudices of the priests and the vices of the populace joined forces against a prince, who was, perhaps, too active in his wish to do good. . . . The Tuscan people did not seem to be sufficiently mindful of what they owed to this great prince."[14] Lady Morgan in 1821 had no doubt that his "impolitic promptitude" betrayed his good purposes, for "he did not perceive that the passage from darkness to light can never with impunity be made sudden." And she added that he introduced a police state: "But even the good effected by Leopold was due too often to means which replaced the crimes they removed by a vileness more degrading. Leopold adopted and improved the Medicean system of espionage; and, governing his subjects like Capuchin novices, corrupted one half the population, to controul the other."[15] Forsyth had the advantage of talking to intimate associates of Pietro Leopoldo; he presented a far more favorable account. Leopoldo's government served Forsyth as a litmus for measuring others. He looked around him and saw the results of Leopoldo's rule in the surroundings he first encountered after landing at Leghorn. The drainage of the countryside, the behavior of the aristocracy, and the condition of farming provided examples that sharpened his awareness of the prince's reforms and of the subsequent changes after his death. At the convent of Fiesole, Forsyth noted that the Franciscans commemorated Leopold's visit there with his brother, the Holy Roman emperor. Someone told Forsyth how Leopold went about, concealed in his greatcoat, to speak to the people and met an old woman at Pisa, whom he asked to tell him about the grand duke: "[She replied:] 'The Grand Duke has a very kind heart but sometimes he does the *berlicche berlocche* [swaps one playing card for another].' 'What the devil do you mean by *berlicche berlocche*?' 'Now he says yes, now he says no.'" The story concludes that Leopoldo "was so well pleased with this censure of himself, that he gave the woman one crown for her *berlicche* and another for her *berlocche*" (382n).

From his conversations, Forsyth built up a detailed image of a ruler who represented an enlightened trust in his subjects, "before the rights of men agitated Europe" (referring to the French Declaration of the Rights of Man, August 26, 1789). Before this, Leopoldo broke down distinctions of rank, saying there were only two *ceti* (orders), men and women: "He immediately opened all the offices of state to all ranks, he brought all men under the same law and tribunals, he suppressed unnecessary courts, he simplified the course of justice, he instituted for Tuscany a penal code of small volume, a code, which abolished torture, mutilation of body, the pain of death and the sequestration of land, yet from steady enforcement rendered crimes rare and murder unknown" (378–379). He reduced the burden on small farmers and producers; Forsyth's account shows minute interest in the Italian specifics of breaking *latifondi* (large estates) into small farmsteads, *livelli* (life-leases),[16] local taxations, *coazioni* (compulsory sales), and brokerages:

> He made commerce free in all its relations, in the free introduction, passage, circulation and sale of goods, of grain, wine and oil, free from the checks which markets, corporations and public brokers had formerly laid on weighing and measuring. The lands he freed from their ancient restrictions to particular corn and oil mills. He abolished all monopolies and *coazioni* [punishing conditions] of hay and straw. He transferred the load of taxation from grain and raw commodities to the materials of luxury. He suppressed the farming [local taxation] of bread, candles, fish, &c. He opened the rivers, freed the chace from restraint, the customs he removed to the frontiers; he threw several vexatious taxes into one; he fixed the sum which was wanted by the state, and left the people to raise it in their own way, yet such were his economy and order, that while he resigned many sources of revenue, he discharged the public debt of the nation, and reduced the annual rate of interest to 3 per cent. (379)

He also promoted projects to improve the culture of his people, abolished the navy, and reduced the military to become a body responsible for public safety (the Community of Florence): "He was the friend of religion rather than of the church. He banished the inquisition from Tuscany; reduced the multitude of idle festivals; thinned the population of the convents, by checking that temerity and that violence which used to stock them with youth; he suppressed those which had lost their monks; he subjected the church-lands to the general taxation, and kept the clergy on good behaviour by a wholesome degree of alarm" (381). These and other good reforms were conducted over twenty years in a manner that belies Lady Morgan's account. According to Forsyth, "All Leopold's reforms were gradual, connected, and led to each other. Nothing was demolished at once, nor did any nuisance cease until better resources were opened to the persons who had lived by it" (381). His inquiry into the state of the nation was thorough:

> He often travelled, not for pleasure or display, but to know his people and their wants. He heard every person; he saw every thing; he registered every notice. The information thus obtained he reduced into a system, which protected him from imposition, and from dependence on his ministers. Thus his knowledge of details surprized thousands who addressed him on their own concerns, and silenced many petitioners. Perhaps this activity was too meddling, too jealous, too constantly at work, for a prince; perhaps he governed his states too much, and trusted the interests of his people too little to themselves; perhaps he left too often the mainspring of the political machine, to watch the action of the minutest wheels. (382–383)[17]

After his rule, much was undone. The rolling-back of Leopoldo's reforms highlighted for Forsyth a deterioration to which the French occupation contributed. Italian society had lost the will to stand up for itself—and not only in Tuscany. Ferrara was falling into decay, Mantua's inhabitants presented "a general stillness, sallow faces," and in Lucca, there was "the worst symptom any town can have—silence" (329, 349, 30). Siena had suffered passively the atrocities of the Armata aretina (Aretine troops), which brutally murdered Jews and suspected Jacobins (1799) in the name of the Madonna (390). Romans presented a veneer of civility; they were the beneficiaries of tourism, or what Forsyth calls "the subsistence which people derive from [the] expenditure" of strangers, which made "courtesy an obligation on all." But under the polite surface was a caustic humor that expressed itself in oblique pasquinades, which they preferred to the "danger attending open attacks" (402). Satire acted as a safety valve in the absence of a collective will to resist.

Another factor that Forsyth saw as contributory to Italian passivity was the role played by the Church in instilling obedience and submission to the de facto power. Here Forsyth differentiated between regions and cities. Pisa showed "no great signs of faith, and so sensible was the present Pope of the Pisans' indifference on that point, that he sent iron crosses to be fixed on their houses, and offered one year and forty days remission of sin for every kiss that should be given them; yet not a passenger could be bribed by this liberal indulgence. At Florence, on the contrary, some favourite altars are worn smooth by the lips of the devout" (367). It was the return of this kind of religious supremacy in Florence that undermined Leopoldo's reforms. The Florentine noblemen had admirable qualities but "their sturdiness of spirit is vanished with the republic. Prone to revolution in that lusty period of independence and hardihood, they have exchanged the more turbulent virtues for meekness, long-suffering, obedience, and every quality that can adorn a slave."

For the first time, Forsyth saw soldiers "disciplined into prayer by the beat of a drum." The Church, in this interwar period, had seized the opportunity to reassert itself. Formerly checked by Leopold and threatened with dissolution by the French, the Church began "to rear her inquisitorial head, and to demand from Spanish piety all the outworks that she has lost. . . . The confessionals of Florence, though indulgent enough to vice, will never remit the three extreme points of religion, abstinence twice a-week, mass every Sunday, and communion at Easter" (366–368). Convents and friaries resumed their power: "Several of those novices were much under 30, the age prescribed by Leopoldo. The church, sensible of the doubts now spreading through her flock, slips in among the distrusts of a divided society, and exerts all the power which a most catholic government gives her over its functionaries, to drive back vagrants to her holy fold" (449). In the secular sphere, capital punishment had been restored and crimes had doubled. Leopoldo's city police were "the organ lately employed by the French for revolution and robbery." (This is possibly why Lady Morgan assumed that Leopoldo introduced a police state.) Farmers once more had to suffer the burdens of local taxes. Each bullock that went into Florence had a levy of ten crowns and each pig ten lire. An excise permit had to be bought for the slaughter (384–385).

Forsyth argued that Leopoldo was "the best prince of his time" and that many of his reforms depended on his absolute power. He contrasted the slow progress of reform in England, where landowners in parliament, with vested interests in maintaining game-laws, effectively blocked the abolition of mantraps. But he conceded that a more democratic government would be safer in the long run: "It leaves us still to desire another form of polity, not so simple, perhaps, nor so cheaply administered, but more safe for the governed, more able to perpetuate itself, and more indifferent to the character of them who conduct it. For want of that perpetuating power, which can reside only in the people, half of Leopold's improvements ceased with his reign" (383). A people could only realize its full potential when there was good government, as we noted in relation to *Marino Faliero*: "Men in the mass are what governments make them, and who can now calculate the powers of the present race if differently directed?" (400) The capitulation of the older aristocracy led to a social uselessness that would also be noted by Mary Shelley.[18] Forsyth noted contrasting examples of aristocratic degradation and the rise of a nouveau riche class. On the road from Pisa to Lucca, there were two "noble postboys," the Cavaliere Seta and the Marquis Bicchi, whose chief amusement was to collect tolls from travelers. The eccentric Seta, "the rich representative of a family as ancient as the Pisan republic," had a large gallery of pictures, which he would not sell but kept in a state of "filth" and neglect. Seta went about playing the fool, sometimes dressed as a mountebank or groom or waiter (425). By contrast, the richest man in Tuscany was Scotto, a social upstart. Formerly a lazzarone from Naples and potboy in a wine cellar, he had retired, having become extremely wealthy by means of usury. Now rich enough from his ignoble gains to turn honest, he was buying up land and had commissioned Roman artists to embellish his palazzi. He kept his "tenements in bright repair, thus employing the poor and shewing the rich how neatness excels their dirty magnificence." But he made no effort to improve his manners and "looks as if he still wore the apron" (i.e., of the potboy he once had been; 440). Which is the less edifying of the two, the noble who disgraces his name, wastes his patrimony, and affects to have low tastes or the authentic vulgarian who uses his ill-gotten gains to patronize the arts, Forsyth leaves the reader to judge.

Elsewhere Forsyth found instances of covert resistance to the French, who were busy transporting manuscripts from the Vatican and works of art from the major galleries to be triumphantly displayed in the Musée Napoléon. Puccini, the director of the Royal Gallery in Florence, had hidden the city's art treasures in Palermo (426). Giovanni Gherardo de' Rossi (1754–1827) was the director of the Accademia Portoghese at Rome, a writer of satirical comedies and a poet. He was a colleague of Ennio Quirino Visconti (1751–1818), the distinguished Italian archaeologist induced by the French in 1799 to be a director of the Louvre. Esteemed by the French, Gherhardo was made the minister of finance until 1800. Forsyth hinted that he covertly protected the Italians: "Rome knows his value, and, in her late adversities, confided her treasury to Gherhardo" (237). Gaetano Marini (1740–1815), "the prefect of the Vatican library and Archives" and an expert on ancient inscriptions, showed Forsyth how the French had taken five hundred manuscripts (the best) by the treaty of Tolentino from the Vatican (203). Marini made his resistance to the French open in 1810. When they transported him to France with the rest of the archives to be their keeper, he declined to act the part and retired into religious seclusion. These and other signs—for example, the secret readings in Pisa, the grumblings about "*dopo i Francesi*" (after the French), the pasquinades of the Romans—show a society that had a growing resistance to the occupation.

Forsyth's maternal grandfather had fought for Bonnie Prince Charlie at Culloden; as his grandson, Forsyth felt some emotion in meeting Henry Benedict Maria Clementi, known as Cardinal York, the brother of the now dead prince. Forsyth indulged no romantic enthusiasm in his sympathetic but clear-eyed account of Clementi, who seemed "an hospitable, warm-hearted, testy old man" (256) but was personally unimpressive: "He says little and in that little is nothing." Nevertheless, he represented a disappearing world of decayed royalty, preserving its meager distinctions. At table, he sat with space "sufficient for another cover" between himself and his guests—Forsyth, "a Neapolitan duke, several Roman noblemen, a bishop and a few prelates." He had different place-servings, but it was a mixture of stoneware, silver, and china "much inferior" to that of the guests. Indulging in Boswellian detail, Forsyth describes his physical appearance: "His dress was an alternation of red and black: a scarlet coif; a black coat lined with scarlet silk; a black silk mantle; a scarlet waistcoat; black velvet breeches; scarlet stockings; black shoes, scarlet heels; a purple coat laced with gold, and a plain episcopal gold cross on his breast" (455). Clementi's society was restricted to a few: nobility, cardinals, the pope and the King of Sardinia. This enabled a ceremonious stateliness in a world cut off from the mainstream. Forsyth was amused at the "Royal Highnessing" that went on between him and the visiting Ernest Augustus, fifth son of George III, King of Great Britain, neither of whom would wear a crown. Dryly, he observed, "This community includes some princesses, yet subsists by begging" (455–456). The letters that Countess Cicciaporci showed Forsyth concerned George III's granting a pension to Clementi of £4,000 per annum.

While Forsyth could be gently satirical with such an enfeebled representative of a bygone order, his criticism took fire with two Britishers abroad, an errant bishop and a self-serving minister. Frederick Augustus Hervey (1730–1803), fourth Earl of Bristol and bishop of Derry, Ireland, was a scandalous talking point: "Lord Bristol, being always on the wing, gave each town in turn an occasion to stare at this *lusus fortunæ* [freak of fortune], whose ambition was to be stared at. His conversation ran generally in support of atheism; yet when others attacked revelation he would for the moment defend that religion which doubled his income" (453). His public behavior was erratic: "With artists he was either close or lavish, never correctly just. Benvenuti told me that he bought his *Judith* when half finished, and ordered it off in that state to a garret in Naples. He would sometimes talk divinely on art, and then relapse into affected absurdity. His conversation was obscenity itself, no modest woman could talk with him, or go up his staircase at Rome, where the frescos were most indecent; neither he, nor his son the first Lord Harvey [*sic*], could create any esteem here with all their liberality. The latter was detested at Florence" (453–454). Sir John Acton (1736–1811), a British naval officer, was prime minister to the King of Naples. According to Lady Morgan, it was he who betrayed to the French the secret that the Venus de' Medici had been spirited away from Florence and hidden in Palermo, away from Napoleon's clutches. Forsyth was staying at Naples when Acton's child-wife gave birth to a child:

> Acton's rise is not more astonishing than his keeping his ground. He first appeared in Tuscany as a barber. At the age of 60 he married a girl of 14, his brother's daughter, or, perhaps, his own; for he was her mother's

> professed cicisbeo [acknowledged lover] long before and after her birth. This child brought Sir John a child during my stay in Naples. An express went instantly to Caserta. The Queen drove into town in the morning with rich presents to the lying-in lady. In the afternoon came the king and made the new-born babe a colonel.
>
> Monteleone estates, largest in Italy, narrowly escaped confiscation. The late Duke died just after sentence of death had been passed on his eldest son, and Acton instantly seized his feuds as forfeited by high treason. The younger son protested against this, claiming as immediate heir to the old Duke; for his brother, being condemned, had been civilly dead before his father died, and was therefore incapable of forfeiting that which he could not inherit. His claims being rejected, he applied to Ferdinand for redress, and obtained the restitution of every acre. The elder brother was pardoned at the pope's intercession, and is now expatriated. (458–459)

Forsyth also was excited by new works of art and sought to meet practicing artists. When he visited the convent of La Verna, he observed "the scenery is now under the pencil" of Jakob Philipp Hackert (1737–1807), a friend of Goethe and Sir William Hamilton. Luigi Ademollo (1764–1849) seemed to be painting frescoes everywhere. The "cathedral at Arezzo was the receiving a magnificent accession. Adimollo [*sic*] was painting there a chapel" (90, 96). Camillo Sergardi told Forsyth how Ademollo "fell into a moody silence, and lay prone on the floor some hours" in order to conceive the execution in Sergardi's palazzo at Florence of "the whole composition of the *Rape of the Sabines*, grouped round a concave ceiling, and exhibiting the same passion in a wonderful variety of expressions" (452). We have already noticed Forsyth's following of Benvenuti. At Rome, he met Angelica Kaufmann (1741–1807), the celebrated artist (240). He doesn't record meeting with Antonio Canova (1757–1822), but he discusses admiringly many of his sculptures in Rome and Venice: the tomb of Rezzonico, Perseus, Creugas, the Graces, Hebe, Hercules and Lichas, Daedalus, two versions of Psyche. "The only Venetian artist that could ever impress my soul or awake its affections is Canova," he wrote (339).

Similarly, Forsyth sought to meet contemporary Italian poets, who seemed to him to "flourish in a second spring," after the doldrums of the seventeenth and early eighteenth centuries. In the knowledgeable chapter "Poets" (18–23), his casual references tantalize us into asking how many he met. In chapter 3, we saw his contacts with Pignotti and a cluster of poets who sometimes met in private ("Some of his best novelle are reserved for private circles" [19]). There are others whom he named. Giovanni Fantoni (1755–1807), the lyric poet, was a professor at Pisa whom Forsyth could have met and whom he praised for his Horatian style but criticized for some overblown diction. Other living poets he reviewed were

Ippolito Pindemonte (1753–1828), Saverio Bettinelli (1718–1808), and Melchiorre Cesarotti (1730–1808; 363), whose forty-two volumes of works began to be published in Pisa from 1800.

While Forsyth was regrettably uninterested in music, he appreciated the other performing arts. In Florence, he went to several plays put on by the company of Goldoni ("a relation of the great dramatist"), where he saw and described Giovanni Andolfati (still alive in 1834) and Petronio Zanerini (1737–after 1802). They were, as he said, "the two first actors of the day" (58), though Zanerini was giving a swan song, for he was to disappear into obscurity soon after these performances. The most extended account Forsyth gives of the dramatic art is also in Florence, at a number of performances (discussed further in chapter 6) by the celebrated improvisatrice Fortunata Sulgher Fantastici (1755–1824), a friend of Monti, Alfieri, and de Staël (49–51). At the first *accademia* (exhibition[19]), Forsyth saw the performance of a "young woman of the same family and name as the great Michael Angelo." She was probably connected to a young man Hobhouse met in Florence, a "Mr Buonarotti" who had known Forsyth and said he was "endowed with a most exquisite taste and altogether [was] qualified to inspect and judge a nation."[20]

In addition, Forsyth attempted to gather intelligence concerning the works of Italy's celebrated men of science no less than its artists and poets. We have already noticed Felice Fontana and Giovanni Fabbroni. Forsyth mentioned that Fontana had a brother who was "yet more generally known than his brother by the title of Abbé" (36). This refers to Grigorio Fontana (1735–1803), professor of mathematics at the University of Pavia, who may have been instrumental in causing the university to order examples of Felice's anatomical models. Forsyth visited Pavia probably in April 1803, on his hasty return. He was still spending time looking for salient features—but skimming—even up to his next stop in Milan, "being rather in haste" but "impatient of anything below excellence" (351). Pavia had been experiencing a violent quarrel about mineralogy and volcanology in which Grigorio Fontana played a part:

> [Pavia] is the present metropolis of Italian science. Though scientific men are in general less irritable than the race of poets,[21] yet the very genius of the place and the aguish air of Pavia seem to have infected its philosophers with a feverous spleen. Spallanzani dispatched poor Scopoli by his scurrility, and fell, in his turn, a victim to the spite of Fontana, who, satisfied with bringing him to the grave, bespattered him with posthumous praise. Fontana himself died lately [August 1803, soon after Forsyth's arrest on May 25, 1803] in the very odour of ill-nature, and has left his character to be embalmed by his enemies. (439)

Giovanni Scopoli (1723–1788) had held the chair of botany and chemistry at Pavia and had been honored by Linnaeus for his work on plants. Lazaro Spallanzani (1729–1799) was celebrated for his observations of the flow of blood in internal organs. Both men also worked in the area of mineralogy and volcanology, where their disputes were said to have shortened Scopoli's life. Ambroglio Soldani (?1736–1808), whom Forsyth met before his visit to Pavia, took issue in turn with Spallanzani and published his observations on volcanic showers in Lucignano d'Asso (1794). He had shown Forsyth one of the stones he collected, which "weighed about three pounds, and contained malleable iron" (118). This iron would not have been produced by the volcano, he argued, and he explained its presence as the result of an electrical vortex in the volcanic shower, mixing clay from the Earth's surface with minerals in the air, which combined to form iron. But another friend of Forsyth's, Padre Ricca of Siena, "the most profound yet elegant scholar in this country" (119), demonstrated to Forsyth that "pyrites and ferruginous matter" were in the soil where the stones fell and that they had come from there and not from Vesuvius, as maintained by Sir William Hamilton (1730–1803). Forsyth met Soldani and Ricca shortly after encountering Felice Fontana in 1802. Probably they told him of the disputes at Pavia, at the same time as they explained their involvement in the arguments about volcanoes. Another possible source may have been Florentine gossip, which told him about Felice Fontana's brother "the Abbé."

Another name should be mentioned. Forsyth makes a passing remark mentioning him when ranking the University of Pisa with others in Italy. He does so with the confidence of an insider rather than a man making his first visit or his first thoughts: "In this university, however, Physics found the earliest protection: it boasts the first anatomical theatre and the first botanical garden in Europe; both created before the middle of the sixteenth century. The botanical chair is now admirably filled by the learned and amiable Santi; yet, in general science, Pisa is declined much below the fame of Pavia" (15). Giorgio Santi (1742–1822) was an eminent professor of natural sciences and chemistry, appointed by Leopoldo and intimate with Fabbroni, Spallanzani, and Savi. The botanical garden where he resided was a particular interest of his, it being used for the study of *materia medica* (medicines), and so linking with the Gabinetto Fisico. Santi reclassified the botanical garden according to the Linnaean system. He had traveled to Montpellier and Paris, meeting Buffon and Lavoisier. He instituted the study of geology, which Forsyth pays attention to in the discussion of volcanic rock. Between 1795 and 1806, he wrote *Viaggi per la Toscana* (Travels through Tuscany), a three-volume study of the plants and minerals of Tuscany.[22] When Forsyth, not a man of extravagant compliment, calls him "the learned and amiable," maybe we should interpret "amiable" as suggesting that Santi was indeed his friend. On May 19, 1802, Isaac wrote that he had received a letter of acknowledgment from "the Botanical Proffessor at Pisa" in return from one that Forsyth "had carried out." Some of the exchange of letters might have been in Italian, since earlier, Isaac remarked, "Nothing but 'most choice Italian' will do—and God help me I have none of that" (*L* 6). So Forsyth had a contact already with Pisa, and maybe it was Santi. Forsyth had been to France before, as we have noted that his visit to the Louvre was his second one, and Santi had also been to France.

The community we have examined—which included artists, politicians, writers, and scientists—was knit together by intellectual exchange. Indeed, we have gone behind the text of *Forsyth's Italy*, which distills their ideas, to raise the phantoms of their presence. As well as this community, there is another: a kind of "hail and farewell" group—persons on the periphery whose light contacts color our own existence and connect individuals with society at large. Forsyth pithily recorded encounters, eavesdroppings, and anecdotes relating to ordinary Italians and sometimes their observations and repartee. A few episodes concern the cicerones and *valets-de-place* (valets who act as temporary guides) hired to show tourists the sights of interest and works of art.

Tourism had encouraged ordinary Italians to act as guides to Italy's works of art, turning their hands from one job to another. While some guides brought profound knowledge of antiquities to the task, others bluffed their way through. When Forsyth asked his *valet-de-place* in Rome to show him the site of the Lago Curcio, the depthless lake into which the fabled Marcus Curtius was supposed to have galloped and, by this self-sacrifice, saved Rome, the guide confidently pointed out a large granite basin, also known as a *lago* (128). At Tivoli, another place on the Grand Tour itinerary, his cicerone was one Donato, who had been a porter of heavy equipment for landscape artists; he had picked up from them tags from Latin poets, which he delivered in a correct accent, together with parroted information (249). When Forsyth challenged him on the details of the architecture of Adrian's villa, however, poor Donato blustered and then confessed, "*Mossio mio non saprei dire*" (252–253; Monsieur, I don't know what to say). He may have taken Forsyth, presumably speaking Italian, for a Frenchman (see later in the next chapter how some of the occupying French troops became tourists too). But the message Forsyth sends is not a warning to innocent tourists to beware of impostures by Donato and his like, which he regards as innocent; rather, he records Donato's good nature, his eagerness to please: "He stopped us at the finest points of view, he lectured, he grinned with admiration, he amused us and was happy" (249).

At Ronciglione, a group of peasants "poured on us . . . the richest ribaldry" (121), though Forsyth provokingly does not repeat it. At Fondi, a Neapolitan advocate in Forsyth's traveling group quarrels on account of a package with a customs official, who happens to be a *castrone* (eunuch). The official asks if the advocate realizes that he is insulting an "organ of government." Yes, replies the advocate, "a well-toned organ . . . the prettiest treble I ever heard in a custom-house." The incensed official promptly orders the package to be sent to Naples express at the advocate's expense (261). An Italian in Rome remarks that some palazzi are simply *facciate* (facades) for show (170). At Fiesole, in the hills that give a fine view of Florence, two old men glory in the sight below but complain how wicked it is that "none of it belongs to us" (77, 77n). Anna Rinieri tells of how, when her father was governor of Siena, a mob of Florentines, who regard the Sienese as vain and flighty and compare them to headless nails, stopped his carriage but, recognizing him, yelled, "Let the governor of the crazy people pass" (391). A mattress-maker laments that his son, who "could not help" murdering a neighbor, has the "misfortune" to be pursued by the brother despite handsome bribes to the police, but if the brother goes on bothering them—just neighbors who wish to live peaceably—it is the will of God that they should murder the brother too (414–415). In Vicenza, a satirical bystander, listening to a rumormonger saying that rebellion had spread from China to Verona, asks which of the two places the man had left that morning, as though both were equally possible to such a teller of tall stories (438–439).

Forsyth's pleasure in liveliness; roguery; wit; good-natured, harmless imposture; and "compound[s] of sense and vice" is a sure sign of his being at ease with the people of the country. This ease encouraged him to add well-drawn observations of Italian life at many levels to his scholarly consideration of cultural artifacts—a rare combination of talents.

5
THE HIDDEN THOUGHTS OF JOSEPH FORSYTH

FORSYTH SELDOM REVEALS HIS PERSONAL side in *Italy* and was commended for this by reviewers, tired of trivial adventures. When he does, we may feel that it is an added pleasure within so much intellection. He can carry his learning lightly and, for example, enjoy the experience of seeing for the first time what he had longed for. Keen to take all impressions, he is delighted by the smallest fact, such as finding on a pedestal of the Blessed Virgin "an inscription at once Latin and Italian" (2) and humorously juxtaposes the two perils of sleeping in a filthy bed "devoured by fleas, and tormented by passengers who could find no bed at all" (1; this harks back to the *letto abitato*, the shared bed mentioned in the previous chapter). After basking in balmy air, he remarks with a Scot's pithiness that he passed a gap in the mountains "where a hurricane" met him "with all the advantage of a blast-tube." Although the book is not an autobiographical account, there is sometimes a vivid glimpse of the author. Noting the mistiness of Pisa, he says that by the Lung' Arno, "I have often perceived my stick and my hair moistened with the descending vapours" (26). At the grotto of Egeria, the water "was delicious, and, finding a large split reed placed over the drip, I used it as a conduit" (139).[1] His observations strike the reader as firsthand, arising from an informed and searching inquisitiveness. He describes digging his fingers in the earth: "I took up handfuls of *pozzuolana* [volcanic ash] so very elastic that, though moist when crumbled, it never stuck to my fingers" (142n). At the baths of Caracalla, he climbs a rickety broken staircase to check that the tessellation is entire (150).

His sense of humor particularly favors the ridiculous—for example, when he reports overhearing Italians quarreling: "*Che tu possa qui cader morto*!" cries a pious wife in a rage to her husband, "*intendo per altro prima confessato e communicato*" (368; May you drop dead, I mean after having confessed and taken communion). At the same time, he reaches out to see the other side of what is laughable. He found that at Laverna, "They particularly adored a tooth of St. Christopher which, an eminent naturalist assured me, came from the jaws of a rhinoceros. I could hardly refrain from an heretical smile, till I began to reflect that the scene before me was the work of faith" (91–92). His footnote to this has a comic mixture of familiar and pseudoscientific terms, inviting the reader to share the joke: "At the Certosa near Florence I saw another grinder of the same holy giant, which approached the sesquipedalian size of Æmilius's teeth. A similar imposition was practised about two centuries ago in France and England, where the bones of an elephant dug up near Chaumont were paraded about as the remains of the giant Teutobochus[2]" (91n).

There is this approachable side to him and also another that he chose to hide. Hobhouse was surprised to find a comment that did not square with his view of the author. He praises Forsyth's succinctness and eye for telling detail and presents him in his writings as an enlightened, restrained scholar. In addition, he calls attention to a passage of forcible and detailed expression of opinion, present only in *1816*, that Forsyth had replaced with a pithy but discreet one-liner for publication in 1813. "A character of the Abate [Carlo Fea]," observed Hobhouse, "which it is clear Mr. Forsyth never could have intended for publication, has been very indiscreetly inserted in the posthumous edition of *Remarks on Italy*." He is right; decency might have suggested that the passage remain hidden, except it was put into *1816* by Isaac for all to see. Forsyth's substitution of the passage with a witty and urbane epigram clearly indicates that in these rejected draft notes for *Italy*, he sometimes therapeutically expressed exasperation or misery or ideas that he might want to put better if they were to survive in print. In the case of Fea, he did put it better. In looking at the passages rejected for *1813*, we have mainly considered remarks that were politically too hot for a book intended to secure his release. We now turn to some passages, not necessarily with a political cast, rejected as well as from the printed text, where we can see an emotional side of Forsyth that he chose to hide.

Hobhouse did not object to the outburst on Fea. In fact, he was delighted to have it because it served his own contempt for Fea's antiquarian remarks, and desire to discredit Fea. Hobhouse refers to Fea's dissertation on the ruins of Rome, *Dissertazione sulle rovine di Roma* (1784), accusing him of not crediting and properly evaluating his sources and glorying in "arriving in many cases at conclusions entirely different."[3] His allusion to Forsyth's critique of Fea is calculated to back up his view that the nature of Fea's research was second-rate.

But what Forsyth had written, although fiercely critical, was more rounded than Hobhouse's dismissive attack. He criticizes Fea for being a self-important scholar, pretentious, and ungenerous. Fea uses his translation of the writings of the great art historian Winckelmann in order to assert his own judgment as superior. He seems a cross between a grub and a bee; he does produce "honey" and is "esteemed for antiquarian depth and sagacity," but on a personal level, he is combative and disloyal, feared and disliked by many Romans, and suspected of theft:

> "This fellow pecks up wit as pigeons pease." A gleaner of opinions, a parasite in literature, Fea lives upon other men's ideas. Whatever you communicate—"Pho!" cries he, "I knew that an age ago," and runs home with it directly to his common-place. His colleague in the Chigi library has enabled him to edit Winkelman with the spirit of an enemy. He is now connoisseur to the pope,[4] the oracle of all new comers, the living encyclopedia of Rome;—Abate Fea the antiquary, Abate Fea the lawyer, Abate Fea the economist, the naturalist, the journalist, the Arcadian, the translator; in short, the grub of literature risen into a butterfly that flutters in every walk, and pesters you into attention. He is a bee which has produced honey and can sting. Esteemed only for his antiquarian depth and sagacity, he was dreaded during the late revolution for his vindictive spirit, and will be ever abhorred for that ingratitude which sought the blood of his generous patron, the pope. He is now entrusted with the care of statues: in the Bracciano cabinet he betrayed too fine a passion for antique. (*1816*, 430)[5]

Forsyth's long tirade on Fea contrasts with his carefully modulated epigram that he did publish in 1813. It leaves the reader thinking that Fea was industrious but was there anything else? It is easy to miss how barbed the printed criticism is: "The Abate Fea, a lawyer from Nice, figures at present as connoisseur to the Pope, and writes upon every subject; but his chief merit is activity" (*1813*, 260–261; *1816*, 237). The unpublished, angry attack gives chapter and verse, showing Forsyth's grounds for the later epigram.

For all his reticence about himself, Forsyth's irony conveys a very strong sense of an individual voice and independent mind. We reread a pithy phrase in case we have missed something, since the text has set up expectations that more lies beneath the surface. The intelligence and resourcefulness of Forsyth's writing makes the reader engage with his text in a spirit of inquiry and a receptiveness to tone. Stendhal found that on further reflection over time, he agreed where he before had differed. He writes, "The only man of sense among you who has written on Italy is the late Joseph Forsyth. I have often differed from him in opinion, but the more I know of the country the more frequently do I give up my first-conceived notions, and come round to those of Forsyth."[6]

Just how difficult it was to penetrate some of Forsyth's views is shown in how he behaves with his family. Isaac Forsyth scarcely has his measure, although it is useful to have him witness in his introduction to the Murray edition how Forsyth was noted for his "gentleness of manners." Isaac says the family had "a secret hope that he would prefer the church" as a profession. The letters between the brothers concerning the death of their mother show that the family was deeply God-fearing. Whatever Forsyth believed as a boy, his numerous anticlerical comments and the lack of any reference to the consolations of religion in his book suggest that his position was that of a Deist or a skeptic who would attend religious services out of good manners or to show solidarity with his fellow countrymen. He could stand outside Christian traditions and remark that "gloomy presbyterians" would have destroyed ancient temples (134), whereas the Catholic Church was a friend to the arts, though an interested one. Isaac had not noticed this side to him or did not wish to notice it. In his letters to Forsyth, Isaac writes with a conscious assurance of his own piety and advises his elder brother on good Christian conduct, along with much that is banal domestic reporting. As it happened, what might have been irksome was just what Forsyth wanted. He asked for more because the normality of such things was a comfort in his exceptional situation.

Murray's editor, who was probably Gifford, was less tolerant of Isaac. By comparing Isaac's manuscript submission in the Murray Archive with the printed version, we can see he was not very impressed by Isaac's pieties. He cut a whole paragraph of Isaac's enthusiasms from the introduction and toned down his language elsewhere. In addition, he did not follow Isaac's recommendation to insert "here a character of [Forsyth's] peculiar literary qualifications, and that delicate sensibility which always shrunk from their display in private or public." The editor showed his skepticism of the upbeat tone in his amendment to Isaac's account of how he tried to reinvigorate Forsyth with "an excursion thro' the Highlands." He replaced Isaac's positive assertion that the Scottish tour did Forsyth good with an expression suggesting the hope was unsubstantiated. Isaac had written, "This aimiable man, and most accomplished scholar, having thus laid the foundation of better health, was on the very eve of removal to another and better world!" In the printed version, "having thus laid the foundation" is replaced with "who was thus thought to have laid the foundation." Isaac's wish to demonstrate the health-giving power of his beloved Highlands glosses over the fact that he also knew that Forsyth had a "tendency to pulmonary complaints [and was] twice reduced by them to the very brink of the grave"; he had written to Forsyth that the Highlands were "where three fourths of the year is very unfit for an invalid" (*L* 27). Maybe he wished to publicly exonerate himself from any criticism that he had harmed his brother. In our reading of Isaac's letters, we may see occasions where he is self-serving and looking for material advantage from his brother under the guise of helping others, such as in letters 28 and 29, where advice to use the Norwich Association turns out to serve him as well as his "friend." Forsyth's polite and indulgent replies give no indication of his awareness of this, but it is likely, from the shrewdness of his character portraits in

Forsyth's Italy, that he was aware. The value of noting this for my present purpose is that Forsyth could be reticent, particularly in the presence of his voluble brother, and did not foreground all he could say. In *Forsyth's Italy*, we should look for what lies behind the restrained language.

The paragraph of Isaac's introduction that was deleted by Murray's editor is worth quoting here, as it gives one of the few personal accounts of Forsyth that might enlighten us about his personality. It shows how his interest in the continent and particularly Italy was a constant passion, involving linguistic study, reading literary classics, and training his eyes to consider architectural design. When he traveled, it was with a mind already stored with ideas and questions:

> While at Newington his cheif enjoyments, and to which he devoted many a midnight hour, were the Classics and Mathematics. His enthusiastic attachment, and extensive acquirements in both, proved a solace and refreshment to his mind after the daily routine, and to him, the innumerable miseries of school life. During this period also he attained a very intimate knowledge of the French and Italian languages, so as to speak them with an uncommon degree of precision, and fluency. In it too he formed his Collection of Books; which for the Judgement displayed in the selection, and the rarity and excellence of the additions in the Classical Department, has not often been equalled by individuals in so retired a walk of life as his. His collection of French, Italian, and German Literature, and the standard works in English, was most respectable; and his Books and Plates in architecture, were numerous and highly valuable. This latter branch of study became the most favourite and incessant object of his attention previous to his departure for the Continent, and his acquirements in it will be easily appreciated by an inspection of his "Observations on the Arts and Antiquities of Italy."[7]

Forsyth himself says that he had not begun his travels with the intention of writing a book, but his journal, which he started only when he got to Pisa, and his good memory allowed him to write in a reflective way in Verdun without access to libraries and museums. Even though his time under arrest in Paris did give him valuable contact with the "outside world," he sent the book to the press feeling cut off. He worried how far his "observations . . . may have lost their interest, or been anticipated in England during my long captivity, I have no means of knowing. My misfortune denies me all acquaintance with the works of others."[8]

In the 1813 text, Forsyth chooses to conceal his purposes in the epigraphs to the chapters. The first begins with an apt quote from Persius's *Satire 6*. In this, Persius presents himself as wintering on the mild Ligurian coast, while Forsyth describes his journey along that coast from Nice to Genoa. Its appropriateness strikes deeper when we note the similarities between the two men, particularly since the epigraph announces that the book will, in a sense, be a satire. For Persius, a stoic, had a delicate constitution and traveled as a keen observer with a satirical sense of the ridiculous. When writing this, Forsyth's own delicate health was in his mind and the inclination to satirize the Napoleonic enterprise was strong, as the rejected papers testify. But to achieve his release as a result of publishing this book, he knew that his censuring remarks should be veiled and also have an innocent application. At the same time, for his own satisfaction, he secretly recorded his own intent, much as a prisoner scratches his name on a wall to assert his own independence. He concealed what only a sympathetic initiate might discover; Forsyth made good his claim to be like Persius in what he wrote.

"Genoa," the next section, has for its epigraph a poem by Saverio Bettinelli (1718–1808) describing the location of majestic Genoa. As the poem has a Virgilian tone and as it comes from *Lettere virgiliane*, it also connects with the previous chapter's discussion of how olives are cultivated in a way that would be familiar to Virgil. There is no hidden subtext, making it more difficult to notice a pattern.

The next epigraph, beneath the heading "Poets," heralds the politically important section concerning Pignotti, the Pisan poets, and others and does have the subtext of resistance to the French, which is reinforced if we restore the rejected passages to their original places. It is from Dante's invocation in the *Purgatorio* (1.7) and is translated as "But here let dead poesy rise again," announcing that poetry can reanimate. Although it will be necessary to travel through purgatory and to record the experience, as Dante does in the company of Virgil, it will make the poets fit to climb to the *Paradiso*. Within the section, Forsyth writes of the Pisan "circle" and how "Italian poetry" seems "now to flourish in a second spring" making it a kind of Earthly Paradise, a "Parnassus of the living." The epigraph works on the level of celebrating Pisa's poetic activity. However, it also hints at an eventual escape from the purgatory of the French occupation, helped by the efforts of the poets. When a section is concerned with a politically sensitive issue, Forsyth chooses epigraphs circumspectly, with their meanings hidden, as we previously saw in his use of Cicero's attack on Verres to obliquely criticize the looting of works of art.

A more obscure reference occurs with the epigraph to the section "Libraries," when Forsyth uses just a half quotation from the Latin poet. This is Martial's *Epigram* (14.184): "They lie together stored in many skins." Martial marvels at how two great epics, the *Iliad* and the *Odyssey* could be compressed into "one volume" of vellum manuscripts (skins). Given the extraordinary length and classic reputation of the Homeric epics, Martial sees it as a wonder that the two complementary riches are held in one place. At first sight, the quotation is a learned embellishment, heading a chapter celebrating the Laurentian library, a magnificent collection. However, it is there to point up a contrast. The Laurentian library had two precious and ancient manuscripts, a Virgil and the Pandects. The Virgil was perhaps the oldest in the world, but it had "disappeared during the late war" (it had been looted from the Laurentian library by the French). On the other hand, the valuable Pandects,[9] the sixth-century manuscripts of the Code of Justinian, the basis for the contemporary rule of law, "were sent to Palermo for safety" (out of reach from the French). Here is the contrast: Virgil, the moral guide to Dante through the cosmic system, and the Pandects, which preserve the rule of law, should still be lying together in the Laurentian library, so that we could rejoice in the same way as Martial celebrates the wisdom and cultural knowledge of the two epics combined in the manuscripts he saw.

Returning to Isaac's "secret hope that [Forsyth] would prefer the church," we find that the edge of criticism of the Church is never too far from Forsyth's lips. However, for it to go into print it must be modulated by wit, so he cut the following passage, where he resorts merely to exasperated name-calling. At the convent of Santissima Annunziata, he observes donations on Whit Sunday of oil in fifteen-gallon barrels brought "on an ass tricked out with ribbands, which enters the church followed by donors, who seem of the same family" (443). In the next example, he uses wordplay to criticize a monastery with a hidden personal involvement. Knowing he is himself a prisoner, we may detect his self-identification with the novices wasting out their youth in confinement and see the passage as revealing his own emotional state under the cover of wit. Forsyth says that at the monastery of Sacro Eremo in Camaldoli, St. Romualdo, who required his novices to live in cells "too sacred and too damp," is "unfeeling." The word carries the double meaning of "inured to pain" and "incapable of feeling another's pain": "The unfeeling Saint has here established a rule which anticipates the pains of purgatory. No stranger can behold without emotion a number of noble, interesting young men bound to stand erect chaunting at choir for eight hours a-day; their faces pale, their heads shaven, their beards shaggy, their backs raw, their legs swollen, and their feet bare. With this horrible institute the climate conspires in severity, and selects from society the best constitutions. The sickly novice is cut off in one or two winters, the rest are subject to dropsy, and few arrive at old age" (87). "Unfeeling" points at the lack of care for human potential and the pity of the waste of youth ("noble, interesting young men"), whose condition, including the waste of years of your life, is much like Forsyth's own when at first he lived in the confinement of a very damp cell in the severe winters of the Vosges Mountains.

A similar concern for the imprisoned youth drives his attack on the hospitality and charity of the monks of Vallombrosa as "the virtue of barbarous society."

It does not solve poverty, but merely palliates it, while the monastic life confines the energies and talents of young men within a narrow compass:

> Such indiscriminate hospitality is, however, but the virtue of barbarous society. Baneful to industry and independence, it feeds poor men, but it keeps them poor; it gives them a lodging, but it weans them from home. Not that I grudge this rich community the means of being so bountiful; I rather grudge it the youth, the talents, and the active powers which the Institution entombs. I grudge it the very virtues of the men whom I found here. Those virtues tend only to palliate its defects, and correct its general influence by the good which they do in detail. (80)

Sometimes Forsyth's criticism is more indirect, undercutting by using an epigrammatic progression from the sublime to the ridiculous. For example, he tells of how despite its eminence in physics, anatomy, and botany, some parts of the University of Pisa have sadly declined: "Attendance passes for merit; time, terms, and the archbishop, confer academical rank." Other times, his criticism is contained in what he refuses to say. In the Laurentian library, he hears orations and poems of a "solemn accademia [recital]," which he does not evaluate; pointedly, he praises something else: "In the gallery was a band of music, the only thing excellent that I heard." And sometimes, he leaves the story to our judgment, as when he recounts people talking about an unnaturally cold Easter. "One reverend meteorologist accounted to me" the reason: "Because it was cold when Peter sat at the High-priest's fire on the eve of the crucifixion." Many of his anticlerical criticisms could be seen as attacks on superstition or bad practice. And he does admit the power of the Easter ceremony at the Vatican that engages so many in an act of faith. However, his skepticism of the Church is always alive. His imagination runs on at the abbey of Vallombrosa to see a more sinister significance in religious objects than someone who was well-disposed to Christianity might have: "Here, too, are preserved all the pastoral staves that the abbots have borne since Gualberti founded the order. The first, a plain black stick, had its head formed like a T; the next head resembled an adze; the next an adze without its pole; and the rest in succession bent gradually into a crosier. In the same crooked manner did the abbots themselves, from subsisting on the charity of a few nuns, creep into territory, lordship, and jurisdiction" (82). Forsyth's last sentence enigmatically refers to the history of how the Vallombrosans came by their prosperity: it was crooked and they crept. In 1039, Itta, the abbess of a neighboring monastery of Sant' Ellero, made a donation to help raise a church for the Vallombrosans. Two hundred years on, Sant' Ellero was forcibly united, under protest, with Vallombrosa. Forsyth's distaste is echoed by a later traveler in 1825. Charles Armitage Brown, writing in the *New Monthly*

Magazine, provides contemporary detail of what was thought to have happened, ending with a quote from *King Lear* that compares the monks to a cuckoo in the nest and, by extension, to the acquisitive and murderous daughters, Goneril and Regan:

> Now mark what followed this endowment [of the founding of Vallombrosa]. The nuns of St. Ilario were at last accused of relaxation of discipline, and in 1255 Pope Alexander IV. transferred them to another convent, bestowing all their lands, buildings, dependent lordships, rights and privileges, on the brethren of Vallombrosa.
>
> "For you trow, nuncle,
> The hedge-sparrow fed the cuckow so long,
> That it had its head bit off by its young."[10]

When Forsyth cut the passage about Leopoldo (*1816*, 378–385), he also cut a disquisition on women that led up to it. Together they make a piece of continuous writing (*1816*, 362–385) where he lets his pen run on to address his own preoccupations and write himself into a better frame of mind. Hanging on his mind are the loathsomeness of prison life—where death, disease, and corruption might lurk—and the moral degradation of the French occupation. What he writes illuminates the conditions in Italy in 1802–1803 but also betrays concerns that he did not have under control.

The impetus for the excursus on Italian women that precedes the passage on Leopoldo seems to have been a part of his account of the Gabinetto Fisico that he excluded from *1813*. Apparently, a fastidious sense of propriety makes him exclaim against letting ladies in to socialize around the anatomical objects: "This awful region, which should be sacred to men of science, is open to all. . . . the gravid uterus . . . is a favourite lounge of the ladies, who criticise aloud all the mysteries of sex" (36). In fact, Forsyth expresses the idea that the Gabinetto is a place that strikes "awe" in the onlooker. Susini's anatomical waxworks, which we mentioned in chapter 4, presented attractive young women as though newly dead. As Forsyth said, they were made with "an accuracy which astonished the Pavians" (39). The two examples illustrated here still exist. Figure 5.1 may show one of those that Forsyth refers to; purchased by Antonio Scarpa for the University of Pavia's anatomical museum, it arrived in Pavia between 1794 and 1795. The organs can be partially disassembled, showing under the intestine a pregnant uterus and the kidneys.[11] The other one (figure 5.2) is at the Palazzo Poggi in Bologna and also can be disassembled. It has been called the "Little Venus" for its good looks and realistic portrayal, with a necklace of pearls and human hair. Many medical anatomies

FIGURE 5.1 Clemente Susini: Pavia anatomy. By permission of Museo per la Storia dell'Università di Pavia.

before Susini's works had been stiff and rudimentary in representing the human body that enclosed the organs. They concentrated on the internal organs almost as components. Susini's represented the human being in an unnervingly realistic way. The wax had a translucency bringing it closer to human flesh than marble. The sense of the women recently being alive is so great that the onlooker may wonder whether in fact they are asleep. But no human could survive the surgical opening of her abdomen. Compelled to see a lifelike human, Forsyth needs to hold onto a view that it is a medical dissection, carried out on the grounds of science, in order to keep at bay the disgust and horror he might feel if it were a disemboweling. In addition, more grotesque images hang on his mind. Moved by their realism, he also writes vividly about the wax specimens of decomposing bodies, which show "every stage of putrefaction—the worm, the rat and the tarantula at work—and the mushroom springing fresh in the midst of corruption" (35). The damp dungeons of Bitche and the maiming of would-be escapees cannot have been far from his mind when he was writing this. We know from his letters that at this time, he was at a very low ebb. On October 4, 1807, he wrote that he felt he had scarcely any identity or connection with society. He was "a thing detached and exiled from his

FIGURE 5.2 Clemente Susini: Little Venus

country" and was keeping away from his "vicious and prodigal" fellow countrymen (*L* 16). Even when he was in a more secure frame of mind, he had a strong reaction to scenes of torture, finding contemplation of the event of the *Massacre of the Innocents* "a subject inexplicably horrible to me," yet one that could be made into "an admirable picture" by the artistic genius of Poussin, who even intensifies the emotion by representing "only one child and one mother, but a mother whose shrieks frighten away her friends" and "the horror is not, as usual dissipated in a multitude of details" (194).

That Forsyth is offended by the sight of women looking at and loudly discussing the wax models in the Gabinetto reminds us how much he is a man of his age and background. Today, what may strike us most immediately is the familiar confirmation offered by this passage of the control exercised by men over representations of the female body, even in an area in which women have a particular interest, the "gravid uterus." What is not so familiar, however, is the detailed frankness of Forsyth's account. Another visitor to the Gabinetto, Enoch Cobb Wines, simply refused to credit that such an affront to modesty could ever be. When *he* went, armed with his *Forsyth's Italy* (thirty years after Forsyth), matters were conducted differently, as he hastens to assure his anxious readers:

> I will not believe that the fair Florentines are so destitute of delicacy, nor that the gentlemen who have the control of this establishment are so regardless of what is due to decency. There were a few ladies in some of the other anatomical apartments, but from this they were carefully excluded. The door was kept locked, and when I entered, it was immediately fastened upon me again. Other gentlemen, I observed, were treated in the same way, and when anyone wanted to retire, he was obliged to rap for the keeper to come and let him out.[12]

However, what also becomes clear when Forsyth's description is placed in its original context is that the passage on the Gabinetto Fisico is the prelude to a meditation on the changes to Florentine society under the French. What affronts him is not so much that *ladies* are admitted to what "should be sacred to men of science" but that they treat the awe-striking place where the scientific mystery is unveiled as a "favourite lounge." This observation is the precursor of many pages of reflection, culminating in the disguised attack on Napoleon through the comparison between Leopoldo and the Medicis. Poverty, superstition, and corrupt practices are part of the troubled brooding, but so is what he perceives as a general decline in Florentine manners, in which loss of female delicacy is only one aspect; French occupiers and a corrupt clergy have played a major role in causing this decline. What the Florentines had been like just before the French came he probably took on trust, but he did have knowledge of its historical heritage: "Such is the influence of power over national taste, that the French have produced a very general change in the exterior manners of the Tuscans, though they remain the object of their secret abhorrence. This change appears in a thousand trifles which are important only in the aggregate, and the tendency of all is to break down the barriers of that dignity, true or false, which once distinguished the politer part of this people" (362). Forsyth's view is a snapshot of 1802 and 1803. Imprisonment kept him from seeing whatever benefits the French occupation conferred. Fergus Robson has written how the experiences of French soldiers occupying Italy "could give rise to dramatically different cultural encounters"; for example, "soldiers frequently behaved like tourists." But despite many mutually enrichening experiences, "soldiers in fact arrived at often remarkably similar sets of stereotypes of Italy and her people." Italian women were seen as "more sexually available and less trustworthy than French women."[13] The license that this would have given to the soldiers must have contributed to the malaise and immorality that Forsyth saw. Forsyth recalls a more worthy past in sympathizing with a nation subject to the forces of oppressive circumstances. He writes that the Florentines are still benevolent and charitable but have lost a sturdiness of spirit and succumbed to superstitious beliefs. Noblemen can no longer write, crowds gather to gape at the slightest thing, and although generous, the people have become slavish with crushed aspirations: "For more than three ages did the Tuscan nobility surpass all Europe in literature and science, as poets, as physicians, as professors. They were the exclusive historians of their own country, and very generally employed as the ambassadors of foreign courts. Dante, Petrarch, Cimabue, M. Angelo, Galilei, Macchiavel, the six greatest Tuscans that perhaps ever existed, were all noble. After this the class of goldsmiths produced the most celebrated names" (375). This is a passage that he considered worth including in *1813*. It gives a succinct view of a noble tradition and contains the subversive caution that the Florentines "were exclusive historians of their own country" (375). There is a sense of Forsyth regaining balance but not enough, yet, to prevent another outburst.

He continues, describing how an Englishman, whose education in "delicacies and decorum" had given him a way of thinking about women that would "tend to throw an elegant drapery over the female mind," would be "apt to stare at the ladies" in Florence (375). But their behavior is the result of social pressures: "Indeed, the female character is, in every country, half the work of men, and where gentlemen require no delicacy in the sex, ladies of course affect none."[14] The Church and social conventions have constricted their behavior:

> The fair Florentines still persist in habits which have been long banished from English society; you will see very elegant women take snuff, spit on the floor, blow their resounding noses in snotted handkerchiefs, clap gentlemen on the thigh, keep conversation continually fluttering on the brink of obscenity and often pass the line. Such are the manners that instantly succeed to the pruderies of a convent education; marriage develops the whole woman at once, and makes immediate amends for the imprisonment of the girl. . . . You meet beauty blended with intelligence, with benignity, with pride, with languishing, with defiance, with devotion; but seldom with modesty. (376)

The custom of a married woman taking an acknowledged lover (a cicisbeo), who often conducts her to church, seems bizarre to him and "wicked"; it often gives way to ludicrous pantomime: "The cicisbeo seems vain of the servilities which his mistress studies to impose on him. I once saw a lady bid her Signor Cavaliere stir up her fire, '*Attizzate il mio fuoco*.' ['Stir up my fire'—Forsyth sees the innuendo.] At the word of command he put his hand under her petticoat, removed the chafing dish, stirred the coals with a small silver shovel which he kept in his pocket, replaced the pan, and readjusted her dress" (377). He had seen this adulterous behavior at close quarters. In a later passage, omitted from *1813*, he describes how Moncenni the banker's daughter married a rich and impotent young man "whom she had never seen, who is imbecile in mind and body, goes sometimes on all fours, and strangles dogs and cats, and is physically unable to consummate the rite. But that the bride is indifferent about; she told my friend Brown on the eve of the marriage that she must first go to Florence to meet her husband; but next day she should enter on all the rights of an Italian wife, and be glad to receive his addresses" (450). The practice of cicisbeism was adopted by Church dignitaries and English tourists alike: "Arciprete Luti, president of the university [Siena], boasted before me in Sa. Catterina Spannocchi's box of the immoral tie which he had formed in the morning. The bride's mother acted like a procuress to her daughter. I saw her encourage her dalliance with Brown, but she complained that English lovers were but birds of passage" (451).

While Forsyth is openly critical of the involvement of the clergy in its pressurizing of women, he turns his irony on the highly erudite and discreetly corrupt clerics of Rome. Most are learned bores, but now and then, one meets a rare minor cleric (*abatino*) who is a true scholar and a gentleman, a modern Renaissance humanist: "No class in the papal state can be more important than the clergy. These, in general, are learned, at least literary men; pretty correct in exteriors and guarded in their debauchery. From the length and rigour of their education, most of them smell of the college or the convent. Yet sometimes you meet an *abatino di città* [a little city cleric], a modern Ruccellai,[15] who may fairly be set in opposition to our own clerical bucks" (404). What does Forsyth mean by "fairly set in opposition"? That the true good breeding, cultivated taste, and discretion of such an *abatino* would shame his British counterpart, a Prince-Bishop Hervey, for example? Or that in blatant debauchery and worldliness, the Italian would be a match for the British clerical buck? Or are all these things true? The *abatino* combines the high erudition and courtly manners of a Rucellai with blatant libertinage, fashionable dress, wit, and a total disregard for his clerical calling? But is "modern Rucellai" ironic? Could there be such a person in decadent early nineteenth-century Rome? It is one of the pleasures of reading *Forsyth's Italy* that at certain points, the reader cannot say precisely what is implied. What his spare prose laconically conveys is the tension between moral judgment and enjoyment of the spectacle. But then he looks around the streets and piazzas and describes in heartrending terms the poverty and starvation of the poor in "all the forms of misery, the sickness, the sores, the deformity, the hunger, which infest the streets, where every beggar is distinguished by his own attitude, tone and variety of the pathetic, while all together present a strange climax of wretchedness" (404).

In his view, the women were being trivialized by being encouraged to be loudly immodest and to indulge in affairs that undermined partnerships: "Let no man tell me that Italian manners should not be tried by English laws. Virtue is of no country. Infidelity is every where vice; nor will its frequency excuse individuals, for individuals have made it universal. Yet female virtue has certainly fewer defences here than in England; and as virtue is ever proportionate to resistance, an Italian beauty with an Italian temperament, remaining faithful to an Italian husband, in the midst of Italian manners, is more virtuous than a English wife can possibly be" (377).[16] In a form of servitude, the Church constricted the young woman in a convent-like way (often actually in a convent) and then encouraged, sometimes by active participation, sexual promiscuity. At the same time, the Church excluded half of its subjects—women—from active participation in the life of the nation and also was composed of men with no experience of women as peers. (His argument here connects with his evenhanded concern for the nuns of Sant' Ellero, whose monastery was extinguished by the male monks of Vallombrosa.) He looked back to when women had a complete social role that also included the "awful region" of medical dissection: "The time is past when Italian ladies wore the doctoral cap, filled the faculty-chairs, preached, dissected, spoke Latin, wrote Greek, and plunged into the depths of science. The time is past when the first women in Italy seemed to live for the historian. What a constellation of female excellence in the single family of Gonzaga! Isabella, Cecilia, Lucretia, Eleonora, Julia, Louisa, all great as princesses, yet amiable as women!" (403)[17]

Under the French occupation, Italian society is at a low ebb, but its men and women are capable of much greater things. Gender is no barrier. Forsyth records his own amicable and instructive conversations in which he learned from intelligent women (whom we have already mentioned in passing in chapter 4). The women he mentions are fewer than the men, but the snatches of conversation suggest warm and sociable relations. He is on first-name terms with the famous artist Angelica Kaufmann: "I have heard Angelica say that the water of Rome revived her powers, and gave her ideas. This amiable woman is the idol of her invidious profession, the only artist beloved by all the rest" (240). He is similarly intimate with Anna Rinieri, who "has the first conversazione here for talents and accomplishments" (579). She tells Forsyth about how she educates her children[18] and introduces him to Signora Fantastici, whom Forsyth admires. Forsyth has a sympathetic and teasing relation with Fantastici during her performance as an improvisatrice (see chapter 6). The Countess Cicciaporci trusts him enough to discuss government letters with him and brings him into the circle of Cardinal York (456).

Notwithstanding the miserable loneliness Forsyth felt in 1807, it does seem that in general, he adopts a particular engaged detachment that often makes him able to stand apart from the conventional and appraise the new. It goes along with his choice to seclude himself in Verdun. Maybe like Henry James's Ralph Touchett, he is constrained by his illness, which had brought him twice near to death, and this encouraged him to be a bystander. Amorous women who preferred his friend

Brown instinctively did not see him as a target. After the moral censure of Florentine society, his empathy for the morally lax but vital society of Naples comes as a surprise. But reading the text again with his personal background at the time of writing as partly a key to understanding him, we should admit that something of the lighter tone for Naples comes from the easier circumstances of Paris compared with darker and more resentful and gloomy period at Verdun: "To a mere student of nature, to an artist, to a man of pleasure, to any man that can be happy among people who seldom affect virtue, perhaps there is no residence in Europe so tempting as Naples and its environs . . . a coast which was once the fairy-land of poets, and the favourite retreat of great men." (272–273).

The description of Naples is a compelling instance of Forsyth's longing to be free. It not only represents an image of escape but also of a happy residence among Naples' merry devils, with Forsyth enjoying the rural beauty of its environs and its association with poets and great men. Virgil, a favorite poet of Forsyth, had chosen to live and end his days in Naples. His tomb was said to be just outside the city above the grotto of Posillipo and was one of the great tourist attractions. Forsyth visited it. Francis Towne's unfinished watercolor of the tomb (1781, shown on the cover of this book) represents the attractiveness of the cliffs above the road that leads to the grotto, an entrance to an ancient Roman tunnel through the mountain. Virgil's tomb stands on top of one of the cliffs, caught in a shaft of light, in the unfinished section of the painting. Its indefinite quality might seem an appropriate analogy for Forsyth's sentiments, as he decided it could not definitely be Virgil's, for it had evidence of holding other funerary urns and Virgil's tomb would surely have been dedicated only to him. So he turned back to be amused by revelers, drunkenly celebrating that they had just seen the actual thing; in mock classical language, he teasingly described them: "I met a party of foreigners full of the God, reeling down from the neighbouring vineyard, between two precipices, to make further libations to the shade of Virgil" (275). His judging mind refused to indulge the fancy that he or they had seen Virgil's tomb and gently satirized the devotions of the foreign tourists. Here we have enjoyment, empathy, and detachment.

The passages taken out before the first edition went to press are often self-revealing, lively, and easy to read. It is easy to suppose that their relaxed delivery reveals the authentic voice of Forsyth, but in fact, they are neither more nor less authentic than the rest. In the case of his character of Fea, he is venting against pretension that dishonors the name of Winckelmann; in his discussion of Florentine manners, his despair of society is being written out. In the previous chapter, we noted that a substantial part of his gaiety in Naples was also cut. He chose to hide his ways of thinking where his strong emotions were involved. It is a trait that he also showed in his letters to his brother, where for most of the time a stoic endurance covers up his agonized state of mind. We only know of some of his hidden thoughts through their inclusion in *1816* by Isaac. In his book, Forsyth writes in opposition to a society that constricts the individual, but in his letters, he makes no direct comment on his sister's ownership of slaves in Jamaica. The nearest he gets to wishing her to change is to ask, "Why will she not be content with a moderate income and return to Britain to enjoy it?" (*L* 13). Otherwise, he marvels at her endurance through many troubles. This accords with the reticence he shows when subjected to Isaac's religious enthusiasm. We do not know what his considerations were in his nonjudgmental conduct with his own family; the inquisitiveness of God-fearing Elgin may have constrained him. His mother was venerated, and people considered her "as almost beatified," and Forsyth's letters "circulated round the village in quick vibration" (*L* 11). In the book, he has more license to wish for freedom from servitude and to criticize religious zeal. Petty behavior in Italy, as much as crushed aspirations and religious superstition, was a target for him.

The epigram on Fea shows that Forsyth would admit you to his hidden feelings and opinions if you were prepared to look further into what he said. This was his preferred mode. Examples of Forsyth's gnomic statements often show not only the active, wide-ranging mind and the terseness admired by reviewers but also a hidden social concern. Comparing the public benefits conferred by a hypothetical private gentleman deriving his income from rented property with those conferred by a monk of the munificent abbey that also derives its great wealth from rents, he observes that the gentleman's revenues "do not return so directly as the monk's into the mass of the people, which is the ultimate destination of all property; but they return through more taxable channels, through cellars and shops" (81). The following question exercises him: Might it be that the charity of the monks in the abbey of Vallombrosa (which depends on the rigorous austerity forced on each member so that the abbey can maximize the amount it gives to the poor) is a more effective means for distributing wealth than state taxes on commodities, which fall on the private property–owning classes and which also benefit the public purse? Although Forsyth notes that the strict control exercised by the abbey over its members provides stability and avoids the squandering of inheritances that may occur among the secular property-owning classes, he does not want to concede that a charitable religious foundation might be more beneficent than they and, without giving supporting evidence, concludes that "the private gentleman, perhaps, spends his income more profitably to the public revenue."[19] What is startling in this otherwise orthodox-sounding reflection is the phrase "the mass of the people, which is the ultimate destination of all property"; Rousseau's dictum, "You are utterly lost if you forget that the fruits of the earth belong to everybody, and the Earth belongs to nobody," resonates in this phrase.[20] Forsyth is far from saying that "property is theft" (a slogan yet to be coined) or from subscribing to the Rousseauvian view that from private property stems civil society and thence inequality and a mass of "crimes, wars, and murders, miseries and horrors." He is not a leveler (nor, indeed, was Rousseau). The distributivism of his friend in the Tuileries is to him utopian, a castle built "very liberally on the rights and property of others" (*1816*, 458). It is easy in one's fancy to be liberal with the wealth of others. Like Samuel Johnson, he does not believe that luxury is in itself corrupting. Compared with the "private gentleman," the monks may be more frugal, but that does not banish the central problem. Their charity is "but the virtue of barbarous society," not that of a civilized commonwealth. The monks' charity "feeds poor men, but it keeps them poor"; property has not found its destination in the mass of people. The spirit of the revolutionary 1790s has not left him untouched.

Again, when considering the usefulness of the Gabinetto Fisico in the hands of imperfect practitioners, he reflects on the speculative nature of science and philosophizes, "Sig. Fabbroni told me that many articles should be melted down as useless; that others were inaccurate; that all, from the yielding nature of the wax, wanted frequent retouching; and that, beginning anew, he could make the system more complete in half the compass. But such is ever the course of experiment. Every new step in science is the correction of an old one. Science may be considered as the art of remedies which originate in defect and end in it" (36). The epigrammatic last sentence would fit well with T. S. Kuhn's Popperian view of scientific revolutions.[21] It also derives from Hume's skeptical view of the nature of evidence: that we proceed on conjecture and end in conjecture.

The precision of his language offers another means of insight into the workings of his mind. Sometimes this is best seen in cases where he uses a term that differs from modern usage. He saw two paintings of Parmigianino in the Palazzo Capo di Monte at Naples. These may have been the *Antea* and *Galeazzo Sanvitale*, which were inherited by the king of Naples in 1798, having been formerly in the Farnese Gallery in Rome. Items from the Farnese collection, which included statuary, had been earmarked for France, but what items had been chosen, when the items went to Naples, and when, or if, they arrived in France is often not clear.[22] Forsyth certainly saw the Farnese Hercules ready for transport and may have seen the *Antea* and *Galeazzo*. They will serve in any case to illustrate how he uses the term *grace*: "Two of Parmigianino's are praised for that grace, which struck me as too peculiar, too characteristic for so vague a quality as grace" (269). The *Antea* and the *Galeazzo* certainly are portraits that have the "peculiar" and the "characteristic" qualities that suggest particular individuals more than a type. Each has an alert bearing with wide-awake eyes, an aristocratically long nose, and an intense studious expression. Specific accoutrements—a gorgeous robe for one, armor and a sword for the other—emblematize their moral as well as social qualities. They answer to the features in the two Parmigianino's that Forsyth saw. However, he says they do not have "grace," which is "so vague a quality"—"vague" having here the sense given in Johnson's *Dictionary*: "unfixed; unsettled; undetermined; indefinite."[23] Johnson has seventeen definitions of *grace*, with illustrative quotations that demonstrate how *grace* may apply to situations that are disparate or contrary, including artificial and natural beauty. While grace is definitely real, it refuses to be tied down to one quality. It has a suggestive power. It cannot be particularized. Other examples of Forsyth's use of *grace* in *Forsyth's Italy* confirm this. He praises Raphael's paintings on two occasions for their grace, as something connected with the tranquility of a great soul, and contrasted with the qualities found in the paintings of Ademollo (105) and Caravaggio (194), who portray the immediate and violent. The particular gets in the way of the sense of the numinous. Canova's Graces have the quality of grace because they belong to such "a world of ideal and uncreated beauty" (238). Too much detail in a sculpture destroys its suggestive power. Ancient Roman sculptors, despite knowing about and using stirrups, nevertheless suppressed representing the detail of the real equipage, because "stirrups would detract from the freedom and grace of an equestrian figure" (132n). Sculpture is removed from an exact representation of the human body in order to reveal grace and sublimity: "Its purpose is not to cheat the eye, but to present to the mind all the truth and beauty and grace and sublimity of forms. Did the excellence of a statue depend on the illusion produced, or on the number of idiots who mistake it for life, the Medicean Venus would then yield to every waxwork that travels from fair to fair" (43). The disturbing realism of the dissected woman in the Gabinetto may also be in Forsyth's mind as he expresses this wish to launch into the ideal beyond the real. The idea has an antecedent in Johan Joachim Winckelmann's earliest work on the aesthetics of Greek painting and sculpture, published in 1755, which was translated into English in 1765: "The imitation of beauty in nature either directs itself toward a single object or it gathers observations of various individual objects and makes of them a whole. The first method means making a similar copy, a portrait; this leads to the forms and figures of the Dutch artists. The second, however, is the way to general beauty and to ideal images of it; and this was the way chosen by the Greeks."[24] Forsyth was both a follower and a critic of Winckelmann. The next chapter will discuss how he reacted to Winckelmann's more developed and voluminous thesis on aesthetics of 1764, *Geschichte der kunst des alterthums* [*The History of Ancient Art*].

6
VISUAL ARTS, ARCHITECTURE, AND LITERATURE

IN NAMING HIS BOOK, Forsyth located it in a tradition of "Remarks" in which places, peoples, and things of note are selected from a tour and give rise to intelligent reflection. The title was intended to confer more learned distinction on his writing than calling it a straightforward travelogue so that his claim to be released as a scholar would have a high chance of success. It was also, I wish to argue, what he could do best, given the kind of mind that he had. This chapter seeks to examine how his work lived up to this title, with particular emphasis on his commentaries on the visual arts, architecture, and literature. The reviews considered him as being within the scholarly tradition. They stressed the originality, strength, and subtlety of his judgments and tacitly accepted that he wrote in the mode of "Remarks." The *Monthly Review* (see chapter 1) had commented that Forsyth had "no tedious journeyings" but instead "the more interesting observations of the antiquary, the scholar and the man of the world."

This interest in observations more than the events of a journey goes back to three authors at the beginning of the century: Addison, Richardson, and Breval. It is likely that Forsyth had read all three, for he had read widely in the literature of travel in Italy, to the extent that he considered it "so beaten a field." He does not directly refer to the titles of their books, but they are probably the commentators he invokes when considering the conflicting opinions on Michelangelo's *Last Judgment*, and they are shown to be constantly in his mind. When watching Andolfati on stage, he thinks of how Addison provokes the "secret intellectual smile."

Addison dedicated his book to John Lord Somers as "Remarks that I made in a Part of these my Travels" and, in his preface, declares, "I have taken notice of several Places and Antiquities that no Body else has spoken of, so, I think, I have mentioned but few Things in common with others, that are not ether set in a new Light, or accompany'd with different Reflections. I have taken care particularly to consider the several Passages of the Ancient Poets, which have any Relation to the

Places or Curiosities that I met with."[1] His book was followed by the Richardsons' perceptive commentary (the title particularly highlights the word "remarks") in 1722 on Italian paintings and bas-reliefs, especially in Rome.[2] The seal was set on this kind of writing by John Breval's remarks on his various tours in Europe, published as doublet folios in 1726 and 1738, each sumptuously illustrated with over forty copperplate engravings.[3] Breval argued for a historical understanding of place—against those who travel "as if there were no more in a Journey to Rome than there is in a Trip to Bath or Newmarket."[4] Placing himself as following in the footsteps of Addison, he proposed to write on a larger scale, since the remarks of Addison were, according to him, no more than a sample. He castigated the aristocracy of his day that looked down on connoisseurship and contrasted how, in former days, one could take pride in the excellent sense of taste of King Charles I ("of blessed memory"), whose magnificent and judiciously chosen collection of artworks had been sold by Puritans with no sense of their cultural value.

Forsyth had the same learned enthusiasm for art as Breval, relating individual works to their history and a sense of place. As we have seen, he was more than ready to engage with contemporary Italy, and often it made him reach back into the past. His consideration of works of art and literature draws on the Italian context and a set of values formed by his extensive reading of its literature and works bearing on its culture—often "Ancient Poetry" (as Addison had called it). Forsyth writes believing his criteria would be shared or at least understood by readers familiar with this tradition, and so his allusive and pithy writing does not foreground them. But even in his day, not every reader was wholly familiar with the underlying values. Brougham in the *Edinburgh Review* had said that Forsyth's observations "had an air of obscurity." They require elucidation for the modern reader as well, as we shall discover in our process of examining those qualities that made the reviewers so admire him. However, a word of caution is necessary: some of the circumstances in which he wrote increase our difficulty nowadays in sharing his ideas. Unlike Breval, he was not able to include engravings, and this requires the reader to have a fine visual memory not only to follow, for example, the descriptive detail of composition and color but even to identify the subject or version of the artwork.

All works of art have an evolutionary history that may include removal from view for a period, substitution, restoration, remodeling, renaming, reattribution to another artist, changes of location and of owner. Many buildings and artworks that the modern traveler sees in Italy are recognizably those that Forsyth saw and described and remain where he saw them. Others have changed beyond recognition or disappeared or are difficult to identify. Forsyth's own nomenclature must be interpreted in this light. (A list of what he saw is given in appendix A as a useful indication of the range of the works of art on which he made remarks and as a record of what could be still seen after the depredations of Napoleon.)

To take one example, when Forsyth visited the cathedral in Pisa, making one of his first encounters with Italy's remaining treasures, he commented, "Even the marble pulpit, fine as it is, impairs the symmetry by standing before a column. This pulpit is supported by a naked figure of most gross design. Indeed, few churches in Italy are free from the incongruous. Here are Bacchanals and Meleager's hunt incrusted on the sacred walls, an ancient statue of Mars, worshipped under the name of St. Potitus, and the heads of satyrs carved on a cardinal's tomb!" (10–11). Visitors today would see a reconstruction of the "tormented expressionism" of Giovanni Pisano's magnificent mannerist pulpit, but that is not what Forsyth saw. Pisano's original pulpit had been dismantled and dispersed after the great fire that destroyed much of the cathedral in 1595. A replacement pulpit was commissioned and completed in 1630, in a new design by Chiarissimo Fancelli, who did not use the original supporting columns. The replacement pulpit that Forsyth saw was a compilation of pieces by Fancelli, using pieces from Pisano and others rather than Pisano's masterwork. This replacement or part of it is now in the nearby church of Santo Stefano dei Cavallieri, which received it as a gift from the cathedral in 1929, and is high up on new tall columns. The *Catalogo Generale dei Beni Culturali's* record of its installation in S. Stefano says that Fancelli had had to combine elements and complete the pulpit ("di ricomporre e completare il pulpito") to replace the damaged one. It took four years and was not in an octagonal shape, as Pisano's had been.[5] What visitors see today in the Baptistery of Pisa is a restoration of Pisano's work made in 1926—conjectural, incomplete, but nevertheless highly regarded.[6] The whereabouts of the columns seen by Eustace and Forsyth are not known.

What, then, did Forsyth see? In 1820, Mariana Starke wrote about the pulpit: "The centre-aisle contains a pulpit of inlaid marble, supported by two small columns; the one porphyry, the other oriental brocatello [bas-relief imitating brocade]; and the first is deemed particularly curious, from consisting of various pieces, so well joined that it may properly be denominated *Breccia porfirea* [aggregate of porphyry]; the second is deemed the finest specimen of its sort in Italy."[7] Pisano's figures were carved from marble, but Starke saw "various pieces, so well joined" in porphyry. Assuming no alteration took place between the late 1790s, when Starke first saw the pulpit, and 1802, when Forsyth saw it, he must have seen the columns she describes. One is not carved with images, since it is made to look like brocade. The other is of porphyry, whereas Pisano's was of marble. Starke says this one is pieced, which could mean that a sculptured figure was part of the support. Eustace briefly mentions that both columns were of porphyry (again confirming that they were not in Pisano's marble) but Starke distinguishes between the two. Neither Eustace nor Starke mention the "naked figure of most gross design" supporting the pulpit. Yet Forsyth's observation is supported by a curious detail in Harvard's fifty-three volume archive of photographs collected before 1885 by Henry Hobson Richardson, architect of the "Richardsonian Romanesque" style.[8] It shows this pulpit low down in the nave of the cathedral, standing next to a pillar, as Forsyth remarks. The shorter columns are, unusually, hidden behind a curtain, something that might have been done if some medieval indecency was indeed carved on one or both of them.[9]

The example of the Pisa pulpit showing Forsyth's distaste for its "gross design" invokes the principle, a cardinal one in eighteenth-century aesthetics, that components of a work of art should be in "keeping." The parts should be consonant with the whole. Forsyth considers satyrs are inappropriate for the holiness of a bishop's tomb, and Mars cannot be hidden under St. Potitus's mask. In Rome, he criticizes the Laocoön's nakedness as being against keeping, since nudity is not required by the story that the statue group is intended to illustrate—that is, the destruction of the Trojan priest Laocoön and his sons by two enormous serpents. However, in this case, keeping is not his overriding concern, or rather, he considers that the Laocoön group fulfils the requirements of another kind of keeping, since the Greeks were accustomed to represent nakedness and the Laocoön is otherwise excellent (229, 290). Mengs infringes keeping by painting Parnassus (an earthbound mountain) in the clouds shown on the ceiling above (222). In the case of the Pisan pulpit, Forsyth notices pagan elements that announce their presence so strongly that what they represent clashes with Christian representation.

At the root of much of his engagement with art is a high value for the artist's ability to portray real individuals. Andrea del Sarto, "though a great colorist, had no poetry in his head, nor pathos in his heart." Forsyth was not impressed when asked to admire the glory of six entwined heavenly angels (he calls them an *innesto*, something that has been grafted on) within Santi di Tito's representation of Christ at table with the Pharisees. They are introduced above Christ in the fresco, showing him with his feet being anointed by "a woman who had lived a sinful life" (sometimes identified as Mary Magdalene): "I, who do not like glories, was more struck by the heavenly benignity which beamed in the Christ" (444). He enjoys a comic St. Joseph holding a book for an angel (198); and while the paraphernalia of an apotheosis of Lewis of Gonzago "may be very heavenly, what pleased me most was the young Prince himself springing out of this confusion in all the beauty of holiness" (184). So high is his esteem for the human that the divine plays second fiddle, and he reflected that a little alteration to da Vinci's *St. John the Baptist* would turn it into a pagan image still worthy of admiration: "So jocund is his smile and so delicate his beauty, that, were the crossed reed transformed into a *thyrsus* and the skin around his loins into a panther's, he might pass for a young Bacchus. How a mere trifle can canonize a figure which, placed in a church, would be worshipped by thousands!" (270). There is not a trace of prudery here. Forsyth could discuss whether a model of a phallus found in Herculaneum signified a brothel and could conclude that it was "probably the badge of the Ithyphallic rite" (305). And noticing the genital bulge on the Termini set "on shafts of oriental alabaster," he observed "where the flower of the marble projects for the sexual distinction" (222).

Forsyth's interest in the technical side of the works of art arises out of his intense observation and his wish to understand the potential and limits of the medium used. An interesting example is his account of scagliola, a mixture of differently colored gypsum (selenite) particles with glue, which is cleverly applied to a surface where it hardens and looks like the most astonishing marble, with colors more vivid than the natural stone. Forsyth's visit to Vallombrosa takes him to the monastery, an important center for the eighteenth-century revival of *scagliola* artifacts that became popular in England with people such as Horace Walpole and John Nash (the technique is kept alive today by a few specialized craftsmen): "Don Hugford, a monk of English extraction, revived the art of *Scagliuola*. This art had been confined to the imitation of inanimate objects, until his improvements gave it the *chiaroscuro* necessary to landscape and the human figure. I remarked at Vallombrosa that all Hugford's pictures are cracked in the outlines, and, on my return to Florence, I mentioned this defect to Stoppioni, who is Hugford's descendant in the art. Stoppioni imputed it to an improper oil used in the first method; as no such flaws appear in his own works, or in those of his master Gori" (83). Forsyth's spirit of inquiry makes him seek out, on his return to Florence, the right person, Stoppioni, with whom he can discuss the matter, as he already knows how the process is achieved. Thinking about it, he compares it in his mind as being analogous to *encaustic* work and better, for "it resists the action of the air, it gives solidity to colour, and the selenite, though inserted like mosaic, is not so subject to dissolution." He knows of five artists working on the revival of encaustic work, which uses wax as a medium, one of them being Quatremere de Quincy, a French artist who publicly opposed Napoleon's removal of works of art from Italy. Related to encaustic is *cestrotum* work, which Forsyth thinks should be regarded as poker work. Sounding arcane now, Forsyth contributes then to a lively debate about a technique described by Pliny but seeming to have three interpretations according to a near contemporary dictionary of fine arts.[10]

Another case of Forsyth's keen interest in process and technique concerns the unrolling of the papyri at Herculaneum. Seventeen hundred carbonized papyri had been discovered in charred rolls. Father Antonio Piagi, an expert on ancient manuscripts in the Vatican library, had invented a machine that unrolled the volumes, but they often exploded into little bits and the writing faded very quickly on exposure to light. When Forsyth visited, an English antiquary, John Hayter, had been commissioned by Ferdinand IV, king of Naples, to try to recover the texts on these precious objects.

> Mr. Hayter follows Piagi's process, but with a greater command of assistants, and has in less than two years unrolled forty volumes.
>
> These rolls, before they are devolved, look like sticks of charcoal. They have no vestige of *umbilicus*, or *cornua*, or an ornament. Their characters are legible only in a certain light, by a gloss and relief which distinguish the ink, or rather black paint, from the tinder. Cut, crushed, crumbled on the edge, and caked by the sap remaining in the leaf, they require in the operator a kind of medical sagacity to meet their variety of wounds; for, in gluing rashly the injured parts, he might reach the heart of a volume, while working at the outside. (287)

The *umbilicus* is the stick to which the papyrus is fixed, and the *cornua* is the ball at the end. Hayter eventually succeeded in unrolling two hundred papyri, which Forsyth would not have known. The writing has faded, so the contents have been preserved as transcripts only. Later, in 1819–1820, Sir Humphry Davy had limited success in unrolling some more, using chemical methods. Attempts to unroll the papyri persisted until the middle of the twentieth century. In this century, x-ray microcomputed tomography is proving more successful in preserving the scrolls, but unfortunately, the means for the computer to distinguish the carbon ink from the carbonized paper has not yet been devised.

In the Villa Borghese, Forsyth saw the statue called the Fighting Gladiator (see figure 6.1). It had been revered since the early 1600s as a beautiful model of fine male anatomy. Forsyth had seen Piranesi's engravings, but there were not enough. He wrote, "The details of a single statue would require fifty, and perhaps the sublime of the original would escape them all" (201). This astute judgment is similar to one made by Ernst Gombrich some years ago, when he argued that an engraver has to select a line to represent the curve of the cheek and the curl of a smile. In a lecture at Cambridge, he spoke of the eighteenth-century equivalent of a coffee table book inspiring the Grand Tourist to see in a statue what the engraver chose to select: a bust differently lit can change expression from the Apollonian to the Dionysiac, but the engraver has to choose which.

Viewing casts often offered a better preparation for seeing the real thing than engravings. In the case of this statue (but not in many others), this was a possibility. Charles I of Great Britain had had a bronze cast made and others appeared in a

FIGURE 6.1 Nicolas Dorigny, 1704: Borghese Gladiator. By permission of Museum of Philadelphia.

number of aristocratic households. But casts were not easily seen by the public at large. They were for royalty and gentry. The small supply was very strictly controlled by the Italian owners. In the later part of the 1700s, Prince Borghese prevented the taking of further molds of the Gladiator, refusing, among others, the Empress of Russia. Nevertheless, Forsyth might have seen a cast of this particular statue. One owner of a copy was Charles Townley, who admitted visitors to view it at his villa at 7 Park Street, Westminster, along with originals in his fine collection of antiquities. At the time, the sculptures from Italy were identified as Greek, but after 1816, when the marble relief from the Parthenon was bought by the British Museum from Lord Elgin, they were reclassified as Roman—excellent copies of Greek originals or in the Greek tradition. Townley's collection may have been one of the means whereby Forsyth educated his taste and enlarged his information about classical statuary prior to his going aboard.[11]

Yet casts, if superior to engravings, would not have communicated the experience of the real thing. They were of varying quality, often rendering detail poorly and losing the particular gloss and feel of the surface of the original. (Although the gloss of a statue in the nineteenth century may not have been what it had been when first made. The Venus de Medici that Napoleon acquired was cleaned at the Musée Napoléon of the remaining colors of gold hair and red lips.) While there was an increased market in statuettes, notably from the studio of Zoffolli in the 1790s, these added the further difficulty of visualizing the dimension. All copies obscured the traces that revealed a restoration and made it more difficult to detect forgeries. Forsyth deprecated the zeal of antiquarians to tamper with the evidence of a statue. In *Italy*, he remarks, "How boldly do those restorers make up dismembered trunks, and affix attributes! Having found at *Præneste* one female body in a stooping posture, they stuck an ancient head with half-shut eyes on the shoulders, set a pail at the feet, and then called the whole a Danaid" (200). He goes on to describe a similar process with a Minerva and a Perseus and then adds a self-mocking conclusion, which strikes a chord with any scholar wrestling with ambiguous evidence: "Thus we lose the freedom of judging on the original trunk, and the pleasurable torment of conjecture." This hits exactly the fascinations and frustrations of scholarship. So Forsyth concludes, "Whoever would know what really remains here of the ancients, must examine on the spot." Even then, the difficulties are large. For instance, "statues of Belvedere have received so much modern work to restore the ancient, that we can hardly distinguish what is original from what is added. Either the old surface is scraped into the whiteness of the new, or the new has received the yellow ivory gloss of the old; while the cement which unites them is so imperceptibly fine, that Persius' metaphor is here realized—their juncture literally eludes the severest nail."[12]

As we noticed in chapter 4, Forsyth opens with an epigraph from Persius as though he were an alter ego. Here Forsyth's nail almost merges with that of Persius.

Apart from the experience of actually seeing the Gladiator in its original marble, of being a witness to its presence, there was another reason to examine it closely. Winckelmann had questioned whether the sculpture really was a gladiator. Perhaps he was a Greek warrior. Forsyth had come inspired by Winckelmann's groundbreaking *History of Ancient Art*, ready to apply its ideas and also to criticize them. French translations had appeared in 1766 and 1781, and Italian translations in 1779 and 1783–1784 (the latter was a revision by Carlo Fea of the former).[13] The book excitingly introduced a new way of appreciating sculpture. Winckelmann tried to make sense of a body of art from the Egyptians to the Romans, "not as a mere chronicle of epochs, and of the changes that occurred within them," for "it is my intention to attempt to present a system" without needing to discuss every artist but "any monuments of art which can in any way elucidate the subject are carefully noticed."[14] Knowledge of the historical background was necessary to understand what the representation was, in order to appreciate the beauty of a sculpture, and a minute description of the materials, anatomical details, and dress would aid a just aesthetic appreciation. Forsyth follows these precepts, paying tribute to the founder of a modern critical theory of art, when he visits the palace of Cardinal Albani: "Here Winkelmann grew into an antiquary under the Cardinal's patronage and instruction, and he projected his history of art, which brings this collection continually into view." Winckelmann, as Albani's librarian and antiquary, knew intimately the Cardinal's magnificent collection. Normally, Forsyth says, "Deep learning is generally the grave of taste. But the learning which is engaged in Greek and Roman antiquities, as it embraces all that is beautiful in art, rather refines and regulates our perceptions of beauty" (221).

Reading Winckelmann was liberating. Forsyth absorbed his findings, sometimes disagreeing with his interpretations, though not in the inimical spirit that the Abate Fea had brought to the task of editing the German art historian's masterwork. For example, "what Winkelman calls the second and third styles of Etruscan sculpture, [belongs] either to Greece, or to the Greek part of Italy" (107). Forsyth criticizes "the group called Paetus and Arria" in the Villa Ludovisi on the grounds that the Paetus looked too ferocious for the character,[15] but neither did he accept the interpretation of Winckelmann, who thought that the male figure was "the Guard who slew both Canace and himself," for "he looks still too fierce for so sentimental a cut-throat" (224).[16] Forsyth also notes, "Amazons are the only female figures that I have seen bound, or rather belted in this primitive way. Some of the Amazons, on the *sarcophagus* of the Capitol, have both cinctures at once. This I also remarked on the Gabine Diana and on some pretended Venuses. I have touched on these points because Winkelmann appears to have mistaken them" (291n). At other times, Forsyth adopts Winckelmann's new ideas without comment. When he saw sea spray scouring the "once-admired group" of the "famous" Farnese Bull, now exposed to the elements, he notes that Winckelmann had downgraded its importance when he said that "most of the shaft as well as the greater proportion of the figures themselves, is new."[17]

In his account of his own visit to see the Gladiator in the Villa Borghese, Forsyth reveals the ardor and pleasure of the seeker at last in the promised land, ready to respond with astonishment and to wonder at the glory and equally ready to examine, compare, and discuss:

> The very porch contains statues which would grace the interior of any palace. What then is within? Within are the Gladiator, the Silenus, the Hermaphrodite, the Apollo and Daphne, each supreme in its own saloon, and encircled with subordinate statues and paintings related to it. In the hall is Curtius starting from the wall, and in the magnificent *galleria* an assemblage of busts which the world cannot match. When dazzled with sculpture and *scagliuola,* the eye has rare basalts, and oriental granites, and porphyries to repose on; porphyry red as blood,[18] and green, and even grey.

In their account of the rising importance of the Gladiator, Haskell and Penny include Forsyth's notion that it is one of those "great preceptive statues" (217), which served at Rome as canons of the art. Along with the Venus de Medici, the Belvedere Apollo, and the Torso, these statues were held as embodying the finest practices of classic art. By calling it the "last," Forsyth registers his sense of the loss of the others to the Musée Napoléon. This sculpture would not stay much longer. It was sold by Prince Camillo Borghese in 1807 to his brother-in-law, Napoleon, and remains to this day in the Louvre:

> But is the figure a Gladiator? On the left arm are straps which indicate a shield, and the head is bare. Now, all gladiators except the Retiarius wore helmets, and the Retiarius had no shield. The elastic bound of this admirable figure was not more appropriate to the amphitheater than to the field of battle. But as the face bears nothing of the heroic or ideal style, perhaps the subject was only a Barbarian Chief, like the Dying Gladiator, for both had shields, but no helmets. Some, I understand, have lately called this figure a Hector: but should Hector ever appear in art without that helmet which gives him a kind of surname in Homer, and affords one of the finest pictures in the Iliad? Hector was for ages a common portrait in Greece, and always young: the person who resembled his portrait so much, and

> was trodden to death by the curiosity of a Spartan mob, was a youth; but the figure in question is a man near 40 years old. (217)

Here Forsyth elaborates and supports Winckelmann's doubts. His judgment that this is a barbarian warrior arises from a combination of areas of learning, all assimilated beforehand and ready to be called to the bar as witnesses. He has knowledge of the detail of the dress and techniques of gladiatorial combatants, a sense of the idealized portraiture of Greek sculpture, an aesthetic appreciation of the statue's pose, possession by heart of the text of the *Iliad*, and recollection of the traditional history surrounding its stories. In addition, he is able to compare it in his mind with the Dying Gladiator that he saw in Napoleon's loot in Paris. That he also identifies as a "Barbarian Chief" (or as it is now called, a "Gaul") shows he is aware of the latest debate and is also on the side of those whose views succeeded. Ennio Visconti originally recorded his opinion that these were warriors[19] when he was acting as keeper of the antiquities at the Borghese, but when Forsyth arrived in Rome, he may not have known this. He does not seem to have met Visconti, who had fled to Paris as an enemy of the pope and was curating the Italian treasures in the Musée Napoléon.

A range of aesthetic, structural, and moral considerations informs Forsyth's appreciation of architecture. The Colosseum (figure 6.2) was almost always mentioned in travelogues of Rome. Breval gives two magnificent double-spread engravings of the Colosseum and furnishes an elegant and relaxed comment on this supremely important building. He tells us the emperors who built the Colosseum were Vespasian and Titus. Then he agreeably quotes a fulsome compliment by the epigrammatist Martial, crediting Domitian (who had no hand in the building of the magnificent structure), and notes that it occupies the supposed gardens of Nero's Golden House. Forsyth is more vigorous and fiercely informed. Everything is observation of particulars and reflection drawn from a wide reading. Accurately discerning stones out of place, "evidently drest for a different purpose," and architectural principles confounded, including arcades that "are grossly unequal" and Corinthian columns that replace the acanthus decoration with "the thickest water-plants," he believes that the two emperors built in haste, fearful of the work being cut short by their deaths. Its engineering principles enabled the building "to resist fires, and earthquakes, and lightning, and sieges" until "barbarians rent that consolidating ring" and, he adds ironically, "Popes widened the breach." When it was entire, "a child might comprehend its design in a moment, and go direct to his place without straying in the porticos, for each arcade bears its number engraved, and opposite to every fourth arcade was a staircase." He examines the whole design, quoting the

FIGURE 6.2 Henry Abbot, Theodòre Fielding, 1820: Colosseum. By permission of NYPL.

architectural specifications of Vitruvius and applauding the Colosseum's ingenious design and safety measures for disbursing crowds after the performance.

His account of the performance, however, provokes a moral reflection on the vices of ancient Rome. The very structures proclaim the enormity of the entertainment, as he notices there are two aqueducts:

> Every nation has undergone its revolution of vices; and, as cruelty is not the present vice of ours, we can all humanely execrate the purpose of amphitheaters, now that they lie in ruins. Moralists may tell us that the truly brave are never cruel; but this monument says "No." Here sat the conquerors of the world, coolly to enjoy the tortures and death of men who had never offended them. Two aqueducts were scarcely sufficient to wash off the human blood which a few hours' sport shed in this imperial shambles. Twice in one day came the senators and matrons of Rome to the butchery; a virgin always gave the signal for slaughter, and when glutted with bloodshed, those ladies sat down in the wet and streaming *arenæ* to a luxurious supper. (147)

The vigor of moral outrage is contained in the clash of two opposing sets of value-laden words: "senators," "matrons," "virgin," "luxurious supper" set against "shambles," "butchery,"[20] "slaughter," "bloodshed." The technical word *arenae* also contains its moral charge, for the Latin originally meant the sand strewn to soak up the blood of the dying and wounded mortals. An additional poignancy is given to the reflection that "cruelty is not the present vice" by the knowledge that Forsyth, himself, was writing this from a Napoleonic prison after seven years of confinement. He knew at firsthand the sufferings of the conquered. Those of the Italian people are also never far from his thoughts, whether writing about the pillaging of artworks by the French, the benevolent reforms of Leopoldo "before the rights of man agitated Europe," which failed because they depended on a single individual and not on the people, or the desolation of Ferrara and Mantua, where sullen silence and covert rebellion against empire showed in adopting revolutionary dress and customs.

The Colosseum also carried a greater charge than mere antiquarian regret for the loss of a noble edifice. It underlined a sense that imperial ambitions of absolute power, involving cruelty, had returned under Napoleon so that the French empire could be content to extinguish the remains of an ancient culture. Forsyth did not witness the good works of de Tournon, Napoleon's *prefet* [chief of the prefecture] at Rome;[21] when Forsyth saw it, whole columns were buried in rubbish, stables were shored up against the building, and it was thought to be on the verge of collapse, such that future generations would never see it:

> Such reflections check our regret for its ruin. As it now stands, the Coliseum is a striking image of Rome itself:—decayed—vacant—serious—yet grand;—half grey and half green—erect on one side and fallen on the other, with consecrated ground in its bosom—inhabited by a beads-man; visited by every cast; for moralists, antiquaries, painters, architects, devotees, all meet here to meditate, to examine, to draw, to measure, and to pray. "In contemplating antiquities," says Livy, "the mind itself becomes antique." It contracts from such objects a venerable rust, which I prefer to the polish and the point of those wits who have lately profaned this august ruin with ridicule. (148)

Forsyth's observation of the aqueducts raised an important question about why so much water was needed. He found his answer in cleansing the blood of the slain. It fitted all that could be seen then, for soil had built up over the years in the arena, and shrines had been erected. After his visit, the arena of the Colosseum was excavated in 1813 by the French, discovering underground passages and cells before closing them up, and it was explored again on a number of occasions. The keeper of the Bodleian Library, John Parker, conducted a huge photographic record of Rome in 1876, following great excavations of the arena in 1874 and 1875. He proposed that some of the underground area was filled with water for the sea fights called naumachia. Writing about the 1813 excavation, he drew attention to the plan that was drawn of the underground passages of the Colosseum that were then exposed: "It represents clearly the passages round it, and two straight parallel channels down the middle of it for naval fights, which were in reality not a representation of sea-fights but of river fights."[22] When wooden covers over the passages were taken away, boats could sail up and down the central channels creating the illusion of a sea fight. His book showed photos of the remains of canals (his plate 10[23]). However, his interpretation has been challenged in modern times. The continuing process of archaeological discovery shows the truth of Forsyth's dictum: "Every new step in science is the correction of an old one. Science may be considered as the art of remedies which originate in defect and end in it."

Turning toward Forsyth's criticism of painting, we should not expect him to write the modern critic's extended analysis of a work of art. He writes for readers "who have already examined the objects I review" (v). This was not an unreal expectation. The popularity of the Grand Tour, with its familiar stopping places and popular sights to see, ensured that a mention of the name of an artist or of the title of a painting thrilled or excited the anticipation of the reader before more was said. Where now we expect more introduction and explanation, less had to be said to engage interest and discussion. An additional consideration was to avoid exhaustive explication. Forsyth follows in the steps of Dr. Johnson, whose notes on

Shakespeare were brief, for "it is natural to delight more in what we find or make, than in what we receive. . . . I have therefore shewn so much as may enable the candidate of criticism to discover the rest."[24] Forsyth's pithy approach was valued by many of his readers, beginning with Hobhouse, who wrote that Forsyth "presents just as much, and no more as serves to present the intended image to the reader."[25] Henry James in his *Italian Hours* wrote in the chapter on "Tuscan Cities" that "most people remember the happy remark" of Forsyth "who touched a hundred other points in his 'Italy' scarcely less happily" regarding the buildings of the Duomo in Pisa: "There stand the Cathedral, the Baptistery, the Leaning Tower, and the Campo Santo; all built of the same marble, all varieties of the same architecture, all venerable with years, and fortunate both in their society and their solitude" (8). James noted that this is Forsyth's frequent manner of writing. Shelley also noted the passage:

> There stands the pile—a tower amid the towers;
> And sacred domes; each marble ribbed roof,
> The brazen-gated temples, and the bowers
> Of solitary wealth[26]

In this case, Forsyth thrusts you into a perspective that is historical. The view is a snapshot into the capital's magnificent past as you emerge from the nineteenth-century world of Pisa's crumbled towers incorporated into "modernized" buildings to see works of art "venerable with years," each fine in itself but made finer by "their society and their solitude," supporting each other in an artistic harmony and surviving apart from the changed city.

In another concise judgment, Forsyth puts us at the side of the tenth-century artist presented with a problem of expressing deep belief. Greek paintings of the Madonna and Child of this period are all uniform because "the mode of painting both [figures] was fixed by the ritual. Painting in that age was satisfied with producing mere forms, and did not aspire at expression or movement. Conscious of her own weakness, she called in the aid of gold, and azure, and labels, and even relief; for these pictures are raised like japan-work. They present all the meagreness, the angular and distinct contours, the straight, stiff parallelism of attitude, the vacant yet pretty little features, which are common to the productions of unenlightened art" (40). The tenth-century artist, who is unconsciously bound by a contemporary convention of drawing that a more enlightened age will expand, strives to give extra significance through other means, such as color and texture.

In a more intimate identification with the individuality of a painter, Forsyth mentions "some pictures of Del Sarto, and among these a beautiful accident of art.

Andrea, having four large saints to paint on the altar-piece, was embarrassed by a panel which divided them into pairs. To cover this defect he carelessly rubbed two cherubs on the board, and was surprized to find these children of chance far more admirable than their principals" (83). This time, Forsyth's perspective is one of the immediacy of solving a specific problem, imputing to the painter what is also his own reaction to the quality of the painting. In the Vallombrosa altarpiece or reredos of the Quattro Santi (Four Saints; figure 6.3), two large boards are separated by a narrow board. The four figures are large and, although natural, stiffly delineated in the large boards, whereas the two putti are put in with a light touch in a compartment in the lower half of the central board with little sense of connecting the two halves. Forsyth's sympathetic response is persuasive. What is to be done with the disparities? How evocative of the artistic involvement are the words he "carelessly rubbed two cherubs on the board"! His emotional response becomes even more illuminating as a result of facts subsequently uncovered that explain the "embarrassment." Accounts differ on who painted what and on what was missing from

FIGURE 6.3 Andrea del Sarto: Vallombrosa altar panels

the central panel.[27] An early copy of the altarpiece, drawn possibly by Federico Zuccaro, shows that it may once have held a thirteenth-century Madonna and Child, a small painting above the cherubs in the central panel. Forsyth does not mention it, and maybe it was lost before he saw it or when the work was removed in 1810 in pieces from the Vallombrosan Chiesa di Romito delle Celle [church of the anchorites] to the Uffizi Gallery. Either way, a blank compartment or an out-of-scale Madonna and Child in a thirteenth-century style would not unite the two large High Renaissance side panels. The panels themselves show a stiff grouping because they try to blend the symbolic with the actual. St. Michael and John the Baptist are painted with clothing and attributes that allegorize them. They are paired with two donors from the order of monks at Vallombrosa—the founder San Giovanni Gualberto and a later member, San Bernardo degli Uberti—who are painted realistically in their contemporary clothing. However, there is no interaction or exchange of looks between or among the two pairs. It would seem that Andrea del Sarto was confronted with an almost unresolvable artistic problem in converting a small thirteenth-century Madonna and Child into a large altarpiece, where he was required to show the saints, including two who were donors, towering over the holy scene. As Forsyth observes, within this difficulty, the cherubs are nonchalantly at ease. One snuggles into the other, who slightly leans toward him.

Forsyth can be equally severe in other areas. At the Royal Gallery in Florence, there is too much to take in. The exhibition is no help to the viewer who would exercise his taste and judgment. Forsyth's account pithily builds up into a memorable and dismissive image of a collection valued and exhibited only for the size of its commercial worth: "The paintings of this Gallery run strangely into series—a series of Florentine portraits classed on the ceiling in compartments of the same form—a series of 850 illustrious foreigners running on the same level in frames of the same size—a series of 350 painters crowded into the same apartment—a series of the arts—a series of the elements, all exact to the same dimensions. Such uniformity betrays the furnishing taste of a tradesman" (41). Many fine easel paintings had gone from the Roman villas that Forsyth praises, but murals remained. The comparison he makes between Guercino's and Guido Reni's *Aurora* ceilings was a familiar way of evaluating both of these great works of art, especially as Guercino's tempera ceiling was painted as a response to the fresco of the established and venerated Guido. The reputation of the two, particularly of Guido, would suffer in 1844 at the hands of Ruskin,[28] who was followed by others, including Berenson.[29] They have not returned to the level of esteem that they had in the eighteenth century. To appreciate the taste of Forsyth's period, it is worth trying to understand why he gives them such a high valuation and also how he makes a distinction between the two. His language is concise but compelling to those who have seen each artist's

Aurora. In his day, they could have been known by the engravings of the Guercino by Francis Pozzi (1780) and of the Guido by Raphael Morghen (1788):

> In another Casino is Guercino's great work of the Aurora [figures 6.4 and 6.5], which covers the ceiling and is detailed into compartments. If compared with [Guido's] Aurora of the Ruspigliosi [*sic*] pavilion [figure 6.6], its composition will be found less obvious and its story more learned. In allegorizing Nature, Guercino imitates the deep shades of night, the twilight grey, and the irradiations of morning with all the magic of *chiaroscuro*; but his figures are too mortal for the region where they move. The work of Guido is more poetic, and luminous, and soft, and harmonious. Cupid, Aurora, Phoebus form a climax of beauty, and the Hours seem as light as the clouds on which they dance. At such ceilings, you gaze till your neck becomes stiff and your head dizzy. They detain you, like the glorious ceiling of the Caracci, the sole object left to be admired at the Farnese palace except the palace itself.

The intensity of Forsyth's gaze that left him dizzy leaves us in no doubt of the huge attraction they both had for a man with his eighteenth-century taste. His description points up the great chasm that occurred, when following Ruskin, such terms as "insipid and sentimental" became common to describe the *Aurora*s. Contained in

FIGURE 6.4 Guercino: *Aurora* overview

FIGURE 6.5 Guercino: Aurora and the Hours, detail of center

Forsyth's praise of Guercino's representation as a "great work" is a sense of its vastness as well as its merit, for it covers not only the whole ceiling but some of the sides. It is painted as though the roof had blown off, taking some of the side walls with it, leaving "compartments" between the pillars on top of which some weeds had started to grow, giving the effect that we are looking up into a vertiginous sky where the figures are foreshortened in an extreme perspective, some emerging from darkness. We see the underside of the horses pulling the chariot, which has had its side sculpted low so that we can see Aurora, who otherwise would have been hidden. Forsyth describes it more sparely as having "the magic of chiaroscuro." His vocabulary is also rather technical in terms of space and personal absorption. He acknowledges the dizzying sense of space in more subdued tones because his focus is more on responding to the painting's immediacy and enjoying the subtlety of the color.

The Guido helps him define the Guercino by opposites: "obvious"/"learned"; "poetic"/"allegorizing"; "luminous and harmonious" / "magic of chiaroscuro"; "climax of beauty" / "too mortal [for heaven]." While we may want to notice other features of description, such as its proto-Romanticism, these judgments are also useful to us. Forsyth immediately recognizes that much thought lies behind the Guercino, who has replaced Guido's Apollo with Aurora in the chariot. What this means is left to us to consider: Guido's Aurora is part of the company of the other

FIGURE 6.6 Guido Reni: *Aurora*

hours, driven on by the sun in the central chariot, confronting dark clouds that half shade her as the dawn dispels the night before the advent of the sun. Guercino's Aurora is central to his story, which, unlike Guido, draws on a particular classical mythical narrative, the *Homeric Hymn to Aphrodite*. Aurora's aging but immortal husband, Tithonus, is wearily being roused from his bed by a cherub who pulls away the blanket that covers him in order to wake him so that he can watch her chariot. (Aurora had successfully petitioned the gods to make the prince of Troy, Tithonus, immortal but neglected to ensure that he would stay forever young. In a preparatory drawing for the painting, Guercino represented Tithonus as older and fatter and hunched, warding off a cherub who pulls him by the arm.) There is great interaction. The two horses leap forward, their proud necks arched, eyes flashing, forelegs prancing to strike the cloud of night with their hooves. Three women ride the cloud in excitement, pointing and gesticulating to each other while another, too near to the horses, flees, looking over her shoulder. A bat disappears toward the broken roof of a cave where a young woman and two babies appear to sleep (see figure 6.7). Forsyth knows these are learned allegories, requiring knowledge of classical authors and Renaissance iconography. When we look at the "obvious" Guido that Guercino is alluding to, it will enable us to recognize that the women on the cloud before the chariot are hours, the figures in the cave are related to Night, and maybe that the cherub over Aurora's head is the morning star. Without it, perhaps we would miss much. It is a point in favor of the Guido that it conveys its meaning more immediately, which Forsyth prefers.

When it comes to considering the particular meanings of the allegories in Guercino, Forsyth says it "will be found less obvious and its story more learned." Although Forsyth himself is learned, he puts this as a mark against Guercino's *Aurora* because the possibilities are many and the choices the viewer makes may in

FIGURE 6.7 Guercino: Night

the end be sidetracked from seeing the work into disputing meanings for their sake alone. The *Iconology* of Cesare Ripa Perugino (usually known as "Ripa"), first published in Rome in 1593 (and so available to Guercino when he was painting in 1623) serves to show why the "learning" of the painting could detain the viewer from the actual seeing. It went into many editions over two centuries, and an English digest by George Richardson, published in 1779,[30] could have been seen by Forsyth. Ripa's book is a compendium of emblematic representations of moral qualities and mythical figures, arranged alphabetically as an encyclopedia. It does not harmonize the entries from many historical sources; the painter and the critic are both free to select the elements that attract them. It is not prescriptive, and so it cannot be used as a decoder but is useful as a starting point. The reader who embarks on this may be startled to find that the woman in the cavern could be seen as Night and the baby in front of her to the left sleeps but the one behind her to the right is dead: Death and Sleep are twins. On the other hand, Night should be a black woman to represent the darkness after daylight. It could, however, be debated. As Gombrich wrote, we should avoid the "impression [that] has grown up among the unwary that symbols are a kind of code with a one-to-one relationship between the sign and the significance."[31] This immediately releases the painter's image-making into something more subtle and less restricted and also gives scope for the critics' scholarly disagreements. Gombrich, Seznec, and Wind,[32] who pioneered the modern study of the influence of emblem books on Renaissance art, disagree among themselves, despite vast erudition.

Forsyth does not venture down the path indicated here, although we do not doubt that he knows it could be done. For him, what is sublime is what can be "taken as a whole" and communicates a "unity of design." This is found in the direct and more "poetic" effect of Guido (10). Despite the distractions of the learned references in the Guercino, he admires the work's "deep shades of night, the twilight grey and the irradiations of morning with all the magic of *chiaroscuro*." The language of his appreciation is subtle and telling.

In its turn, the Guercino illuminates the *Aurora* of Guido. It too is a highly individual work. Guido refuses perspective and the effects of trompe l'oeil. We see his fresco on the ceiling as though it were a wall painting. It is surrounded by an ornate frame of plasterwork, with a female figure carved in basso relievo (projecting at a low level) at each corner. This is just a setting; we look past it to see a brightly lit group of figures in gorgeous color, moving as though they were in a stately Roman procession. In fact, the women who follow the chariot are taken from a Roman sarcophagus in the "Ruspigliosi pavilion." Guido's *St. Peter and St. Paul* (which Forsyth saw in Bologna) revels in the drama of chiaroscuro, but here the luminosity is a major part of the ethereal effect that Guido conveys. Energy of light and shade is replaced with serenity and formalized gesture, where each character strikes a pose representing a mood that would later strike a chord with those brought up in the eighteenth century on Boydell's Shakespeare gallery. They are not overtheatrical but seem to represent an internalized expression of mood, for heads are turned away or look past a neighbor. Each occupies a personal space, like singers expressing their predicament in an ensemble. Stendhal said of Reni that he had "absolument la sensibilité à la Mozart" [definitely the sensibility of Mozart].[33] There is no interaction, even in the women who loosely hold hands. Each gesture seems to have come at some significant moment and prompts us to identify the women as the hours and to know that the Apollo, the sun god, drives the chariot and therefore Aurora must precede him. The painting hints at classical allusions and the viewer readily makes the connections. Such a language was second nature to Forsyth, who lived with classical literature in his mind all the time and used remembered passages, as we saw with the epigraphs, as a way of defining events and situations. A literary sense works all the time with Forsyth. In continuation of his comparative way of thinking, here he uses one painting to help define another.

As we have seen with Forsyth's comparison of the lifelike waxwork to the distilled beauty of a Greek sculpture, the *Aurora* of Guido, with its poetry and harmony and clarity of significance, gains over the intellection, energy, and business of the Guercino, where the interactions "make it too mortal for the region where they move." Earlier we noticed how Poussin's *Massacre of the Innocents* enabled Forsyth through its artistic process to bear the horror of the subject. This was done by removing the confusion of many kinds of deaths and agonies to focus on the intense distress of just a few figures, who represented the event sufficiently and enhanced his sympathetic reaction. Poussin learned how to compose his painting by studying Guido's version of the same subject, *La strage degli innocenti*, which had already drastically reduced the numbers of murders of this often-painted scene to focus on a few. One of Guido's women, who is being pulled by the hair, is very like Poussin's central figure, whose hair is similarly grasped. It is a pity that Forsyth could not have seen that Guido in Italy; it was the first on the list of paintings that the French took under the Treaty of Tolentino, one of thirty-one fine paintings listed as having been looted from Bologna.[34]

We find that Forsyth is challenged by Michelangelo's *Last Judgment* (figure 6.8). We have seen him as the learned, skeptical, and ironic seeker. Here he is the observer, conscious of his own limitation and open to what is new. He is also the learned scholar reflecting in his "Remarks" on the opinions of others. The reputation of the fresco had raised controversy. The Richardsons had not enjoyed it, for it seemed to flout respectable notions; it was "full of Choquing Improprieties, and Absurdities, though some of These have been Corrected since by other Hands, by covering with Draperies what was most Offensive; but the wrong manner of Thinking in other respects could not be so easily alter'd, unless by demolishing the Whole Work."[35] Miscellaneous ideas did not cohere together: a beautiful thought "to express the Terror of that Day, the Blessed Virgin, (even She!) clings close to her Son" is destroyed because "other Saints do not express the like Terror, or indeed any Degree of it." Charon has been given the face of the pope's master of ceremonies because he criticized Michelangelo's picture, and there are other improper allusions. Such incidents betray the fault of the conception and the design: "The Composition of this Picture is no better than the Manner of Thinking, and absolute want of Harmony; and the Colouring of This and the rest of *Mich. Angelo's* Works in this Chapel is Black, and Harsh, so that the *Tout-ensemble* is very Disagreeable."[36] Smollett, in his tetchy tour of 1766, saw the "whole together as a mere mob, without subordination, keeping or repose."[37] But Reynolds in his farewell lecture to the Royal Academy (1790) proclaimed Michelangelo's genius as vigorous and imaginative, although wild and capricious. His sublime achievements provided the fire that energized the perfection, beauty, and taste of Raphael.[38] Forsyth includes the contending adverse criticisms in his account of the fresco. He too is at a loss in front of a work that challenges his received ideas. But he is too good a critic to retreat into stock notions and a comfortable downgrading of the artist in order to preserve his

FIGURE 6.8 Michelangelo: *Last Judgment*

preconceptions. At the outset, he has the technical knowledge to recognize that the color has been blackened by the smoke of candles, just as he did when interpreting the frescoes of Herculaneum, also faded by fire and time. He tries to be fair and address the work as though it were newly painted. What strikes him is the thought contained in the fresco:

> This immense work of the resurrection is too learned for me. I revered it rather as a monument in the history of Painting, and the cause of a great revolution in the art, than for any pleasure that it gave me. It includes too many pictures in one. The separating figure of Christ gives order and even

> symmetry to the upper region of the work; but plunging downwards, I was lost among Gods and men—angels and demons—in air, on earth, and the waters under the earth. In this dingy field, you stop only to smile at singularities, such as Peter restoring the keys with grim reluctance, Dante's devils, his Minos and his Charon diabolified. (203)

He meets the fresco with respect and begins to interpret and order the upper regions according to a harmony he understands. But his reading of its subject is intense and sweeps him off his feet, plunging him downward until lost in the nether regions. This is a perfect rendering of the passion of the work and the unsettling vision it contains. And there is nothing niggling in his reading. He is undisturbed and even amused by the passages of personal reference. And he connects it with another great Italian genius: Dante. This provides him with the following illuminating comparison:

> How congenial the powers of the poet and the painter! Bold and precipitating, they dash on to their immediate object in defiance of rules and ridicule. One critic charges this mighty master with anatomical pedantry, stripping every thing to display the muscles. Another condemns the intermixture of epic and satire, of Scripture and profane fable: a third, the constant repetition of the same Tuscan figure: a fourth heaps on him all the sins of the sublime—gloom, harshness, negligence—the fierce, the austere, the extravagant—tension, violence, exaggeration. In short, had we any doubt of that one transcendent merit which could atone for so many faults, the very multitude of his critics would dispel it.

The very disturbance of the work, provoking differing condemnations from other writers of "Remarks," validates its worth.

However, exhausted by the experience, Forsyth turns to Raphael and finds "this is passing from Homer to Virgil." The painting that catches his attention is *The School of Athens* (figure 6.9). His attention to the detail of the painting is minute, showing that he was capable of close analysis and detailed description of a painting in the manner of Ruskin, not just pithy, distilled, suggestive remarks. He applies an extensive knowledge of the individuals depicted and the appropriateness therefore of their expressions and considers whether its anachronism is appropriate, remembering that Dante had done a similar thing. Raphael's painting is full of "meaning" but not dependent on the abstruse collocations of allegory: "*The School of Athens* is a composition perfectly encyclopedic. Every head is a portrait, and every portrait is finished with a fidelity which usually enslaves; yet what variety of expression here! Every science is separate, yet what a chain of groups! No principal action prevails, yet how harmonious the whole! How superior such mortals, both in interest and effect, to the genii of allegory! How pardonable the anachronism which brings

FIGURE 6.9 Rafaello: *The School of Athens*

such a family together! Perhaps the divine painter caught his first idea from the divine poet" (205). A parallel to the preference for Raphael over Michelangelo may be drawn with the preference for Pope over the metaphysical poets in the eighteenth century. It is very interesting to see that in the case of Forsyth, this was not owing to a blindness to what the allegory represented but a preference instead for "decorum." It may be difficult for us, as post-Romantics, to recapture the sense of decorum that Michelangelo disturbed. But a useful coda is Forsyth's own commentary on a painting he saw in Venice and compared with one of Tintoretto's. He had seen Tintoretto's *Last Judgment* in the Palazzo Ducale and then moved to the next room to see another on the same subject by Palma, il Giovane (the Younger): "Palma's *Last Judgment* [figure 6.10] is another immense composition, but more intelligibly detailed. These artists seem fond of introducing their friends into such pictures. In one part of this work you see Palma's mistress in heaven [figure 6.12], in another the fickle lover sends her to hell [figure 6.11]" (338). Tintoretto's painting is a crowded long panel, one of the world's largest canvases at 74.1 feet by 29.9 feet. Palma's solo work is similarly wide but more ordered. Not as large as the Tintoretto, the canvas is as wide as the 60-foot wall it covers. The eye has difficulty taking in the whole expanse as it does with the vertiginous *Last Judgment* of Michelangelo. To overcome this, Palma's *Last Judgment* pictured an ordered frenzy of activity. Small reproductions cannot convey the scale and movement of the composition. Christ in majesty attended by the Virgin, surrounded by brilliant light, sits in the center at

FIGURE 6.10 Palma il Giovane: *Last Judgment*

FIGURE 6.11 Palma il Giovane: Falling woman, detail of *Last Judgment*

the top of the painting. Three angels encircle his throne, pressing souls toward him. The upper zone has the community of the already saved and Moses, with horns assigned by tradition[39] and his tablets of the Ten Commandments, is on the right. The lower zone is where the judgments are being carried out. With his right hand, Christ commands the elect to heaven and with his left casts the damned to hell. Six angels, sounding the trumpets of doom, dive into the multitudes, to separate them to the left and the right. Events match and contrast. The angels twist and turn like swimmers plunging, unsynchronized. Four angels in the center converge on the place of division. Further to the left, an angel in a light-crimson garment plucks a soul into heaven. Further to the right, an angel in an ochre garment and with a sword casts down a woman in blue skirts who is in free fall. She is the figure Forsyth identified as the painter's bare-breasted mistress, tumbling prone above one devil who has clawed hold of her leg and another who plucks at her dress and hair (figure 6.11). The same woman, as Forsyth noted, appears on the left, hurrying to heaven upright, on foot and covering her nakedness with her arms, now a penitent Magdalen (figure 6.12). Standing back from the detail, you see another harmonious arrangement. On the left side, the flesh tones of bare arms, necks, faces, torsos, and legs form a Blakeian swirl above the Magdalen in serpentine movement toward the

FIGURE 6.12 Palma il Giovane: Saved Magdalen, detail of *Last Judgment*

glory at the center and the top of the painting. The careful guidance of the eye by such elements of the composition is what makes it "intelligibly detailed" in contrast to Michelangelo's *Last Judgment*.

Forsyth's facility in the Italian language enabled him to also fully appreciate the Italian stage. Most of his contacts, as we have seen, were Italians with whom he could discuss and discover contemporary matters. His command of the language was excellent, so he could experience the language of the streets; we see him being amused by the "richest ribaldry" poured on him as he travels through Ronciglione and thinking the Venetian inflection was like the Welsh. He was a frequent theatergoer, admiring the comic actors Andolfati and Zanerini. He said Andolfati could "thrill the heart as well as shake the sides," although in at least three comedies, he had seen grotesquely inaccurate parodies of English aristocratic dress. He was at home with literary figures, talking to such people as Pignotti and Sacchetti, Alfieri's secretary. So he was well prepared for his encounter with the celebrated improvisatrice Fortunata Sulgher Fantastici, a practitioner of extempore poetry whom he heard several times.

Smollett had commended the talent of the improvisatore for its "wonderful fluency and precision. Thus, he will, at a minute's warning, recite two or three hundred verses, well turned, and well adapted, and generally mingled with an elegant compliment to the company."[40] Eustace was less astonished; he was simply amused by the performance that he saw, concluding, "The exhibition was perfectly new to us, and while we enjoyed it, we could not but agree that such an ease and versatility of talent, might if properly managed be directed to very great and very useful purposes."[41]

Forsyth's long account of his encounter has all the elements of sympathetic listening, openness, critical acumen, historical perspective, and a sense of multiple effects. He begins with recognizing the tradition of *poesia estemporanea* [extempore poetic composition]: "So early as the fifteenth century the two blind brothers Brandolini excelled here in singing Latin extempore. The crowned and pensioned Corilla drew lately the admiration of all Italy, and Signora Fantastici [figure 6.13] is now the *improvvisatrice* of the day" (49). A humorous lightness enters his description of the *convegni* [meetings] that she arranges "whenever she chooses to be inspired"—a kind of willed spontaneity. Despite the detached irony, he is caught up in her *estro* [fire of genius]; she "astonished me by her rapidity and command of numbers, which flowed in praise of the fair poetess [a previous performer], and brought her poem back to our applause." His ear is attuned to Italian metrication and flexibly responds to changes of mood. He observes, "Her numbers, however, flowed irregularly still varying with the fluctuation of sentiment; while her song corresponded, changing from aria to recitativo, from recitativo to a measured recitation" (50).

On two occasions, he proposes a subject. The first is a gift to her, for he suggests her fan and he appreciates her Pignotti-like description of "this little weapon" of coquetry, tracing its origin and use. In fact, all her renderings of poetic subjects show extensive reading in the classics, including "a minute acquaintance with the Argonautic fable." So the second subject he proposes is to test her range, and those familiar with Cowper's *The Task*[42] will readily sense his amusement in his punning reference: "Tired at last of demi-gods, I proposed the sofa for a task, and sketched to her the introduction of Cowper's poem. She set out with his idea, but, being once entangled in the net of mythology, she soon transformed his sofa into a Cytherean couch, and brought Venus, Cupid and Mars on the scene; for such embroidery enters into the web of every *improvvisatore*" (50). There is no dismissal of her talent when he catches her out. Instead, he launches into reflection on other improvisatori and the connection of their art with *vers d'occasion* [verse written for a particular occasion], such as laureate odes. He believes much resides in the enthusiasm and

FIGURE 6.13 After Angelica Kaufmann: Fortunata Fantastici, 1794

immediacy of the performance, for the poems in cold print do not live up to the remembered experience: "Judging from her studied and published compositions, which are dull enough, I should suspect that this impromptu-exercise seldom leads to poetical excellence." The art particularly flourishes in Italy because "an Italian *improvvisatore* has the benefit of a language rich in echoes. He generally calls in the accompaniment of song, a lute, or a guitar, to set off his verse and conceal any failures. If his theme be difficult, he runs from that into the nearest common-place, or takes refuge in loose lyric measures. Thus he may always be fluent and sometimes by accident be bright." Such improvisation is no small achievement and connects with a noble tradition: "In attending to the Italian *improvvisatori,* I began to find out, or perhaps only to fancy, several points in which they resemble their great predecessor Homer. In both may be remarked the same openness of style and simplicity of construction, the same digressions, rests, repetitions, anomalies. Homer has often recourse to shifts of the moment, like other *improvvisatori.* Like them he betrays great inequalities. Sometimes when his speech is lengthening into detail, he cuts it short and concludes. Sometimes when the interest and difficulty thicken, the poet escapes, like his heroes, in a cloud." A lengthy footnote buttresses the idea with relevant quotations from the *Iliad* and the *Odyssey.* But his account finishes with a lightness of touch in an amusing anecdote, showing his relish in small matters as well as the grand: "I once thought of Homer in the streets of Florence, where I once saw a poor cyclic [i.e., Homeric] bard most cruelly perplexed in a tale of chivalry. He wished to unravel; but every stanza gave a new twist to his plot. His hearers seemed impatient for the denouement, but still the confusion increased. At last, seeing no other means of escape, he vented his poetical fury on the skin of his tambourine, and went off with a '*maledetto*' ['curse it']" (51–53).

Such an extended examination, with its varied interest and nicely modulated tone, shows how capable Forsyth was of writing a well-honed essay worthy of a book of "Remarks." Similar praise can be given to the range of the discussions of the Borghese Gladiator and of the Colosseum. But this was not felt to be a consistent virtue of his book as a whole. In 1825, the *Edinburgh Magazine* said that despite many good things, *Forsyth's Italy* contained "inadequate and desultory notices." Too much of the Murray edition was unstructured. Such a perceived failing of a writer, eminently capable, should draw our attention to what we now consider to be important: the second edition was unfinished and Forsyth was not responsible for the desultoriness of the inserted passages. He would not have simply added his rejected notes to the end. We know this because his self-editing of *1813* was rigorous and shows that he wrote with a clear conception of how it should appeal to his audience. That book's primary purpose was to liberate him from prison by showing him to be a scholar writing in the reflective tradition of "Remarks" on cultural matters. As we have seen, it also served to sustain him in various ways under the constraint and anguish of prison. It helped him both endure prison and enjoy a kind of mental traveling. But he said he was dissatisfied with what he wrote for *1813.*

The manner in which it was produced had disadvantages leading to weaknesses he felt might be in the book. Forsyth tried to deflect criticism by referring to them in his own advertisement prefacing *1813* (v). He had not set out to write a book; he felt that Italy was "a beaten subject," and his journal was not designed as a source for that and was begun late in his travels. Other than having an excellent memory and a keen mind, he did not have the best materials before him to furnish his reflections. *1813* is not a thematic survey or the kind of comparative study that brings together critical traditions from other writings, even though it does recall a number of debates. It has different virtues. It owes its shape and tone to the circumstances of its production. Forsyth chose a chronological account of his travels in order to profit from his own journal, written without a book in mind, as it was what he had in prison at the beginning as the prime source for the re-creation of his experiences and for reflection on what they meant. There were no adequate library resources to hand in Verdun. It is remarkable how much he was able to recreate and how fresh his responses are. This is thanks to his intense studies before going to Italy. It is also a major achievement that he was able to manage the strong emotion and moral outrage provoked by his reflections so that the therapeutic value was there for him and also so that he was still able to write a skillfully concealed satiric commentary on the political state of the nation. Inevitably, his chronological approach meant that he would be less systematic in his critical dissertations. In the final pages, he would have less to dwell upon, for that was the time when he was hurrying to escape from the prospect of being caught up in a war: "My stay in Venice was short. We make the tour of Italy, as we make the circuit of a gallery. We set out determined to let nothing escape us unexamined, and thus we waste our attention while it is fresh, on the first objects, which are not generally the best. . . . We run through the last rooms with a rapid glance. Such a feeling as this will account for the hurried manner in which I passed through the few final towns of my journey, and this feeling was enforced by the dread of an impending war" (341). In terms of the book's initial purpose of gaining his release, the final pages telling of his haste serve his emotional appeal well, leading up to the final sentence, which shouts rather than belonging to the quieter tones of the study: "The next day I was arrested as a British subject, and I am now passing the TENTH YEAR OF MY CAPTIVITY" (356). Before this hurry comes his last view of a great painting, Guido Reni's *St. Peter and St. Paul*, discussed in chapter 3 for its fineness and as standing as a marker for his sense of his own prematurely aged condition. We can see that placing this backward glance near the end has an artistic shaping in the Cadell edition of 1813. Isaac added in the Murray edition pages, almost a quarter more of the whole text, after that original end, thus concluding it with the weakest and most fragmentary rejected passages, the ones that Forsyth had been most likely leave out altogether. And so the book acquired a miscellaneous and unstructured quality, and it comes to a lame conclusion. Forsyth did not live to see this, but it does underline two things about the edition published after his death. The miscellaneous scrappiness of the last part of *1816* did not improve it as a representative of the considered reflections of the tradition of "Remarks." However, it supplied additional raw material that could have helped fill out a different one that did. Parts of this material already had been commended in the reviews.

While Forsyth did not explain the reason for his dissatisfaction to Isaac, I think we can say that, like some of the perceptive reviewers, he thought it was too thin, rather like Breval thinking Addison's book a "sample." The evidence for this is in what he was doing to prepare *1816*, although what it implies has to be conjecture. He was going to do more than just correct the many errors he found in the first edition; *1813* was to be a base text that he would use to produce a better book, for he had his rejected papers beside him, already sorted into three sections and titled for use. And from November 1814, he had the collections of the British Museum, where the reading room had become a vital resource. It had been moved to become two rooms to accommodate a growing collection of newspapers and journals and had about four thousand annual attendances. This is where he would have access to other contemporary accounts of travels and art and also reviews that would inform him of what standards of taste had become. In addition, he could renew his knowledge of the works of art by various means. He had brought back from Scotland in April 1815 his books, which Michael Anderson, the Edinburgh bookseller, called "an excellent collection." Much of this, such as the etchings by Piranesi and the writings of Winckelmann, would assist the expansion of his reflections on the works of art. The British Museum also had a fine collection of prints and drawings, recently augmented by the Cracherode bequest, which Forsyth could consult. The collection had already become fine and substantial enough to tempt in 1806 a print dealer, Robert Dighton, to steal prints from those that were lightly tipped into guard-volumes [covers that protected the prints]. He was able to do this for eighteen months, partly because the collection was big enough for the loss not to be noticed and also because it had not been cataloged by the keeper, who was subsequently sacked. Most of the prints were recovered. There was also another improvement that would have encouraged Forsyth to use the museum rather than write in his library at home. While Forsyth was imprisoned in France, the museum's collection of casts and originals of classic sculpture had grown. Townley (d. 1805) bequeathed his collection of about three hundred sculptures to the museum as a nucleus of a rapidly expanding department of antiquities.

What would *Forsyth's Italy* have become if Forsyth had lived to complete it? We can agree with the reviews that we should have liked more art criticism, noticing that reviewers thought Forsyth well capable of giving it. Part of his dissatisfaction with the first edition must have been that on a personal level, the looting denied him the chance to appreciate many great works he had hoped to see in their Italian setting. His experience of traveling in Italy had been diminished by their absence. In the context of the postwar years, an enlarged discussion of these missing works would have been timely. While it was formerly a good device to present himself to Napoleon as simply a traveler, experiencing for the first time a longed-for journey to Italy, we know that he had more experience and information than he had included in *1813*. He had been to Paris before 1802, and he had gone again then, knowing what to look for in Italy, such as "the admired Peruginos," which he found were no longer there. After the wars, he was free to compare his pre-Napoleonic impressions of the Paris collection of art with the Napoleonic style of 1802, for he had actually made a study of what was there. As he revealed in his revision of the text for *1816*, when he was in Paris before he traveled to Italy, he was "engaged by the great museum, and the revolutions which that capital had undergone since my former visit." When under house arrest in Paris, did he go again when he visited the Tuileries? In any case, he had information about the missing works of art that he could write about. He lived to see the first steps made to dispossess the Musée Napoléon of its extractions; when he died, in September 1815, Canova's mission to negotiate for the return of Italy's pictures and sculptures was nearing completion. Only slightly over half the looted paintings were returned, and some were never restored to their original owners. The best known of the returnees were Laocoön and the Venus de Medici. Within a month of his death, the first wagons bearing returned art treasures were rolling toward Milan.

If we restore the excised passages to occur within the book in the order they were conceived, we see that Forsyth's gifted appreciation of the works of art in Italy often expands into reflections, expressing a regard for its people and an involvement in their world. These suppressed passages show the fertility of his mind. His account of Leopoldo, drawn from Fabbroni and Fontana, had led him further into speculation about princes and the difference between a benevolent despot and a mercenary adventurer. Under the constraint of prison, he had to omit these subversive reflections and do the same with other passages that strayed into areas that would have displeased an audience of French arbiters. This cramped the book he was impelled to publish in prison. In the postwar period, he could expand on his ideas and also research contemporary publications to address issues they had in common with his. Formerly, he had felt the lack of this and had expressed a wish he had been able to consult others, as he explains in his advertisement prefacing *1813*: "I design my observations chiefly for them who have already examined the objects I review: but not without anxiety, which the lateness of their appearance is but too well calculated to excite. How far they may have lost interest, or been anticipated by publications in England during my long captivity, I have no means of knowing. My misfortune denies me all acquaintance with the works of others and may perhaps claim some indulgence for the many defects of mine" (v–vi).

When he was in London again, he was already reading the reviews and maybe looking to see whether he might write for one of the journals, such as the *Quarterly Review*. We know something of that sort was said in a letter now missing because Isaac replies that he is sorry that Forsyth would not make money with them; either the reviews did not pay well or there was no opening for Forsyth: "Your account of the mode of conducting Reviews in Lond^{n} astonished me, so very little do we at the extremities know what is doing in the centre. It not only surprizes me but disapoints me sadly, for I had in my own mind reckond on your taking at least a couple of Hundreds from that Source, annually" (*L* 29). As well as getting information about contemporary publications on Italy from the reading room, Forsyth appears to have attended coffeehouses, many of which had journals and newspapers for customers to read. One of Isaac's blandishments to Forsyth to come again to Isaac's home in Elgin is "You must consider yourself as in a Coffeehouse with us" (*L* 32).

Forsyth's adjustments to his tone of irritation, noted in chapter 3, showed that the revised edition was not going to be simply a more complete version of what he might have written in prison. His irritation over certain follies, errors of taste, and political infighting, all of them Italian, had cooled. On the other hand, he had lost eleven years of his life. His emotion regarding this would have driven his political analysis and filled the space in the text where paintings and sculptures looted by Napoleon might have been discussed. A number of things he had already noticed might have caused him to reflect further on the contemporary political situation in Italy. This would accord with the wishes expressed by Palgrave and the *Edinburgh Review* that writers would address the "political aspect of Italy [which] is alone sufficient to excite our most intense regard." For example, there was his entrée to a network of Italians unhappy with the regime; his particular knowledge of the resistance in the universities of Pisa and Pavia; his remarks on the state of the population in Florence, Siena, Rome, Naples and Pavia; his analysis of the precedent of Leopoldo's Tuscany, which showed what might be done by an enlightened ruler; and his knowledge of other anti-Napoleonic acts and sentiments (Puccini's concealment of Tuscan art, the citizens' contempt for Monti as a turncoat, their abhorrence for the French, the covert reference to Napoleon's restoration of clerical power as the whim of "a young man"). All these might even have led him toward tentative hopes for a united post-Napoleonic Italy, fragmented as it now was.

The passages concerning Cardinal York, Bristol, and Acton might have become illustrations in a philosophical disquisition on titles and privileges, just as his thoughts on property arose from his visit to the abbey of Vallombrosa. Some passages he might have discarded as too trivial, yet they enliven the final pages of the Murray edition. We hope that he would not have dropped the anecdote of the Venetian senator, who, on being told that the astronomer at the University of Padua had sufficient instruments to make his observations and needed only a good horizon, exclaimed, "Why, then we must send to London for one" (439), or the curious information, collected at Milan, that "a young Genevese, named Du Pau, used here to cut portraits without looking at his work. He could make his dog bite a slice of cheese into a correct profile of Voltaire" (461).[43]

The unfinished second edition already tells us much about the cultural life of Italy. Had Forsyth finished the revision, it might have told us more, and the book would have had more coherence and elegance. Fortunately, some of the most revealing and suggestive of his working papers were preserved for posterity, thanks to the financial canniness of an affectionate and respectful brother, who stuffed the suppressed papers in at the end.

THE LETTERS OF THE FORSYTH BROTHERS

THIS COLLECTION, AN INCOMPLETE SERIES of Forsyth's correspondence with his brother from 1801 to 1815, illuminates more of his personal side and the conditions of the Napoleonic period. Extracts have been cited throughout the preceding chapters. The greater detail here gives the readers an understanding of context and enables them to judge the character of the extracts from how they interact. It may be that readers will discover overlooked leads to understanding more about matters discussed in this book.

Forsyth's "more famous brother, Isaac" (a phrase I heard in Elgin), is more easy to trace than Forsyth. He was a civic worthy (figure 7.1) who left much evidence of his charitable and socially philanthropic activities in societies and bricks and mortar. His grandson Isaac MacAndrew wrote a biography,[1] and he frequently is mentioned in *Elgin Past and Present.*[2] Isaac and Forsyth were two of seven children of Alexander Forsyth and Anne, née Harrold, his second wife. She figures considerably in the letters and is described by MacAndrew as "no ordinary woman" and "of superior understanding, great firmness of character, and exalted piety."[3] The memorial plaque on the wall of the Elgin Cathedral burial ground, raised by Isaac, provides an epitaph on her and six of Alexander's children.

SACRED TO THE MEMORY OF
MRS ANNE HARROLD,
SECOND SPOUSE OF MR ALEXANDER FORSYTH, MERCHANT IN ELGIN.
SHE DIED ON THE 17TH JULY, 1807 AGED 81 YEARS,

1. I. F. MacAndrew, *Memoir of Isaac Forsyth Bookseller in Elgin 1768–1859 by His Grandson Major-General Isaac Forsyth MacAndrew, Bengal Staff Corps* (London: Kegan Paul, Trench, 1889).
2. Herbert Bannermen Mackintosh, *Elgin Past and Present* (Elgin: J. D. Yeadon, 1914).
3. MacAndrew, *Memoir of Isaac Forsyth*, 6, 8.

FIGURE 7.1 Ernest MacAndrew after Innes, 1851: Isaac Forsyth. By permission of Museum of Elgin.

AFTER FULFILLING THE DUTIES OF LIFE
IN THE VARIOUS STATIONS OF
A WIFE, A MOTHER, AND A FRIEND,
WITH THE VIRTUES PECULIAR TO EACH.
ALSO ARE DEPOSITED HERE
THE REMAINS OF HER CHILDREN,
ALEXANDER, JAMES, ANNE, JEAN, CLEMENTINA, AND
JOSEPH.

THE MEMORY OF THE LAST, WILL BE BEST PRESERVED
BY THE DURABLE MONUMENT HE HAS LEFT,
OF REFINED TASTE, JUDGMENT, AND CRITICAL SKILL;
IN HIS REMARKS ON THE ANTIQUITIES, ARTS, AND LETTERS OF ITALY
COMPOSED IN HIS VISIT TO THAT CLASSICAL LAND.
PASSING THROUGH FRANCE, IN HIS WAY HOMEWARD,
THE INDISCRIMINATING FURY OF WAR, THEN RAGING,
DETAINED HIM MANY YEARS IN WASTING CAPTIVITY;
AND THE SLOW RETURN OF PEACE
YIELDED HIM BUT A GLIMPSE, FOR A FEW MONTHS,
OF THE FRIENDS AND THE SOIL THAT WERE MOST DEAR TO HIM.
HE DIED 21ST SEPTEMBER, 1815, AGED 52.

Except for Joseph and Anne, none of these are Anne Harrold's biological children. They were the children of Alexander's first wife, Margaret Ross, who had fourteen children by him. One of the half sisters—maybe Jean, or Clementina, or one whose name we do not have—was a restless, stubborn character who pops up suddenly in the letters. A slave owner in Jamaica, she moves between Caribbean islands and makes a stormy voyage home on seas where convoys are sometimes necessary against the French. Brother John, who also figures, is Forsyth's half brother, who settled with his family in Sherriffston, which Isaac uses as a periphrasis—for example, "our friends from Sherriffston."

Isaac was a bookseller in Elgin, having been apprenticed in Aberdeen and London as a bookbinder. In 1780, he established the earliest "subscription" (circulating) library in the North. In 1801, he married his cousin Catherine Forsyth, daughter of William Forsyth of Cromarty. (In the letters, his "second mother, Mrs Forsyth," is his mother-in-law.) He owned a farm and was a founder member of the Morayshire Farmers Club (1799) and its secretary from 1800 to 1827.[4] Isaac also tried various manufacturing ventures, such as the thread manufactory mentioned by Forsyth in the letters, and another for straw hats. But he always lost money on them. In character, he was very different from Forsyth: pious, self-righteous, canny, always on the lookout for shopping and business opportunities. But he was also affectionate and humorous, taking pains for others, and his love of domestic detail was just what Forsyth needed in the long exile of eleven years. So too was the talk of farming, judging by Forsyth's acute observations of Leopoldo's improvements to Italian agriculture in *Forsyth's Italy*. Isaac would lecture Forsyth on

4. MacAndrew explains that it was then common for businessmen in provincial towns in Scotland to maintain small farms, and carry on two professions.

pious proprieties and on writing prompt and full letters (while confessing he had great difficulty in filling the pages himself). He seems unaware of Forsyth's skeptical temper and his understated emotion and ironical disposition. Despite knowing that Forsyth twice before his imprisonment nearly died from his chest complaint, he is stunned when he does learn the degree of bronchial illness his brother suffers, although we can guess about it, reading between the lines of Forsyth's letters. Isaac's rude health allows him to make light of Forsyth's perilous sea voyage to Morayshire and allows him to think that nothing can be more bracing than a joint walking tour to Staffa, at the end of which Forsyth died. Of course, Forsyth was quite at liberty to refuse his brother's eager attentions and coolly responds in his letters to blandishments of buying properties in Elgin. In essence, Isaac was in awe of his brother and overplays the pious mode. Forsyth would easily have seen the psychological mechanism at work but makes no demurral and seems also fondly attached.

Other characters make their appearance in the letters. Many are walk-on parts and some are big guns who do more, such as the Marquis of Huntly (of the Gordon family), Castlereagh (the famous statesman, whom Byron and Shelley were later to revile as "that intellectual eunuch" and the personification of Murder, respectively), the Leslies (a distinguished old local family),[5] Mrs. Cuming,[6] Lady Grant of Monimusk, and General le Febre.

The conditions for an English detainee such as Forsyth make for interesting reading. There is a variety of prisons: the terrifying dungeons of Vauban's citadelle de Bitche, the concentration camp muster of the fortress of Verdun, the relaxed house arrest of Paris with libraries and museums to visit, and the supervised detention of Valenciennes with rides into the country. Deprivation of human contact, of freedom to walk and to read, are at one end of the scale. At the other, almost a normal life. Even though there are the bitter winters of Verdun with morning and evening *appel* (roll call), wives may visit. A couple of people escape and turn up at Isaac's house. There is some access to funds in England. Servants and wine may soften existence there, but the English prisoners, "vicious and debauched," may make the constraint too obviously painful. Always letters will be read by some official, may prompt punitive action or be thrown away. Post is unreliable and slow, and franking is expensive. A prisoner never knows whether something like the

5. Isaac Forsyth published in 1798 *A Survey of the Province of Moray; Historical, Geographical, and Political.* A William Leslie was co-author. Mrs Leslie frequently is mentioned.

6. Probably a descendant of Cumming, the best friend of Forsyth and Isaac's maternal grandfather, Harrold, who had fought with him at Culloden Battlefield.

Terror may return. In Forsyth's restrained and wary letters, the signs may be seen of increasing despair and declining health.

Social events are also recorded over the course of the letters' twelve years. There is the rise and the fall of the value of the pound and the bright festivities of Napoleon's marriage to Marie-Louise at St. Cloud. After the war, there are the negotiations with Murray via George Smith for the publication of the second edition of *Forsyth's Italy*; the reflections on the shabbiness of Cadell and on cliques of booksellers, including Blackwood; the astonishment of the provincial at the way reviewing is conducted in London; a wish for a report of that great actor, Edmund Kean.

These transcripts are taken from a collection of photocopies of letters that I was given access to in the Elgin public library and from which I was permitted to make photocopies. The originals are untraced. They are numbered in pencil in a modern hand, in sequence of date, up to 33, with another letter unnumbered. From this categorization, there are items missing: numbers 1, 3, 5, 7, 8, 9, 10; part of 11, 15, 19, 20, 22, 23, 24, 25, 30, 31; and part of the unnumbered one. The subject matter of the remainder suggests that the numbering of the whole group is based on their concern with the relation of Forsyth to Isaac. In support of this, the letters we do have allude to others that are not in the collection.

The table below shows all the letters known to exist from these manuscripts. Those in roman are reproduced here. Those in italic are not in the collection but are mentioned in a letter (which is identified by its number in a square bracket). If one of these missing letters has been acknowledged to have been received, it is marked "recd." These missing letters cannot be assumed to have been in the collection as numbered. An attempt to hypothesize that they were included in the count when someone penciled the numbers discovers that there are too few between numbers 6 and 11 and too many between numbers 17 and 21.

No.	From Isaac Forsyth	From Joseph Forsyth
		Letter from Aberdeen [2]
2	October 19, 1801	
	December 25, 1801 [4]	
4	January 18, 1802	
		N.d.; recd. May 1802 [6]
6	May 19, 1802	

(*continued*)

No.	From Isaac Forsyth	From Joseph Forsyth
		December 14, 1805; recd. [11]
11	February 10, 1806	
12		April 28, 1806
	August 2, 1806; recd. [13]	
13		September 23, 1806
14	July 22, 1807	
		September 14, 1807; recd. [16]
16		October 4, 1807
17	June 23, 1809	
		March 1810 [18]
18		April 22, 1810
		June 1812; recd. [21]
	July 2, 1812; recd [21]	
	August 1812 [21]	
		January 2, 1813; recd. [21]
21	February 1, 1813	
		Autumn 1813; recd. [26]
	Autumn 1813 [26]	
		May 28, 1814; recd. [26]
26	June 2, 1814	
		June 20, 1814; recd. [27]
27	June 30, 1814	
		October 8, 1814; recd. [28]
28	October 20, 1814	
		November 3, 1814; recd. [29]
29	November 20, 1814	
		March 15, 1815; recd. [32]
32	March 27, 1815	

The photocopied images are faint and imperfect. They do not have sufficient contrast to show the edges of the paper, including the many holes. Show-through of text on a page underneath can be mistaken for continuation of the writing on the page being examined. Some detached scraps of paper holding text have been misplaced before photocopying. Some text is cut off where the original document has not been scanned in its entirety.

CONVENTIONS OF PRESENTATION

The following symbols indicate different aspects of the condition of the MS:

<word>	Letters/words missing because of a hole or cutoff. Roman letters within indicate a guess at what was there. Italic *hole* or *cutoff* distinguishes the two.
[word]	Letters/words missing through imperfect scanning (misaligned or faint). Roman letters within indicate a guess at what was there.
[[word]]	Letters missing because of a blot or a covering flap. Roman letters within indicate a guess at what probably was there. Italic *blot* or *flap* distinguishes the two.
«word»	Letters on a displaced flap returned to their original place
^word^	An insertion point with the word on a line above
[*?*]	Word following is an unsure reading
~~word~~	Canceled, legible
~~*illegible*~~	Canceled, illegible
{*space*}	A space on the same line to indicate a kind of paragraph break. It indicates a new topic but saves paper for the writer and so the cost of franking.
/	A page turnover in the MS

October 1801 *Forsyth journeys to London*

LETTER 2: ISAAC TO JOSEPH, OCTOBER 19, 1801

Elgin 19th
Octo^{r} 1801

Dear Brother

I had the pleasure of your Letter from Aberdeen yesterday, and we were all much gratified to find that you proceeded on terra firma towards London. These two days have been so boisterous that our mother has not ceased sending up ~~th~~ her thanksgivings on the occasion.

I hope this will meet you safe at Mr Dax's.[7] Your Horse only came last night (Sunday) and the carrier is not yet arrived. The Hyre to Abdn is 20/-,[8] but how much the cost on the road I cannot exactly say 'till Keith[9] returns, perhaps 10 or 12/-. My Mother begs you would not think of sending a rope mat from London. Her own was sent back on Monday last, & she has no use she says for another. I do not know of a single scrape of news since you left us worth writing. The meeting at Inverness did not turn out so brilliant as was expected. No Dukes & only one Dutchess.

Our Mother has held out pretty well; for a day or two after you went I observed a weakness in her voice & Cold hanging about her, but being perswaded to put on her flannel shift again she has recovered from both & is now in her usual way. /

Baine of the Inverness came last week & with him I certainly expected the Box from Newberry's people but was disapointed. If their House should lye on your way at any time I beg you might give them a philippic on carelessness.—

I am further to give you the trouble to call on A.W. Barkly London Str, N° 9—or N° 6. and request him to desire a fr^{d} of his of the name of Dunbar to send me ^to

7. Forsyth's lawyer.
8. There were "20/- [shillings]" to £1.00. The equivalent of £1.00 now (2018) would be worth £69.90. The value of the pound peaked to £81.90 in 1802, fell back to its lowest point in 1813 at £59.90, and rose again in 1815 to £68.00. In these letters covering this period, the 2018 equivalent values are given when mention is made of a sum of money using RPI from the website Measuring Worth, accessed October 18, 2018, https://www.measuringworth.com/calculators/ukcompare/index.php. The site discusses different ways of calculating the amount.
9. Keith is a small town near Elgin. This seems to be a local landowner from there, even though it is also the family name of a line of lords Marischal, in Scotland.

first ship^ a Hoh^{d}[10] of his very best <u>Brown Stout</u>. This Mr. Dunbar, it seems, is famous for his skill in Porter, and as Mr B. has influence with him, I know for the sake of his Cromarty friends as well as my own he will exert it. If you pay Mr B. & put it to my D^{t}[11] I will be obliged. Your great coat is <u>safe arrived</u>, but vastly too small for our fr^{d} John.[12]

I beg you would purchase & put in the Box with the black muff & tippet for Kate a black lace Veil of the patent kind they come cheaper & look as well as the others.[13] /

By this mornings post I see the intercourse between England & France opened up,[14] and suppose you will not long remain in London. I depend on hearing twice from thence; on your arrival, and when you depart, the latter with a detail of your future plan.—You will mention where I am to write you.

My mother renews her prayers for your safety & health, and both sides of the street very cordially join in them. My Catherine[15] begs to have a place in your remembrance.

I pray you give my sincerest thanks & good wishes to M^{r} & Mrs Dax for all their kind offices. I wish it were in my power to do them or any of their friends a service.

I remain with affectionate regard
My dear Brother
Yours truly
Isaac Forsyth

I have occasion to write Mr Miln[16] tommorrow's post & will not omitt to thank him for the attention you experienced.

10. Hogshead, a large brewery cask of a regulated size. A hogshead of stout would have been fifty-four Imperial gallons (sixty-four US gallons).
11. Short for "debit."
12. We have no physical description of Forsyth, but by this, we can assume he had no great stature.
13. Cannyness over the bawbees characterizes Isaac throughout. See the indirection of his queries about insurance in letters 28 and 29.
14. Private travel to France had recommenced with the announcement of the Treaty of Amiens on October 1, 1801. The treaty was ratified on March 27, 1802.
15. Isaac's wife, daughter of his uncle, William Forsyth of Cromarty.
16. A granddaughter of Alexander Forsyth by his first wife, Margaret Ross, married a James Miln. The Milns become the focus of a dispute about a will in letter 6.

November 1801	*Forsyth travels to France and Paris*[17]
December 25, 1801	*Forsyth arrives at Nice*
January 18, 1802	*Forsyth embarks for Leghorn*

LETTER 4: ISAAC TO JOSEPH, JANUARY 18, 1802

London 16 February 1802 Received & forwarded by

Yours truly

A. Brander[18]

Al. Sigre Giuseppe Forsyth
Gentiluomo Inglese
Posta restante
Pisa,
Tuscana

Recd 28th March at Pisa

The Eliza sails from Falm°[19] 11hrs:-[20]

Elgin 18 January 1802

Dear Brother

On the 25th Decemr I wrote you addressed to the Post Office at Pisa,[21] I sitt down again to write, tho' I have little to say, because the oportunity of your

17. Forsyth says, "I left England in November" (*1816*, v). Isaac says it was on October 12 in his intro (*1816*, 3), but he is probably wrong. He makes other mistakes. He is wrong by a day about the date of Forsyth's initial arrest (May 26, not 25, 1803) and by a year about the date of Forsyth's removal to arrest in Paris (1810 not 1811), and is confused about the days of the week and date of Forsyth's death. November 12 is a possibility, since on October 19 (in this letter), Isaac thinks that Forsyth still has time to fulfill his commission to purchase a hogshead of the very best brown stout.
18. These three lines are written upside down. Brander's note suggests it has taken nearly a month to get to London or he has had to wait for the next suitable boat, the *Eliza* (noted in another hand). Forsyth records receipt in Pisa. Brander may be related to Pitgaveny in the next letter.
19. Falmouth.
20. These two lines appear upside down.
21. So Forsyth was not expected to stay long in Leghorn.

friend Pitgaveny[22] to London, perhaps nearer to your residence, presents itself. {*space*} The first article in point of precedence of communication respects our Mother, & by my last (for I will presume on your recieving it) you would find her recovering from a very severe cold. I am now happy to add that she has continued to recover, 'till yesterday & she was then able to present her acknowledgments again in the new chapel,[23] and perhaps again to lay in the seeds of more distress. But she will have it so, & thinks her life well spent in such sacred employment. I do not percieve that she has suffered anything by being out. She is chearful & happy, but ancious to hear from you. I pray you do not omitt any opportunity of giving her such a comfort. {*space*} Our other fr^{ds} are all well, and all beg their kindest remembrances to you. Nothing material has occurred since Christmas. We have had a most severe & close winter since the 1^{t} of Novem^{r}, except 14 days in that month,'till now. The roads have been blown up,[24] the mail carried on mens shoulders, and 2 posts often in arrear. We have been / often pleasing ourselves with the idea of your being in a warmer climate, where these impertinent intruders, frost & snow are not found.[25] Yesterday & to-day the wind has blown fresh from the Southwest with mild weather, which has carried off the Snow & ice & broken up the Ɨ rivers. I hope after two months suffering we shall have pleasant weather again.

The Blow-up which hung so heavily in expectation on our minds, has taken effect, and we are at ten thousand miles distance in the friendly regards of the Milnes.[26] During the most pompous farce of a funeral which has perhaps ever been played, at least ever in Elgin—we were punctual attendants, and like "merry mourners"[27] gaily put on all the trappings of woes. From the then apparent cordiality, I was decieved into a hope that we might go on with the same smooth hollow friendship we had begun. But no! it was convenient and determined on to renounce the poor Brother

22. "Going" or some such word is apparently omitted. Pitgaveny may be John Brander, laird of Pitgaveny and founder of Branderburgh, whose daughter was to marry in 1822 Sir Archibald Dunbar of the neighboring family in Duffus.
23. This shows that the Forsyths' mother worshiped at the "Free Presbyterian Chapel" in Elgin (Robert Young, *Annals of the Parish and Burg of Elgin* [Elgin: Printed for the Author, 1879], 455). Her sons evidently did not approve.
24. He means that they have been ruined, presumably by the terrible weather, an obsolete sense (see *Oxford English Dictionary Online*, s.v. "blow, v." 25a, accessed June 26, 2019, http://www.oed.com); a *blow up* could also mean to have a violent quarrel, in which sense Isaac uses it some few sentences later.
25. Isaac was not alone in this misapprehension, though Pisa had (and still has) mild winters on average.
26. Mentioned in letter 2.
27. Probably alluding to John O'Keeffe's short piece *Modern Antiques; or, The Merry Mourners, a Farce in Two Acts* (1792).

entirely; not only to strip him legally, but after having in a fit, or an affected fit of generosity declared to several people that she meant to be "a kind sister and a liberal friend"—deprive him of what in equity & justice was his own, and as a cause for doing so, imputed it to the machinations and duplicity of the Forsyth's!! {*space*} Stephen has written our Brother a very pretty Letter, which also contained a copy of one sent by the same post to James Miln in a style of manly indignation, with here & there a touch of the most poignant but delicate sarcasm. He wishes to know from my Brother / whether by the Law of Scotland His ffather[28] could deprive him of the Heritable property, and whether his ffather was reported in a sound mind att the date of the Deeds. My Broyr very properly refferred him to Mr Sellar[29] here, as the proper person for such information, and for conducting any enquieries and business he might have to do.

Mrs Donaldson & her Doctor have gone to Paisley—Miss Agnes[30] is with "The Marquis"[31] at Huntly Lodge, so that <*hole*> Park is deserted; whether there is an intention <*hole*> <*hole*> it to the Hammer[32] I know not yet. <*hole*> I told you I had little to say & you see how I verify <*hole*> sayings—for I am fairly aground. Mrs James Roberston[33] had a son 'tother day. My Box of Prints have not yet appeared. I have written Mr Dax to enquire at Scales about them.

Accept our united Love & affections,

& beleive me unalterably

Dear Brother

28. That is, "Father." The custom of using *ff* instead of an initial capital *F* "prevailed amongst engrossing clerks and writers in attorneys' offices to within the last forty years, and in some instances even later" ("The Double 'ff' or Capital 'F,'" *Notes and Queries* 12, no. 305 [September 1, 1855]: 169–170).
29. Probably a local lawyer. He is dealing with legal affairs in letter 6.
30. Unidentified but sounds as though she is a young family member.
31. Alexander (1743–1824), fourth Duke of Gordon, was created Baron Gordon of Huntly and Earl of Norwich in 1784. He held the title "Lord Superior" of Huntly, which in previous times, was "Marquis"—this is probably why he is given quotation marks in this letter as "The Marquis." There are some tantalizing coincidences of interest with Forsyth. He visited Italy in 1761. He became in 1793 lord chancellor of the University and King's College, Aberdeen, from where Forsyth graduated in 1779. MacAndrew wrote of Isaac's "oldest and most influential friends, such as the Duke and Duchess of Gordon" (*Memoir of Isaac Forsyth*, 132).
32. That is, to auction it off. The park has not been identified.
33. Probably a neighbor and not mentioned again. Isaac is casting around for news.

I paid our Mother £10—& placed it to your acc[t] agreeable to our arrangement. On the first of July I shall pay her other £10 on my own acc[t]. I.F.

Yours
Isaac Forsyth

February to April 1802 *Forsyth in Pisa*

April 1802 *Forsyth in Florence*[34]

LETTER 6: ISAAC TO JOSEPH, MAY 19, 1802

2/6 paid

Al Sig[re] Giuseppe Forsyth
Casa Rosa Baldi, N° 116, Via della Crocetta,[35]
Firenze,
Italy /

Elgin 19 May 1802

My dear Brother

A few days ago your long expected and most welcome Letter from Florence made its appearance. I cannot tell you how much misery & distress it relieved my mother & me & all your friends. We thought you had quite given us up. I thought you had taken some umbrage at me because my Letters had not reached you. Now all is right again; & pray be more frequent in your communications. Don't for one moment think of the postage; I don't value it a rush, and if I did I could clear something handsome by charging a shilling a head for a sight of your Letters which would willingly be paidd. {*space*} To begin with the usual routine—Our mother has stood out pretty well since I wrote you, & ~~at~~ is at this moment in tolerable health. My entreaties, and I am afraid even yours will not have the desired effect of lessening her visits to the other side of the town. Her attachment there is too deeply rooted to be moved by any mortal influence. She sends you her thanks for the account of

34. He had moved to Florence by mid-April, for he was there for Easter Day, which was the April 18. He writes of "the pleasure I enjoyed 'at evening from the top of Fesolé.' . . . All the world, just released from the privations of Lent, were fresh in their festivity" (*1816*, 76). Isaac received a letter of Forsyth's from Florence before writing his letter of May 19.

35. Via la Crocetta is now Via Giuseppe Giusti, near Santissima Annunziata.

Religion in Italy & blesses God that she is so near Mr Ballantyne![36] My Broy[r] & family (except Miss Grace[37]) are quite well. She has been sadly distressed by violent headachs—swelled face—pained stomach—and many of the "ills that flesh is heir to". I must not quote now, no, not even from Shakespeare. Nothing but "most choice Italian" will do[38]—and God help me I have none of that.[39] {*space*} My dear Catharine goes on charmingly, and joins all the family strong in attachment & love to you.

From Jamaica we ^lately^ had 3 long Letters of the 3[d] Feb:, our sister is thank God in good health and having released herself from the drudgery of school Keeping is now enjoying the produce of the labour of her negroes, and the proffits of leting her large House to lodgers.[40] How this scheme may do I can't tell, but in my answer I did not offer any observations on a subject I was not capable of forming a just opinion. She complains much that you left England without writing her. We all assured her that that could not have been the case, as you promised our Mother to do so, & you had mentioned in a Letter from London to me your intention / of doing so, and that your Letter must have miscarried. I have not heard anything respecting Stephen's affair lately.[41] Sellar sent a memorial to Counsel at Edinb[r] on the subject who gave a decided opinion on the practicability of establishing his right to a full legal share of the moveables, but that he was best judge whether that would be an object better worth his attention than the provision of £100 p an: which the latter claim, as to himself, but not his son, would invalidate. I suppose our friend will continue to hold what he has. We stand with the worthies here in the same state of gloomy alienation & distance as ever. Dr Stephen was much pleased with your compliment to his Peninsula. He would fight the man who would take but an

36. William Ballantyne had been recently installed (1801) as minister to the "Free Presbyterian Chapel" in Elgin. He was "an able and energetic preacher, very zealous in discharge of his duties," whose sermons attracted large audiences. Differences between the congregation and himself over governance (he leaned toward the less hierarchical Independents) led to his dismissal in 1804 (Young, *Annals of the Parish*, 455). Forsyth's letter had evidently contained a vivid picture of Catholic rituals and/or the clergy.
37. Half sister to Forsyth and Isaac.
38. *Hamlet*, act 3, scene 2.
39. As the last quarter of the second edition was supplied by Isaac from Forsyth's journal, this admission is a pointer to where errors of transcription may have occurred.
40. That the labor of black slaves enables their sister to have an independency and enjoy freedom from the "drudgery" of keeping a school is an irony seemingly lost upon Isaac. His grandson testifies that he was an abolitionist, but gives no further details (MacAndrew, *Memoir of Isaac Forsyth*, 136).
41. Perhaps about the will mentioned in letter 4, four months ago on January 18 of the same year.

ounce weight of sand from it, but he will never spare a penny for that embellishment of which it is highly susceptible.

Pitgaveny went, we are told, with flattering hopes to Malaya, what his realities have been is not told, tho' we hear of his intention of soon returning, tho' like the man, undetermined whether by sea, or by Paris.

Don't be angry that I follow the outline of your Letter, I am so barren of extraneous matter, that I must stick close to my text, & spin well too to get my Paper filled.

Dr Walker's Farm remains in the most unprofitable state of Wildness you last saw it; not one stubble is yet turned down![42] The Demararian's dependance being on a sickly wifes fortune, she has departed to the other world, and he to the torrid zone—and left his avaricious Lordship his uncultivated acres to reproach his rapacious greed.

The Prints came soon after I wrote to you last—they are charming. Mrs Leslies finery came safe too,[43] & please highly.—Pray write me from Sienna, from that cool Grotto, where you will have tension enough of fibre to recount all your proceedings in Florence, & all your adventures in Italy not yet communicated. Be assured the last particular that respects you & them will be most interesting here. I have never seen ~~*illegible*~~ so cool a season as this; our fibres are tightened to trembling by an intense frost, a northerly wind, and daily showers of Snow for 16 days past.

Your words shall be faithfully delivered to friend Roberts on his return from Keith whither he has been ever since they arrived. He has as / Letters of acknowledgement for those you carried out, from Miss Watson & the Botanical Proffessor at Pisa,[44] which the Captain has most industriously displayed in confirmation of the high respect he was held in there.

I had a long letter this morning from my friend John Innes[45] in London announcing his becoming an <u>equal</u> Partner with David Scott and two other Gentlemen in

42. This and other farming information that Isaac communicates belies Forsyth's professed lack of interest in such matters in letter 12. This reinforces the view noted there that he was conscious of the need for caution, since his letters were being read. No more is said of Dr. Walker or the Demararian family.
43. If this was the "black lace Veil" of letter 2, it corroborates the idea that Forsyth did not leave for the continent until November.
44. Miss Watson is unidentified. I suggest in chapter 4 that Giorgio Santi is the professor. It seems there had been some previous contact between Elgin and Pisa.
45. John Innes is mentioned with some reverence by Isaac several times. He is clearly wealthy and a partner in a shipping concern (letter 17) in London, with David Scott, Mc Callum (this letter), and possibly Barclay, Grant Allan, and Chas Grant (letter 20). He

that immense House on the 1st of this month. Since the death of Lennox which happened suddenly in December last a new arrangement had become necessary, & such was the extent of his talents & industry that they were indispensibly needed, & thus handsomely rewarded. McCallum retires from the concern with £8000[46]—his share of the Profit (& a small one he held) for 16 months that he was in the former House. This will give you some idea of the prospect that opens to my friend John.

The Peace has had some agreeable effect on the Thread business <*hole*>«demand has»[47] encreased & the prices have advanced & I hope <*hole*> "still more" advance. We have sent a considerable parcel to <*hole*>«& expect to» clean out our Warehouse bye & bye.

If the «weather» would but permit us we should now go to the Cottage I mentioned my having taken for the Summer in my last, near Myreside, and at the bottom of the fine ridge that rises so prettily above the Lake of Spynie & commands so fine a view—perhaps not quite Italian—but yet very agreeable to Morayshire eyes.

Miss Duncan Moristoun,[48] was married 'tother day to James Roe Esqr of Geddes & has left many a young man wearing the willow—. No other news of any consequence.

I shall as you desire draw on Mr Dax for the £10 paid my mother in Jany on your acc^{t}.

I again entreat of you to be write us frequently, and with united best wishes from every one here I remain

always, Your affectionate

Isaac Forsyth

August to September 1802 *Forsyth in Siena*[49]

September to January 1803 *Forsyth in Rome*

has an entrée to high society through the Brodies to the Marquis of Huntly (letter 26) and is a longtime member of the prestigious Highland Society (letter 28).

46. Worth £655,200 in today's currency.
47. Words with « » appear misplaced over the right-hand hole. Here they replace the show-through of a hole on the left-hand side.
48. Moristoun and Roe are unidentified.
49. He was in Florence at least until early July, for "on July 9th, St Zenobio's relics were again exposed for three days" (*1816*, 446). He "set out for Rome [from Siena] after the first rains of September" (*1816*, 118).

January to February 1803	*Forsyth on Naples excursion*[50]
February to April 1803	*Forsyth in Rome*[51]
April to May 1803	*Forsyth makes a hasty journey to Bologna, Venice and Milan, as relations break down between Britain and France*
May 26, 1803	*Forsyth is captured at Turin*[52]*; after an abortive escape in Marseille, he is forced to march in winter to Fort de Bitche (or Bitsch, Moselle) in the Vosges Mountains and imprisoned in its dungeons*

LETTER 11: ISAAC TO JOSEPH (INCOMPLETE), FEBRUARY 10, 1806

10 Feb 1806

Your thrice wellcome ^& languished for^ letter of the 14th Decr. came to my hand yesterday. I have not had a day of greater enjoyment for many a month. Our venerable mother ^too^, how happy it made her! To be informed from your own hand that you have not had ^a cold of^ a weeks standing since leaving us—~~a~~ that your aguish ~~I~~ Complaint of which we had heard from Dr Scott[53] & Mr Dax had not troubled you for a long time ~~*illegible illegible illegible*~~ and in fine, that during the severity of such a winter as this you have no Physical Complaint whatever, is good news indeed! The pleasure it gave to every one connected with you in my family & in my Broy^{rs}[54] was really great, and it has circulated round the village in quick vibration. Pray endulge us frequently in such enjoyments.

50. Forsyth was in Naples for the "Bacciamano," the kissing of the hand celebrating King Ferdinand IV's birthday, on January, 12, 1751 (*1816*, 406). He was at Portici, where Hayter had been working for "less than two years" (*1816*, 287); Hayter began work in 1801, so this is early in 1803.
51. He was in Rome for Easter Day, April 10, 1803 (*1816*, 395).
52. "I arrived at Turin on the 25th May, 1803. The next day I was arrested as a British subject" (*1816*, 356).
53. Isaac, writing to Forsyth, calls him "your old companion," according to letter 17 (1809). But he also says he saw him in person at the time of this letter (1806). Scott is not mentioned in James Lawrence's narrative. It is likely Scott was admitted to Verdun as a visitor and was not an imprisoned companion.
54. Isaac uses the old-fashioned symbol *yogh* for "th." So this is "Brother's."

I wrote you two Letters on the 18th Jany. under much distress of mind from the Complaints you made to M^{r} D—of my forgetting you, when God knows how frequently & ^how^ anxiously you were the subject of my thoughts & of my pen.

Our dear Mother has always been the prominent figure in my correspondence to you—in all my former letters her health & situation were the principal objects of communication. It gives me peculiar satisfaction to be able to say that the swelling I mentioned on the 14 Nov: has almost entirely subsided, she is able to use her common shoes, & tho' she very properly never ventures out of doors, she is yet able to walk about her house freely. Except that Constitutional cough with which she has a battle every morn^{g}., ~~I~~ ~~*illegible*~~ and that weakness incident to persons of her advanced age, I do not find her ~~*illegible*~~ affected by any positive ~~complaint~~ ailment. Her mind & temper are most chearful ~~& pleasant~~ & her conversation is almost entirely religious & the only anxiety she feels is to be occupied in the / service of her Master. In this ~~every faculty~~ grand object every power of perswasion, rebook,[55] example, experience, and encouragement is employed. And she is most successful.

The people who associate with her, look to her with veneration, they consider as almost already beatified, and recieve her counsels & advise as those of a superior being.—

We who are near & dear to her have much to answer ~~for~~ if we fail in improving so precious an oportunity. My little ones are the particular objects of her delight & instruction. The Oldest has a mild gentle affectionate temper & clings closely to her, she has a good memory too, and ^her grandmother ~~*illegible*~~^ has it ^already^ well stored with Hymns & good words ~~by her Grandmother & Jean Lamb~~. Ann is full of humour & playfulness, with a little spice of her daddys keeness of temper, ~~and besides having~~ and being able only to rattle off a sort of nursery jargon that don't yet amount to language, is not such a favourite as Eliza. She is however a very constant attendant on the lesson, but more from love of the pudding that follows than the learning that is conveyed. Such is the anxiety to have even her well begun that they have given her[56] an Evening prayer which she is not little ostentatious of. She sends her best gift to you—her blessings; and regards[57] a frequent & direct communication.

55. Almost certainly a late instance of the pre-seventeenth-century spelling of *rebuke* (see *OED Online,* s.v. "rebuke, n.," June 2009, accessed June 25, 2019, https://www.oed.com/view/Entry/159285?rskey=qeoYSU&result=1&isAdvanced=false#eid, which also gives *reboot* as a Scotticism for *rebut* ["3b a check, a stop. Scottish"]). The word is clear in the original.

56. "Her" is repeated.

57. That is, "regards highly."

If my Letters of the 18th ~~N~~ should reach you they say all that I yet know of our sister. I have not heard from her since she left Jamaica in Jany. 1803—& I have only once heard of her from Mr Rob. Henry of Kingston[58] the substance of his Letter I gave you before to this effect. That she left their Island to proceed to Charleston or Savannah with her Slaves, but being overtaken by a Storm the Vessel was Stranded in the Gulf of Mexico & she found her way to the House of the Governor & was retained by his Excellency ~~as~~ to teach music to his Children! I wrote her formerly, & on the 6th of this month I wrote[59]

April [*?*] *20, 1806* *Forsyth is transferred to Verdun*

LETTER 12: JOSEPH TO ISAAC, APRIL 28, 1806

winter in Lond^n^, [*?*] Sandy

Verdun 28 April 1806

My dear Brother,

I have at length the pleasure of writing to you from Verdun where I arrived a few days ago. You may easily imagine the advantages of this removal—a large town full of resources—the society of respectable men, and the renewal of former acquaintances—Our correspondence now will not be subject to the same delays and miscarriages; and I therefore request from you, on the receipt of this, some account of yourself and of our common friends. Let me know particularly how our dear Mother has completed the winter. Your last described her most affectingly, at your Christmas dinner—an effort which placed her in a very endearing light.

Of Bitche I have nothing to complain. I enjoyed every indulgence which the situation would admit.[60] The agues which attacked me there have only improved my constitution. The air of the Fort was friendly to my old complaint, and the climate superior to what I have yet experienced at Verdun. But here, I have the power of

58. That is, Kingston, Jamaica, not then the capital but the leading mercantile town.
59. Letter ends here.
60. A typically terse and elusive statement. It has some satiric touch for, knowing that being thrown into the dungeons of Bitche was used as a threat to coerce the prisoners of Verdun, "indulgences" would have been very little like luxuries. Forsyth has a similar tone in saying that among Fea's accomplishments, his "chief merit is activity" (*1816*, 237). The constriction of Bitche may be imagined from the advantages Forsyth sees in Verdun (a place of misery for Forbes): society, freedom to move about, resources to study.

choosing between the upper and lower town, / that situation which will best suit my health. I have already fixed on a very comfortable lodging of two rooms, at two louis a month. I mess with some gentlemen whom I have long known,[61] and for an excellent dinner and a bottle of good burgundy, pay about 3/9—Not having yet found among the Prisoners a servant that will suit me, I pay the people of the house for their attendance—We are served in the English style—the English fashions prevail here—there is an English chapel, where a Mr Gorden, an amiable friend of mine, officiates—there are English charity schools—English taverns—and sometimes an English play.[62] But I speak of things that must be already known to you—only because I have nothing to say particularly of myself.

When you have occasion to write to London let Mr Dax know where I now am. You may address to M. F. Prisonnier Anglais, Verdun sur Meuse, France.

Continue to send me as interesting letters as your last; but more frequently. Be as minute in regard to our venerable Parent, a subject so supremely interesting to us both. Write How you go on. How does the Inverness concern succeed?

Is there any possibility of resuming your thread manufactory / at a more auspicious period? How does the Palmer-cross (or what is the name?) go on?—are your buildings all erected? is the machine in full activity?—As for the ferme ornée opposite to you—nothing can be more remote from my views. I need not tell you that I have no knowledge of agricultural improvement, nor any taste for the thing;[63] and, even had I both, I should hardly wish my own property to embellish another's.

In the event of an exchange, I see the propriety of my fixing ultimately in some part or other; but I scarcely think it will be Scotland—At present, I can determine nothing and reserve even the thoughts of such a subject for a period <whe *hole*>n I shall be able to judge and to execute—Surely I nee<d not *hole*> add, that wherever I may be—in liberty or in bondage, at home or abroad—I retain the same affection for

61. Group dynamics seem to have made Forsyth regard his three years of confinement as a very long time.
62. In *Forsyth's Italy*, Forsyth refers to "our" English china (*1816*, 75) as though he shared English nationality. His long sojourn in London and the South may have acclimatized him to thinking in this way. Here the matter is in the balance. In letter 16, he distances himself from the "vicious and prodigal" Englishmen in Verdun.
63. Forsyth's remarks on Leopold's agrarian reform (still in the papers he put aside) belie this. Possibly, his constant awareness of his letters being opened and read has made him guarded.

you, the same attach-ment to my friends—again I invite you to have free recourse to me in any difficulty—and to believe me ever—

your most sincere friend
and Brother
Jos Forsyth.

LETTER 13: JOSEPH TO ISAAC, SEPTEMBER 23, 1806

My dear Brother

Your last letter of various dates from July 17 to Augt. 2^{d} has been detained a long time on the road hither, as I received it only a few days ago. Sorry I am to learn the declining state of our Mother's health. Your very particular and affecting account of her leaves me room to fear that I shall never see her more. I beseech you, while you still continue to enjoy her among you, to give me, as frequently as you can, the satisfaction of knowing how she wears through the winter that will soon approach. If she inquire after me, tell her I keep good health and am as comfortable as a person debarred from his friends and country can ~~be~~ expect to be. Assure her that she is very frequently in my thoughts, that she is the chief object for which I regret my captivity,—that my most indecent prayer is once more to see her, or if that be denied—that her passage may be smoothed to a better existence!— /

I had a letter from Dax, which is sufficiently satisfying. He seemed rather hurt at ~~being~~ our suspecting he might be unprepared for any demand and assures me that he is always ready to honour any draft or order of mine that is given regularly and fully.—You know how punctilious he is. I have always found him very friendly—and should be exceedingly sorry, situated as I now am, to break with him.—His balance comes about £10[64] short of my~~a~~ account—but I am confident it is very fair; for I forgot one or two orders which he sent to Italy for friends of mine &c.

I am very sorry to hear of the law-suit in which our Mother is engaged, and am most anxious to learn the issue of it. Let me know also whether the Bank Directors have done justice to his application.

64. The value of £1.00 was the equivalent of £74.40, a fall from the peak of £81.90 in 1802.

Is there no prospect of resuming the manufactory?—not even in the event of a peace?—I Pray how does your Inverness concern go on?

—I heard of it from a young man now a prisoner here, who brought with him a copy of your Provincial History.[65] I thought I had been the most northern of all the unfortunates; but there are several Highlanders here, such as the Mr. McKenzies from Dingwall—a Major Falconer—a McFarlane from Inverness &c &c. /

How diversified the life of our poor Sister! what an incessant struggle for independance! how much I admire her spirit, her object, her perseverance! what nerves, and what a constitution she must have! Surely she must have acquired some property in her adventures. We know of old her economy—why will she not be content with a moderate income and return to Britain to enjoy it?—

I shall be anxious to hear a good account of your own dear wife, to whom I offer my warmest acknowledgments for her attentions to our venerable Mother.—I think that within the circle <of our *hole*> own family & friends you will find material for a very l<on *hole*>g <letter *hole*> which, if it is not already on the road, I request you will sit down to as soon as you receive this.—I am, my dear Isaac,

yours most affectionately
Jos Forsyth

Verdun sur meuse
23^{d} September 1806

LETTER 14: ISAAC TO JOSEPH, JULY 22, 1807

A Monsr Monsr [*sic*] Forsyth
Prisonier Anglais,
Verdun,
in France.

Elgin 22nd July 1807

My dear Brother,

I wrote you lately thro' the medium of a friend in London which I trust has reached you in the last month, and from the ample detail I ^then^ gave

65. Probably John Grant and William Leslie, *A Survey of the Province of Moray; Historical, Geographical, and Political* (Aberdeen, U.K.: Isaac Forsyth, 1798). The book was known in Elgin as "Muckle Isaac."

you respecting our venerable Parent would prepare your affectionate mind for the melancholy task I now have of communicating her death! {*space*} This lamented, tho' by her much-wished-for event, took place on Saturday morning last, the 18th current at 2 o'clock. ~~*illegible illegible*~~ Her sacred remains were yesterday deposited in "the narrow house", attended by every respectable inhabitant of the place. She has left behind her a character of the most unsullied purity and the most emminent piety. It will long be held in remembrance by all her acquaintance, and must be cherished by us with the dearest affection. In my last I informed you so fully of the state of her health and the circumstances of her situation that I shall not now resume them previous to that period. Soon after I wrote, she felt much anxiety to try the benefit of the Country air, seeing its effect so visible in the improved condition of our children who had gone out early on account of the Hooping cough. With some difficulty we got her out to my Cottage in the Haughland. You cannot concieve the happiness I then enjoyed in seeing our aged & respected Mother placed in the midst of her family, the very youngest of which seemed to vie with the eldest in every attempt to gratify and please her. She Slept better, had more appetite, and really seemed better for the change. But at her period of life no radical improvement could be expected; and objects then however interesting for a time lose their power over the mind—She wished / to be at home again, & after a residence of 10 days we got her back to her own bed & her own room, pleased with everything that had happened & promising to spend a fortnight with us during the Harvest.

She continued tolerably easy for some time after her return home, but about the beginning of this month her cough & expectoration visibly encreased, and conjoined with her extreme weakness, was the cause employed by Providence to remove her from a state of great distress to the possession of that Heavenly Inheritance for which she so anxiously prayed, and so diligently & so successfully prepared herself. "'Tho Dead she yet speaketh" a powerful language to us my dear Joseph, to follow her footsteps, that thro' the faith & patience of which she was so bright and shining an example, we also may with her inherit the Eternal Glory!

You will not doubt that I have done every thing in my power to testify my respect to her memory, in conforming to all the established usages of the place on such melancholy occasions. In this I have been very readily assisted by our worthy Brother John, his wife & family, by her two nephews Alexander & John Jack—her cousins Wm Gordon & James Anderson of Linkwood—by our connections the Milns—and indeed by many unsought who were with me zealous to shew forth their affectionate regard to such precious remains.

As[66] In her temporal concerns I have not yet been able to do anything.

She expressed long since to me a wish that her furniture should be sold by auction to pay such debts as she might owe, her funeral expences, and the legacies I shall afterwards mention, and to keep the Balance, if any, to myself. I solemnly assured her that I should never sell one article that belonged to her; that I should faithfully pay her debts & funeral expences, and all the legacies she mentioned. That the furniture should / be valued by a sworn auctioneer and if the amount exceeded the Claims on it I should hold myself accountable to you & our Sister for equal thirds of the residue.—With tears of satisfaction she acquiesced in this plan, & I shall religiously carry it into effect. I must however in justice to myself mention that all the principal peices of Furniture were purchased by me when a Batchelor for the improvement of my Mothers accomodation and my own and have since remained in her possession, tho' never understood by her or me in the light of her property. It is besides my intention & I hope it shall recieve your approbation, to give to her faithful attendant Jane Lamb, who has served her with an uncommon degree of affection and tenderness for 8 years past——the Bed & bedding her Mistress slept in & as much more as will make out a room's furniture. This with remembrances to her poor friends & favourites will occupy a good deal of her furniture. The Legacies are Twenty pounds[67] to the Missionary church here of which she was a member, & to which she felt a very warm attatchment. Five Pounds to her servant Jane Lamb—ten shillings to a poor Cousin John Richards—and 10 shillings to two other poor persons. If there is anything of her furniture, or personal articles, that you would choose as a rememberance of so dear and respected a Parent, be so good as mention it soon, that I may carefully preserve it for you. I should in the mean time enclose a small quantity of her hair, but that I am affraid to trust so precious a relicque to the present very uncertain chance of this letter being ever received by you. Unfortunately there was too small a quantity of it taken off, & this circumstance combined with the former induces me to place it in my scrutoire 'till the communication between us is more safe, or 'till the happy moment shall arrive that may see you again on your native land. {*space*} Alas! when that happy moment does arrive, I fear there is now no attraction for you in this point to which once your warmest affections poured. But let me not endulge in such melancholy ideas as these. I will / hope, that tho' the great connecting link is removed, yet that Elgin & its inhabitants—that myself & my family shall still be objects of regard & interest with you. To us everything that relates to your happiness, your liberty, your

66. "As" squeezed in front of "In," representing a later addition, probably.

67. The equivalent value of £1.00 being £73.00 in 2018.

temporal and eternal good are objects of our fervent prayers—our most anxious thoughts. I have this day written our poor sister an account of what has occurred. I have also written to Mr Dax & requested him to communicate it to you, that by two different channells you may the better chance of recieving it. I pray you write me. I have not had a line from you for 12 months past.[68]

The want of intercourse ^with you^ was very sensibly felt by her who can feel no more.

[Address here running sideways, from bottom to top]

Our dear Mother was born 10th Novemr 1726—died 18th July 1807 & buried in our Father's Grave on the 21st July 1807. If you should employ your mind on an appropriate inscription to her character & memory, I will most gladly concur in the expence of a plain simple unostentatious (like the life of the Christian saint it ~~illegible)~~ I ^shall^ commemorate) marble—for that purpose. Ever Yours while[69]

Isaac Forsyth

LETTER 16: JOSEPH TO ISAAC, OCTOBER 4, 1807

Verdun 4 October 1807—

My dear Brother

An opportunity being offered me this moment of sending a half sheet to England by a secure conveyance, I embrace it, to inform you that, immediately on receiving the fatal tidings of your last letter dated 22d July, I wrote in reply (about the 14th Sept) by the surest channel I could then find. As nothing material for me now to date has transpired since that time; I shall just, for fear of that being miscarried, repeat what was most essential without returning upon the painful reflections which the ever-lamented event then excited.—I never received from you any account of our dear and venerable Parent's illness previous ^to the^ change which has removed her to a better state of being. I had not heard from you for a year past,[70] and during that time I had written to you repeatedly.—Your

68. That is, since July 1806, but we have Forsyth's letter 13 of September 23, 1806, to show this exaggerates.
69. No word seems to be cut off here; just an inadvertence of Isaac, perhaps. The words are crammed in.
70. That is, since October 1806. We have Isaac's letter of February 10, 1806 (letter 11, a fragment), so Forsyth may have had another after that. This letter is written in an uncharacteristically small hand in order to get the most out of a half sheet.

affectionate conduct to our beloved mother during the long course of years you ~~have~~ lived together must be now a source of heartfelt consolation to you. Your disposal of her property I cannot but approve in every particular. As eldest son, I beg leave to pay her legacies, debts and funeral charges—as soon as you can send me the amount of them, I will desire Mr Dax to remit you the money. I will most ~~red~~ readily join in erecting a marble slab to her memory and leave to you the epitaph, which I am confiden[t] none could give better than yourself. My prospect of returning home being now more remote and unreal than ever,[71] I cannot beg of you to reserv[e] for me any of her furniture; but will be thankful for any small <*hole*> matter as a memorial, which I should cherish as a second relic—a book, for instance, or any little object that she may have expressed a wish of my possessing. You do right in not trusting the hair to any conveyance, for at present nine letters in ten from England are lost or stopt. Sometimes, indeed, ladies venture over hither to their husbands; but your situation precludes you from catching such an occasion. You seemed to doubt that this melancholy event may detach me in future from Elgin. My last letter, if it reach you, will have assured you of the contrary; as far, at least, as a thing detached and exiled from his country can give assurance of the kind, concluding that I should return to Elgin when released and settle there, you proposed to me last year the purchase of our Brother's property in the town—I hope you received my answer, which would convince you that I could not possibly enter into such a measure till I return to Britain, if at all.[72] I am anxious to hear what he is now doing, how you go on in town and country, what accounts you may lately received from our poor sister and any thing that may ^have^ taken place or be projected in our family since you wrote me. I am indebted to Mr. Kitchen of Nairne[73] for occasional notices of you. He calls on me frequently and is now in good health, He is one of the very few young men here who are not ruined since their captivity by a society of Englishmen the most vicious and prodigal I ever witnessed on earth[74]—I continue in good health—I ride out every day—I mess with one companio[n] and see very little of the world or desire to see—Some time ago I applied for leave to reside

71. In letter 12 (April 28, 1806), Forsyth had imagined but dared not plan where he might settle on returning. Now he is more despairing.
72. "If at all" is added in an even smaller script, showing that deeper reflection made Forsyth almost without hope.
73. Possibly a James Kitchen, who was born in Nairn on June 1, 1785, and died in Kingillie, Nairn, on June 8, 1862. He became a lieutenant general in the Madras Royal Infantry. It is not, however, known if he was a detainee or prisoner of war. See Moray Council Local Heritage Centre, "Libindx Online Genealogical Search," accessed October 18, 2018, http://libindx.moray.gov.uk/people/people_report_view.asp?REF_ID=NM089953.
74. Isaac remarked in his introduction that Forsyth "lived almost in solitude" except for meeting his own countrymen because of his repugnance for this behavior (*1816*, 5).

in Paris in order to continue a study which requires access to public libraries and museums. The interest used for me would have obtained for me that permission, had ^not^ my adventure at Marseilles been brought into the Minister's notice.[75] My friend at Paris has not given up the point and still encou*<cutoff>* [and] *<cutoff>* [my dear Brother] believe me unalterably *<cutoff>*

LETTER 17: ISAAC TO JOSEPH, JUNE 23, 1809

A Monsr Monsr Forsyth
Prisonier Anglaise
Verdun
Sur le Meuse

London 23^{d} June 1809

My dear Brother

You will be surprized to find me again addressing you from this great city. I did so about 6 years ago. The occasion of my coming hither just now is cheifly on our Sisters account, who after the dreadful fire in Trinidad, which burnt her & thousands beside quite out,[76] caught a most distressing and general Rheumatism over her body & limbs, in consequence of damp accomodation. She is advised to try the effect of a Sea Voyage & the Medical assistance of Lond^{n}, and proposed being here by this time, I find that the Fleet has been detained for 10–12 days, for Convoy, & may not arrive before the 10th July. I have about 10 days business of my own, but shall then be very much on the fidgetts if she don't come in. I already wrote her urging her return to Elgin to spend the remainder of her days in the bosom of my family in quietness & rest, & not continue any longer that buffetting ^with^ ~~of~~ Fortune which for so many years she has carried on unsuccessfully. Her answer was in the old independent spirit, that she was determined to persevere, & had no doubt of ultimate success if she had her health which she reckoned on as certain on arriving in England, & wishes me much to come hither & see her. I shall try her yet once more tho' I have little hope of success; if she agrees, I shall do everything in

75. Probably Forsyth was considered to have broken his parole and received unsympathetic treatment from officials who did not know him. See letter 21 about parole. According to Isaac, Forsyth was liked and respected by French officials who had contact with him (*1816*, 4–5). His wish to study is presumably for his book and predates October 4, 1807 ("some time ago").

76. In a great fire of March 23, 1808, three-quarters of Port-of-Spain, capital of Trinidad, was destroyed, but only two people died.

my power to promote her comfort ~~scr~~ and endeavour to give her Twenty pounds[77] a Year of an <*hole*> If you could spare her something, with the triffle she has left of <*hole*>, & she might be able to keep a snug ~~scribb~~ establishment for herself, & I should think would in every way be more comfortable & respectable, than wandering over the face of the Earth as she has hitherto done.———I was most happy yesterday in falling in with two Gentlemen who escaped from Verdun 24th April last, Mssrs Baird[78] & Fulton, & who, the former particularly, gave me the most interesting accounts of your situation, appearance, & health. Since I ~~*illegible*~~ saw your old companion Dr. Scott, I have not had so much satisfactory information respecting you. I was truely gratified to find that your health then & for several months before was excellent; Mr Baird said you had been unwell last Autumn; but now perfectly restored, and that you contrived to bear your restraint with as much patience as possible, & enjoy all the comforts your situation permitted. I was glad to find you received my letter thro' General le Febre.[79] I have not had a line from you since yours of October 1807! This is the more distressing as Young Mr Kitchen contrives frequently to get Letters over to his Worthy Parents in Nairn.[80] To / him & to them I am particularly obliged for the only knowledge I have had of you in all that long period. {*space*} My good friend Lady Grant of Monimusk[81] is here just now, and engages to forward another Letter to you thro the medium of General Le Febre, & to accompany it with one from me to her descriptive of your period of confinement &c, &c—, this she is to back strongly herself to the General, in

77. The pound had fallen to an equivalent value (2018) of £66.00 below the £69.90 of 1801.
78. John Goldworth Alger mentions Baird but his Fulton seems to be not this one (*Napoleon's British Visitors and Captives 1801–1815* [Westminster: Constable, 1904]).
79. This appears to be Charles, comte de Lefevbre-Desnouettes (1773–1822). He had been aide-de-camp to Napoleon and distinguished himself at Napoleon's victory over the Austrians at the Battle of Marengo (1800). He became a general and "Count of the Empire" in 1808, but was taken prisoner by the British in the Peninsula War in Spain that year. In 1809, he was living at Cheltenham on parole. As a gallant general close to Napoleon and himself a prisoner of war, he was a likely person to act as a conduit for Forsyth's letters, but how this was managed is not known. In a curious counterpoint to Forsyth's case, Lefevbre broke parole and escaped from England to France, and at the restoration, he escaped again, this time to America.
80. Some corroboration that Forsyth was treated more harshly than others.
81. Another instance of a family drawing its wealth from the slave trade. The Grants of Monymusk, Aberdeen, owned a large sugar estate in Clarendon, Jamaica, also called Monymusk. It is still working and has one of the island's few remaining rum distilleries. Lady Grant is probably Mary, wife of Sir Archibald Grant, the fourth baronet, or Lady Anne Grant, sister of the Earl of Seafield, who in 1820 was living at Grant Lodge, the jointure house of the Elgin family, which Isaac appears to have supported politically (MacAndrew, *Memoir of Isaac Forsyth*, 129–131).

the hope that he will interpose his influence with the Government in your favour, if not to the extent of procuring your release altogether, at least your removal to Paris, which seemed sometime ago, & Mr Baird informs me still is an object of desire with you. {*space*} This Letter goes thro' the medium of a conveyance to Rotterdam which Mr Baird is possessed of, & which he has kindly allowed me to avail myself of. My other, which will be nearly a copy of this, Lady Grant forwards, I believe, from the Treasury[82] here to General le Febre, enclosed in a strong one from herself, verifying my information respecting you. How far this may be advantageous, or even prudent, I am uncerta[in]; it has only the merit of good intention in us.

In the Letter which you recieved I mentioned the death of ^my^ second mother,[83] my best friend & councellor—Mrs Forsyth of Cromarty. Mrs Forsyth spent the Winter with us at Elgin, but in a very poor state of health. Mrs F. & she accompanied me to Edinb^{ro} in the hope that the jaunt might be useful to our sister, & that we might consult the most eminent of the Faculty there. They put her on a course of Medicine the good effect of which was visible before I left them, & have given her such assurances of ~~*illegible*~~ established & confirmed health for the future, that her hopes & spirits were much raised. They go down to Cromarty in company with one of the Proffessors of St Andrews who is a townsman & friend of theirs. / Before leaving home we sent out our four young misses to my little Farm to graze.[84] I hear every week of them; they ^are^ in charming health & spirits & very diligent scholars under <u>Jane Lamb</u> who was long the faithful servant & companion of our venerable mother. We are fortunate in having a creature so attatched & so capable as she is, and them.

Our Broy^{r} enjoys admirable health at his new Farm of Sherriffston & his wife & daughter are very fond of it too. Alice has gone to China in one of my friend John Innes's Ships. I have not yet seen M^{r} or Mrs Dax (being only 3 days in town) but the moment I knew of this conveyance to you I wrote him a Note in case he chose to avail himself of it by writing you. If any Letter comes in I shall enclose it. {*space*} Our relation Stephens is still at Chelsea, & still writing, tho' I believe more for <u>Bread</u> than Fame. {*space*} All your early friends in & about Elgin are well & <*hole*> to make very anxious enquiries about you, & to express <*hole*> desire to have

82. The mention of the treasury suggests that Isaac was attempting to engage some very powerful interests on Forsyth's behalf. The head of the treasury was the chancellor of the exchequer, who, in June 1809, was Spencer Perceval. He became prime minister in October of that year.

83. His mother-in-law.

84. Isaac "the farmer" speaks!

you among them again. This to [[me *blot*]] would be one of the greatest sources of happiness that could [[*blot*]] be opened; but I am affraid your habits & ideas are so changed with your long residences on the Continent, that the monotony of our existence would not & could not satisfy you. Your Books at Elgin are perfectly safe & I mean on my return to unpack some of the cases, to examine them more particularly. I believe there are two trunks or boxes of yours here under the care of Mr Rob. Dunbar, I shall enquire about them, & if you wish it send them down to join the others; or let them remain to meet you here when the happy moment of your liberation arrives. What a pity you have been deprived /of such a fountain of enjoyment as your admirable Library would have proved during a period of so much leisure.

Let me hear from you my dear Joseph, for your safety & happiness is I assure you the second object of my heart.

Ever Your affectionate Bro$^{y^r}$

Isaac Forsyth

March 1810 *Forsyth is transferred to Paris*[85]

LETTER 18: JOSEPH TO ISAAC, APRIL 22, 1810

Paris 22^{d} April 1810

My dear Brother

I wrote to you about six weeks ago from Verdun, and informed you of the interest which M^{rs}. Cuming and Major Kingston were making to obtain my removal to Paris. I have now the pleasure to inform you that they have succeeded. I arrived here a few days before the great fête.[86] I feel myself infinitely obliged to M^{rs}. Cuming on this occasion. She is perfect[ly] well, but sets off next Wednesday (the 25th) for Holland along with her son, a very accomplished young man. I have found her really what you described her, a most obliging and amiable woman.

I was preparing to settle here & pursue some studies, when the unexpected apparition of a commissary for the exchange of prisoners has agreeably deranged[87]

85. Isaac misreports the transfer as happening in 1811 (*1816*, 5)
86. The celebrations of the civil marriage of Napoleon with Marie-Louise at Saint-Cloud, April 1, 1810, followed by a religious ceremony on the next day.
87. The first indication of Forsyth's emotional turmoil, which he tries to suppress in this letter.

my plan and drawn my thoughts to objects far more pleasing than those of Paris. Were I not half ashamed to confess, after so many disappointments, that I can still hope, I should think myself now nearer home than ever. I had a letter today from that excellent young man Kitchen, who is full of the same anticipation & hope—What pleasure to me should we really meet in the course of this summer! but seven years of captivity has so completely altered my features that you will hardly recognise your brother. [[An *blot*]] immense crowd of strangers who have flocked hither for the present fêtes make private lodgings very [[difficul *blot*]] t to be got in a good quarter; and, unfortunately for me, the library & museum which <I wo *hole*>uld wish to live near to, are situated in the most fashionable part of the town. In the hotel where I lodge at present I pay four louis a month for a single room on the third floor; at Verdun I had four times the accommodation for myself & servant on the first floor, for half the money. It is expected, however, that on the reflux of the present crowd, things will return to their former prices. I cannot say that my health is improved by the air of the capital. At Verdun & even at Bitche, though sometimes attacked by an ague, I was free from any complaint in my breast; but here I feel some return of my old asthma and find the mounting of their immense staircases very laborious—no colds however—my lungs are much sounder than when I left you.—Happy should I be to find our poor sister even partially recovered—& to meet my ~~ne~~ old & new relations in good health & willing to receive the straggler back!

Mrs Cuming begs me to send through you her best respects to Mrs. Leslie, to whom she wrote last March by Major Falconer, and she requests he will send his answer to that letter under cover to the house of ^Major^ Jacques Laferre & Co Banquiers—~~No. 1 Rue Napoleon~~, Paris. At the same time remember me very kindly & gratefully to Mr Leslie.

I have always abstained in my letters from any public subject and it is still more ~~prud~~ necessary to do so ~~he~~ now. For any thing that regards myself I have nothing to communicate that deserves mention. I keep aloof from all public companies. I had gazed & gaped my fill of Paris & was just settling to my book when the account of McKenzie ~~derang~~ unhinged me.[88] Should his mission terminate favorably, we shall soon meet & I will not be long in Britain without seeing you.—Remember me most affectionately to all my sisters & young friends on the farm—God bless you—my dear Brother! yrs most faithfully Jos. Forsyth

88. Colin Alexander MacKenzie, whose negotiation of an exchange of prisoners ended in failure (see chapter 3).

July 24, 1811 — *Forsyth is transferred to Valenciennes*[89]

June 1, 1812 — *Forsyth dates his first edition of his book before sending the manuscript to reach Cadell*

LETTER 21: ISAAC TO JOSEPH, FEBRUARY 1, 1813

Elgin 1 February 1813—

recd 26 March
Repd 2d April 13[90]

My dear Brother,

Your interesting Letter of the 2nd. Jany. is just recieved and I hasten to reply to it. I never recieved any subsequent Letter from you since yours of June last, untill now, alltho beside my Letter of 2nd July which you acknowledge, I wrote you again in August. Since then I have also written Mr Tweedie[91] but am without any reply from him too. I am extremely distressed to find you so great a Sufferer from your stomach & asthma.[92] It is the more painful to me as from the tenor of your last Letter I had throughout all this winter thought & spoke of you as residing in the more genial climate of Nice or Nismes, and hence secure from those dreadful complaints which are so oppressive to you. I read with the most poignant regrett the affects of this severe Winter on your health and constitution, and trust in God that an early & warm Spring will renovate both more speedily than you could look for. {*space*} Our sister has had a very severe turn lately, but got through it wonderfully, and is now again in her ordinary state, occasionally very much distressed by Rheumatism, particularly in damp weather, but still utterly unable to walk or make any use of her limbs without the assistance of her servant. {*space*} My wife has been an invalid too, a very unusual thing with her, for the last three months; she is now thank God much better and with the returning Spring I trust will be restored to her usual Strength and activity. {*space*} All our children are in excellent health. The two eldest are at an excellent Day school lately established here; Eliza is very well forward in her branches [*?*], & promises to have some taste & execution [*?*] on the Piano. {*space*}

89. Isaac's introduction (*1816*, 7) explains that Forsyth was visited by two gendarmes on the 22nd as result of tightening of conditions for POWs. They gave him two days to remove from Paris, either to Verdun or Valenciennes (another town fortified by Vauban). Given the dissipation at Verdun (and the exploitative governance), Forsyth chose the latter.

90. Forsyth's annotation.

91. Not identified.

92. More evidence of Forsyth's stoicism.

Our good sister takes the trouble of preparing them all for this school, and they are infinitely obliged by the pains and attention bestowed on them by her. {*space*} Our friends at Sherriffston[93] are quite well. Our niece came down last Autumn from Edinb^r^, and left a fine little boy with her mother to nurse & care for. She has lately returned to her husband. The youngster thrives well. He is named / John Alexander, after her Grandfather & Uncle. {*space*} Your old worthy cousin Miss Nelly Gordon died about 10 days ago. Her Brother, the Milns, Pitgaveny,[94] Mr Leslie and all your other freinds are well, & constantly enquire about you. {*space*} I dined yesterday at Mr Thos. Cuming with your friend Mrs L. Cuming. She is always so kind & particular in her enquiries about you; that I shewed her your Letter. She regretts your bad health exceedingly, & feels for the anxiety under which you labour at present, and desired me to remember her to you in the kindest manner.

Affairs, I am affraid are not with her, as I could wish, or ^as^ her merits seem so highly to deserve. She is an amiable & intelligent woman, to whose society I am more attatched than any other (my own good wife's excepted) that I know. I have in every way in my power endeavoured to pay some of your obligation to her friendship.

[Blank space of three lines]

In regard to your uneasiness about the publication of your name in the List of those said by the french Minister of Marine to have broken their parole of honor, I have entered with considerable warmth, and acted as I trust will meet your ideas on the subject, and compleatly exonerate you from so foul & false a charge with every one who knows you & shall see what I have directed to be published in all the daily Papers in Lond^n^ where the List appeared. In the Morning Chronicle of the 26th Ult^o^ there is a very strong & angry Letter from Sir James Crawford (whose name had also been in the List, which bye the bye I never saw, tho' I read the Courier & Chronicle daily) denying the accusation, and daring the Minister to any thing like prooff of his having broke his Parole. {*space*} Now what I have done is this:—By this days post I wrote my particular freind M^r^. George Tod extracting that part of your Letter which relates to this business, and adding from my self what farther is necessary, and intreat him to show all to <u>The Editor</u> of the Morning Chronicle with whom he is in the closest / habits of freindship, requesting that he will mould the whole into the form of a letter with <u>my</u> signature, or a paragraph, as he shall think most effectual to the end in view, and publish this in the Courier, Chronicle,

93. The family of half brother John.
94. This is the Pitgaveny who went to London (letter 4) and to Malaya (letter 6) with the "intention of soon returning."

Times, Post,[95] & every paper in which tha [*sic*] abominable List appeared. {*space*} When it is compleated I will forward you a copy of these publications & doubt not but it will prove satisfactory.

[Blank space of three lines]

I have by this post ~~scr~~ written M^{r}. Tweedie whose silence has suprised me too, very much. I have taken the liberty of enclosing your Letter as the most effectual thing in the world to rouse him to attention to your wishes, and urged everything from myself I could think of, requesting him to write you; & write me, immediately on receipt, in what state the matter entrusted to him stands. I still hope good will come of it, «that»[96] he can offer sound sufficient reasons for the seeming delay that «has happened». I shall be most happy to read the book[97] eith[[er in print *flap*]] «or MS and» be careful of it, if in the latter state.

[Blank space of three lines]

There is little news here of an interesting nature. Corn & [[Wheat *flap*]] which are the staple commodities of this Country are at almost unprecedented prices. Wheat £3[98] per Bdl, Barley £2.10/, Oats £2.5/s, Potatoes £1.10/ Tho' these things do great good to the farming Body, who to be sure, are the cheif, in Morayshire; yet they also bear very heavily on the poor, and much privation & suffering must be the consequence.

Pray dear Joseph write me soon again, I shall be very uneasy untill I hear how your health is, & must therefore strongly enjoin you not to lose a week or even one day in being particular respecting it. {*space*} I shall write you soon with the result of our publication in Londn., & I hope with an answer from Mr Tweedie.

God bless & preserve You, Ever Yours faithfully

Isaac Forsyth

95. The leading London papers. The *Courier* was a Tory-supporting evening paper, under the ownership of Daniel Stuart. One of its former editors, James Parry, was a détenu who died in Verdun. Its most famous contributor was Samuel Taylor Coleridge. The *Morning Chronicle* was the leading Whig newspaper, then under the editorship of James Perry; its most famous contributor was William Hazlitt; the *Times* was Tory-leaning; The *Morning Post* was also owned by Daniel Stuart, and rival to the *Morning Chronicle*.
96. Words with « » are on a flap obscuring part of the right of the page. They have been torn from the left side, leaving a hole behind.
97. This seems to be the first edition of his book, published by Cadell in 1813.
98. The equivalent value (2018) of the £1.00 had fallen again to £59.90.

Autumn 1813	*Forsyth is transferred successively, as Allies advance, to Mons, Orleans, Blois*
April 6, 1814	*Forsyth, in Orleans, hears that allies entered Paris on March 31*
May 1814	*Forsyth arrives in England*[99]

LETTER 26: ISAAC TO JOSEPH, JUNE 2, 1814

Joseph Forsyth Esqr
at Thomas Dax Esqr
28 Queen's Square, Bloomsbury
London

Elgin 2nd June 1814

My dear Brother,

Your Letter of the 28th Ult^o from London gave us all a most agreeable Surprize. It arrived last night & I hasten to express my happiness & congratulations on your safe arrival in this land of liberty and health. I was looking to hear from you last night but it was from Paris in answer to mine to you there of the 15th, that I expected it. I wrote you under great anxiety & alarm, & am now much relieved by yours from London. Rest, good advise, & mild weather will speedily restore you. What precious freinds are Mr & Mrs Dax; and how doubly is the kindness of such freinds felt under your circumstances. Mrs D's attentions & society will do you as much good as Dr Walshman's prescriptions. Bye the bye I really wish you would see Dr Babington. I have more confidence in that man than any other of the Faculty I ever saw in Scotland or England.

I shall look again anxiously for your promised Letter of this week, when perhaps you shall have been able to form some plan. If, as I trust, the very air of this "Blest Isle" becomes bracing and balsamic to you, and you gather strength and firmness as fast as I hope, then we will expect you in the "Montpelier of Scotland" early in July. I cannot express how desirous of this meeting your sister and myself, and very many more are. If you would find a land journey too fatiguing either to Edinburgh, or even from Edinburgh northward, I would recommend your taking a passage in the Smack Hero, Swanson master. A man whom I know very well, /

99. Isaac's introduction to *1816*, 8.

who would be attentive to you, ^has excellent accomodation,^ and ^would^ land you at Burghead. If, as I hope your strength and your curiosity will induce & enable you to take a highland tour from Edinb^r I will meet you there, at any time you fix, and travel north with you in the most deliberate manner you choose. {*space*} Your Query about the Name & residence of your married neice is another prooff how many of my Letters have never reached you. I have told you in least half a score, that she was married to Adam Longmore Junr Esqr of the Exchequer, lived at 22 London Street, near Edinb^r, and has a lovely boy (John Alec) about 18 months old. Should you come to Edinb^r, I will fix on a particular Hotel where I shall be before you, & act as your ciciron to <u>"Auld Reekie"</u>. When you return to Italy you will do the honors of <u>Rome</u> for me.

I saw your friend Kitchen for a few minutes lately, and frequently during a 3 days stay with his Aunt here some time before. He is a most aimiable, intelligent young man, & extremely attatched to you. Our conversations were solely occupied about you, Verdun, & France. He shewed me your Letter from Orleans which he recieved at Morlaix. I saw by it too another prooff of the irregularity of my letters to you. You there desire him to mention that you had written me to interest some of the Gordon family[100] in your release by an application to Lord Aberdeen. I recieved your Letter & instantly addressed The Marquis of Huntly, as the most active and persevering friend of that noble House, the very inheritor of his mothers qualities in this respect. His Lordship entered <u>instantly</u> into the business with great warmth, but as the Armistice was broke up before <u>Your</u> Letter arrived here, he wrote Lord Castlereagh,[101] then (September last) at Dover Castle. The Marquis was pleased to send me the Ministers answer which was most polite but declared in the frankest manner his total inability to be of any Service to you. This Letter I enclosed to you, & sent it thro' your friends near the Mansion House to your address in Valenciennes. I am thus particular, for this reason, that I think you / should wait on Lord Huntly to pay your respects & acknowledgments. I mentioned the probability that you would do so to my friend Mr Innes, and asked him to be your master of ceremonies. John's intimacy with Mr & Miss Brodie procured him the honor of being the only other Gentleman present at the marriage ceremony, except the immediate parties. He must hence be well qualified to make you known to The Marquis.

100. Possibly related, since Isaac mentions, in letter 21, "your old worthy cousin Miss Nelly Gordon."

101. Robert Stewart (1769–1822), Viscount Castlereagh, was foreign secretary and in 1814 represented England's interests at Chaumont and then Vienna.

[Blank space of one line]

Don't talk of going to my sisters for she has no bed, tho' excellently well accomodated herself; nor don't talk of my making you a man of consequence, or our finding you an incumbrance. All this is very unkind & unlike you, and very distressing to my feelings. Pray who is there on earth that has such a claim to, or such a possession of my heart & my house (my goodwife and bairns only excepted) as you. We have two spare bedrooms & a Drawing room on the upper floor, one of these & the drawing room as a Study will always be yours, and be a saf<e *hole*> retreat <from *hole*> the din & noise of a half a dozen misses <*hole*> as to < *hole*> he was mentioned when I believed you to be <*hole*> a hale <& heart *hole*>y man. Now you shall use him or not, when and whence you please, for he is very nearly an idler, & <*hole*> ~~scribble~~ ~~*illegible*~~ devoted to your service.

[Blank space of one line]

My sister & my wife & the Children all join in expressing their joy at your arrival, earnest prayers for your speedy recovery, and affectionate regards to you——

I am ever My dearest Brother

Yours faithfully

Isaac Forsyth

I cannot omit mentioning a dream which Mrs F. had the night before your last letter arrived. We had been talking much of you for the past fortnight, and I had calculated your Letter from Paris would arrive as last night, all this must have led to the dream which she told in the morning. She dreamt she saw my clerk coming from the Post Office with Letters & newspapers, that she went down stairs & took them from him, & on my opening a small Letter addresed by you, we found only a Poem enclosed congratulating You on your arrival in London.

LETTER 27: ISAAC TO JOSEPH, JUNE 30, 1814

Joseph Forsyth Esqr
at Mr Falkener's Plumber,
~~at Thos Dax Esqr~~
Hampton, Middlesex
~~22, Queen's Square, Bloomsbury~~
~~London~~

Elgin 30th June 1814

My dear Brother,

Your Letter of the 20th is an agreeable prooff of your convalescence. The Country has done you good. What may we not hope for from native air & the best of the season, which I trust is still before us, for hitherto it has not been steadily good. {*space*} That was another unfortunate rencounter with those rattling sovereigns you had. But now every danger of that kind is gone bye, and I hope with them your evil genius is gone too, and that nothing remains but radical and permanent reestablishment to your health and spirits.

I see you are determined on a voyage. Perhaps in the present degree of your strength, and liability to cold, it is the safest as it certainly will be the easiest mode of conveyance. I am very happy to say that my favourite Smack & Captain will be ready for dispatch at the time I should think the most convenient for you; on the 15th July, the Hero, Swanson master, will start from Downe's Wharff for Burghead. I happened to be writing John Mason Monday last, and begd of him to be informed respecting the first smack, & to communicate to you. Since then I hear the above & nothing of the kind could give me more pleasure, as I hope you will experience all the comfort & accomodation you can reasonably expect in such a conveyance. Swanson will bring to at Lossiemouth and put you ashore there, where you will find my wife, who goes down for 2 or 3 weeks on the 3rd July, and who will send up for a chaise & be most happy to accompany you home. I reckon on this happening about the 20th or 22nd, by which time I expect to be returned from / a Journey to Abd^{n}, Stirlng, Glasg^{w}, and Edinb^{ro} for which I sett out on the 2nd July. {*space*} If you have anything to say to me in Edinb^{r}, or anything that I can do for you there, a Letter will find me at Messrs Constable & Co, Booksellers, from the 16th to the 20th. On the 22nd I hope to be in my own house.

You amuse me with the state of society at Hampton. I suspect we are everywhere geting too much into their mode of determining a man's merit; by the extent & capacity of a man's show. I am surprized at your want of success in search of a habitation in so wide a field of enquiry. I have always said you would pitch somewhere within a dozen miles of London, & I think ~~it~~ that is the best circle for you in the Island. But my dear Brother before fixing, would not you do as well to trust to Lodgings for the first Winter, that you might ascertain whether everything in the situation, society, and a thousand other necessary considerations were to your mind, before you went to any expence in finishing, furnishing &c &c. {*space*} I hope & know you will give me Credit when I say that no settlement by any other individual on earth could bring so much satisfaction to me as yours would in Elgin; but I am not selfish enough to sacrifice (if I could) your best chance for steady health & mental enjoyment, to a wish for your residence here, where three fourths of the year is very unfit for an invalid and where the State of Society is yet by no means on a level with your desires. /

I hope you will make another attempt at seeing His Grace,[102] and The Marquis. They are both very aimiable Noblemen, and from the interest they feel in the happiness of others, richly deserve all the respect that can be bestowed on them.

As to our cousin Stephen I am really at a loss to point out his residence, tho' I am sure you will make another effort to reach it before quitting town. I think it very likely Mr Mason can inform you.

My goodwife & the bairns are all busy & well, this is the day of their annual examination at school, tommorrow the Magistrates give all the Youngsters in the place a Bal[[l *blot*]] in reward for their application & progress—and next da[[y *blot*]] all hands rush away from the trammells of Schoolkeeping to the Country & the seaside;—Ours go to Cromarty, & they are all in the clouds about it.

May God almighty bless & preserve you my dear Joseph and give us a happy meeting.

Give our affectionate regards to our estimable friends M^{r} & Mrs Dax. Our sister sends her Love. She is a little way in the Country for change of air, but gets on very slowly.

I am ever yours faithfully

I^{c} Forsyth

Mrs Jack particularly wishes you to call on our relation Mrs Burns—somewhere in the City road. John Mason will find the address. Mrs Peter Gordon has been enquiring particularly about you, pray call on her; she lives, 8, Barnsbury St. Islington. Her eldest daughter is married, & will be happy to see you. I have no commissions for you except one. You'll remember the large map of the Province of Moray I once tormented you so much about; it is in the hands of the engraver, Barrett 289 Holborn, if you can possibly obtain it from him, & send it to George Smith[103] at

102. That is, Viscount Castlereagh.

103. George Smith, who in 1814 was a clerk for John Murray (see note 12 to chapter 1 and note 4 to chapter 3 for more information and for the speculation that he is the "Smyth" in the John Murray ledgers to whom Forsyth's play *The Condottiero* was passed in 1829). He seems

Mr Murray's, Bookseller Albermarle Street, I shall be glad. Pay no more postage, or I won't open your Letters.

July/August to September 1814 Forsyth visits Isaac[104]

LETTER 28: ISAAC TO JOSEPH, OCTOBER 20, 1814

Mr Forsyth
at Mr Dax's
28, Queen Square
Bloomsbury London

Elgin 20th Octor 1814

My dear Brother

Your long expected Letter of the 8th relieved me from much anxiety. I had no idea that you could possibly be 16 days on your Voyage. The weather here for 12 or 14 days after you left us was beautiful, tho' the winds certainly were unfavourable to your purpose. But to be baffled 5 days off Fraserburgh, cooped up 2 in the Humber, and then almost thrown away in Yarmouth roads, with the episode of a Gallopping horse in the Storm never once entered into my contemplation. I saw however soon after your departure enough to make me smile at the Sagacity of my cousin & myself in predicting a rattling Northwester to you which would land you at Downe's Wharff on the 5th day. Thank God however, alls well, and that you have found the same kind friends you expected.

I have little to say but that we are "all well" here—that Mrs F. found her little Grandson recovering when she arrived in Edinbr, that he is now almost quite recovered, and that we expect her back soon. About a week after you went Mr. Innes arrived, & I daily regretted your departure. I should have been so happy to have made you better acquainted with a very worthy fellow. He was here about 10 days, and dined in a different house every day. He gratified me by taking his first dinner in Morayshire with us, & was afterwards in the Evengs. & Morngs. as much with us as the kindness of his numerous frds would admit. He is to be in Town about the 30th inst, & says he will find you out as soon as he can, & hopes you will see him

---

to have been then living at 23 Doughty Street, Mecklenburg Square, where Isaac directs letter 32 "as I have no frank today." He will later advise on the suitability of the second son of Mrs. Burns for the bookselling trade (*L* 29). He was a conduit for the publication of the second edition of *Forsyth's Italy*.

104. For two months (*L* 28, 32) or three months (Isaac's introduction to *1816*, 8).

frequently. If you should wish for any information or any service within his power at any time I know he will be gratified by your free & frank application to him. I mentioned that I had suggested to you as a material thing worth the seeing for once the first meeting of the Highland Society (in March) / He said he was an old member & that it would give him the greatest pleasure imaginable to introduce you as his frd. This, I should much rather like than your going with "the Minister at War", & you can mention it to Mr Innes. Since you left us the Scite of Gray's Hospital has been fixed.[105] I think the situation will delight you. There is a little rising green bank behind & to the westward of M^{rs}. Spence's house, divided from it only by a road leading to D^{r}. Stephen's property, & formed into a sort of tongue by the road that leads to my farm. I think you & I looked at it as a fine situation for a Cottage. It will be a noble termination to the Street, & to the view from our Parlour & Drawing room end windows. The plan of the Hospital and two Elevations are given in by Mr Gillespie of Edinb^{r}. The medical people speak of the plan as most excellent, & the Elevations look admirably. The whole can be done within £6000.[106] and the Trustees have readily agreed to allow £7000 for ^its^ exteriour walls round the ground, forming the Grand &^{c} &^{c}. Gillespie has agreed to force Marywell into every room in the House by a pump, for £100, & half an hour a day's labour from the House Porter. There is now an application to the Lord Chancellor for the money to go on with the Whole, & we expect it will be begun next Spring. M^{r}. Innes, who was here at the moment, can give you everything about it. I am happy to say that I succeeded beyond my expectations in a hive of fine heather Honey for M^{rs}. Dax. There never was such a scarcity seen. This hive contains about 2lb^{s}[107] of Honey of a very fine Quality, grown on the banks of the Spey. It was shipt by the Fame on 14th. inst and addressed to "Thomas Dax Esqr., 28, Queens Square Bloomsbury London". I hope it will come safe, as I gave particular directions to keep the top uppermost. When M^{rs} D wishes to get out the Combs, I recommend her drawing (with a shoemakers pinchers) the four cross sticks on which the Bees form their Combs. She will then get each of the Combs to come away seperately and entire. The ends of the sticks project beyond the ^outer^ sides of the Hive. / When you write (which I expect will be soon) you will do me a favour by mentioning if there are any Elementary Books for the French language superiour to those in common use in this Country, by which the Children in France are taught the Grammar &^{c}.

105. Endowed by Dr. Alexander Gray, who made his fortune with the East India Company. The infirmary opened in 1819.

106. The pound had picked up slightly to £64.20 in 1814. This is equivalent to £385,200.00.

107. A guess, since the writing looks more like "26th."

A friend of mine has applied to me on this subject & I could give no information, beyond Pomey, Chambaud, Scott, Levizac &^{c}, but all this he was familiar with, & thought something purely french might be had & would be superiour. Of this pray inform.

I beg to know particularly where you are settled, how you like it, and what your plan of life is. Even, the minutest information, about your self will be highly interesting & gratifying. Have <*hole*> Smith privately, & has he pointed out the <*hole*> <*hole*> you to apply in regarding the business Channel for [*?*] talked of. I am most anxious to know your procee<d *hole*>ings. Poor Mr. Tod has been in miserable health, but we were all rejoiced to learn that he had made a most wonderful recovery. Our worthy fr^{d} Parson Gordon has lost his eldest son James. He died on this day s'enight of Water in the head, & very suddenly. This is a very heavy affliction. Fortunately his Wife keeps well. Marriages are the order of the day here. Mr Warden marries Miss Dunbar of Duffey tommorrow. Tom Brander, Miss Leslie next Saturday; and others are on the tapie.[108] M^{rs}. Cuming gives way to the happy pair on the 22nd, & leaves this about the 25th.—Would you ask either of the M Dax what their opinion ~~scr~~ of the Norwich Union Life Association is, as to its responsibility—It is a Life Insurance Company on the same principle as The Equitable, & proffesses to insure at 10 p^{r}. Cent less/annual Premium, but my freind who enquires, is desirous to have the opinion of a Gentleman likely to be informed, as to its Stability & final Responsibility.

My goodwife & the Bairns with Miss Grace all desire to be remembered in the most affectionate manner to you.

I was very angry with you on my return from Burghead to hear of your most unnecessary Profession!!

God bless you Ever Yours
Is^{c} Forsyth

LETTER 29: ISAAC TO JOSEPH, NOVEMBER 20, 1814

Elgin 20 Novem^{r}. 1814

My dear Brother

Your long & kind Letter came while I was on a business Journey thro' Sutherland, Ross, Nairn, Moray & Banffshire. I have only yesterday finished that & the little

108. "Sur le tapis": on the tablecloth—that is, "for discussion."

bustle connected with it, & now (Sunday) I take the first leisure hour to thank you for so interesting and Brotherly a communication. {*space*} Since then our worthy friend Tod has gone "to another and a better Country"! M^{rs}. Spark here, too, followed him on the 7th. day after. Their complaints were alike, their duration alike, and their termination nearly at the same time. His attatchment to her was such that he has left her £300 & £200 to her 2 sons. His other bequests are alike judicious & generous. We felt here so much attatchment to him, that ~~scribb~~ his loss is mourned like a Brother. The Morayshire Club at their first meeting on the 2nd Decem^{r} are to appear in mourning, as a tribute of respect to his memory.

I am just informed of another death in which we are still more interested, and which involves great distress and inconvenience to a very helpless family. Our relation poor Mrs Burns is no more! Her husband writes me that she died after rather a sudden illness on the 5th. ins^{t}. She has been for many years in delicate health, & without the means of much care or comfort for herself, her constitution has been broken with excessive anxiety & fatigue in rearing a very numerous family, of which seven are still alive. He says it was his wish & intention / to have communicated this event to you & requested your presence at her funeral, but unfortunately he had not your address.

Catherine & I are much concerned about the children, and anxious to ascertain how they can be carried thro' without the care of such a Mother. {*space*} I hope you will see Burns soon (at the Book Office India H^{o}.) and enter a little into his plans & his affairs. He does not seem to me to have had one friend among all his relations, & on every difficulty in his situation (& these have not been few) has always applied to his wifes connections. He is a good "saarless" sort of fellow, with no action of mind or body, & seems fit only for a drudge in a public office. Between his Wife's, his sister, and his own embarrassments in life & business, they have cost John Forsyth Esq his sister Mrs McK., & myself, upwards of £600. Still we cannot see the Children go to misery without extending a helping hand.

It strikes me that M^{r}. Innes, M^{r}. Barclay, M^{r}. Grant Allan, & M^{r}. Chas Grant would all lend a hand to get them into some of those numerous hospitals where board, education, & apprenticing are provided for such helpless creatures;—if the pride of their Father & Aunt will admit of such a provision. {*space*} The eldest son William (17) is now in a Bankers Counting Ho; the second (about 13) was intended by his mother for a Booksellers apprentice, and if you'll send for George Smith & consult with him about the practicability of geting him into a respectable place for 7 or 8 Yrs to receive board & washing, I shall be glad that he succeeds. If George cannot find such a situation, and that the lad gives it ^still^ a preferrance to any other, I should try to find room for him here, provided George Smith after examining into his talents, education, and disposition, thinks he would answer my purpose as an apprentice; otherwise, I beg neither you nor he will mention this matter, which I do not allude / to in any Letter to the Father this day. The other four boys are under 12 years, & it is for them I could wish to interest you.

I have the greatest repugnance to involve you in any such matter more especially under your present distressing situation from asthma,[109] but the case is clamarous, & you will have pleasure in doing good. Your account of the mode of conducting Reviews in Lond^{n} astonished me, so very little do we at the extremities know what is doing in the centre. It not only surprizes me but disapoints me sadly, for I had in my own mind reckond on your taking at least a couple of Hundreds from that Source, annually. I hope, however to hear soon that you are engaged in Something of importance, that you will enter on Con amore. I am certain a little moderate employment of your mind will also be useful to the Body as well as the purse,[110] and that everything will go on pleasantly when that is the case. {*space*} Without having any prying impertinence in my disposition[111] I yet feel that anxiety about my friends, and above all others in your final arrangements, that you must consider me as looking with desire to the period when you can properly make them known. {*space*} We are all hands looking forward to the green fields & sunshine of May to tempt you back again to us in the Country. There is a probability of West Park being to be Let soon. Col: Hay is a very anxious candidate for Main,[112] & if he succeeds, the former might be had. Would it be desireable to you? You know the accomodation, the rent, & can suppose the taxes, & expence of keeping the Garden, & an establishment for such a place. There is a situation at the east end of Bishopmiln, on the top of the "Brae", which possesses a beautiful view of every object in the / vicinity of Elgin. The area is about 150 feet by 60 with the same hanging bank that Captn Anderson has for his Garden. This could be had for a small fee or duty I believe, & you could have the satisfaction of building a Classic Cottage after your own taste. I see no prospect of your geting the aimiable widows House, unless you take herself with it.

109. Evidence of the permanent damage to Forsyth's health.
110. A healthy mind in a healthy body . . . with a healthy purse!
111. Isaac's defensive comment that he has not "any prying impertinence in my disposition" may be protesting too much!
112. The word clearly reads "Main," but "Nairn" may be intended.

Thanks for your entertaining information regarding our fr^d Stephen. I believe what he says respecting the produce of his pen is stricktly true. I thought his noble patron would have been more bountiful.

Pray have you fallen in with M^r. T., and how was your letter taken?

I am much obliged to you & M^r. Dax for the information regarding the Norwich Association. As well as for the friend I alluded to, I have some idea of insuring a thousand pound or two on my own life for the benefit of my family, & I should like to know which Office was reckoned in London the most sound, & where the business was also done on the most moderate terms. It is seldom however that both these advantages are, or can be, combined. Did your freind the Lord Mayor insist on your presence at the civic feast on the 9th ins.? {*space*} Have you seen Kean? Pray give me your opinion of him.[113] I beg my kindest regards to your worthy Host & Hostess. Are they gone to Acton, & do you still occupy 38 in Queen's Square? My Fire side send each & all even little Kate, their love & duty to you. So does the Goodwife of Sherriffston & Miss Grace. Pray write me soon again and in the same agreeable manner.

Yours ever Isaac Forsyth

November 1814 — *Forsyth studies in the reading room of the British Museum for revision of his book*

LETTER 32: ISAAC TO JOSEPH, MARCH 27, 1815

Joseph Forsyth Esqr
No. 23, Doughty Street,
Mecklenburgh Square.
London.

Elgin 27th. March 1815

My dear Brother

I am very pleased with the expedition and the contents of your reply. {*space*} M^rs. Forsyth continues to mend gradually & the young ones nearly well.

113. In this year, 1814, Edmund Kean's demonic Shakespearean acting exploded on the London stage at Drury Lane Theatre. That year, Kean played the roles of Shylock, Richard III, Hamlet, and Macbeth. *Macbeth* opened on November 5. Since this letter is dated November 20, Isaac is undoubtedly enquiring if his brother has seen Kean in the Scottish Play.

M^{rs}. Mack. has kindly remained with us 'till now, but goes in 10 or 12 days. Her presence has been of infinite consequence to her sisters recovery. Eliza is flattered by your compliment, and Anne is straining to share in your good opinion. {*space*} I am most happy at the issue of a certain interview; it is exactly what I anticipated.

Now that you have your Cash from Cadel[114] I am glad too. I really think you ought to consider of a new Ed^{n}.; and as these folks have behaved so shabbily, I would sell it to Longman & Co., or any of those Houses (Murray perhaps) who would give you a handsome sum down for it. Smith can better advise the proper channel than I, and I am convinced he would gladly take every trouble for you in the business. {*space*} Be so good as say to him that I received his Letter of the 20th and the Courier he was so kind as send.—I was alarmed lest he had had a return of his Spring illness and Confined altogether, as he did not acknowledge any of a String of Letters & comissions for a long time past. Now I see the cause clearly, & am much obliged by the attentions he has given to several of them, particularly that to a little namesake friend of mine who I am /breeding a Sailor with a view of bringing him out in the India Country trade.[115] {*space*} George can explain the matter to you if you should think it worth the trouble. {*space*} He has however said nothing respecting Six Historical Prints of Woolett size after West &c,[116] in frames (black & Gold) which I asked him to enquire the prices of & write to me respecting. Pray put him in mind of this, & if you can be of any service in the business I will thankyou; the best subjects, & the quality of the prints you must be master of. They are for our friend Wm Young Esqre of Inveragie. If they did not come too high in price I believe I should purchase another sett for my friend Mrs Mackenzie ~~scr~~ who feels so deep an interest in our family and takes such a burthen of them. Like Young's I should wish them to be of the very best impressions and Choice Subjects

114. Cadell published the first edition in 1813. Presumably they held Forsyth's payment until his release.

115. The Indian country trade, also called "local trade," was the term for highly lucrative private trading, often carried out by members of the British East India Company, typically between Indian and Chinese ports; for an account of its workings from the perspective of American participation, see Lisa Sturm-Lind, *Actors of Globalization: New York Merchants in Global Trade, 1784–1812* (Leiden, Netherlands: Brill, 2018), 48–50.

116. William Woollett (or Woolett; 1735–1785) had been royal engraver by appointment. His most celebrated prints were published by John Boydell, of Shakespeare Gallery fame, and included historical scenes taken from the painter Benjamin West. The Royal Academy's copy of Woollett's engraving of *The Death of General Wolfe* (after West) is given as 427 millimeters by 590 millimeters (16.8 inches by 23.2 inches; "The Death of General Wolfe, 1 January 1776," Royal Academy Collection Online, accessed October 18, 2018, https://www.royalacademy.org.uk/art-artists/work-of-art/the-death-of-general-wolfe). Presumably this was "Woolett size."

from the History of England & Scotland, to match in Size and if the subjects were in pairs so much the better; tho this latter circumstance is not essential.

I write this for G.S. here as I have no frank today & really have no time. If you have leisure to co-operate with him in the Choice, he will manage the bargaining part of the business finely. /

I now turn to your proposal. Be fully assured that nothing on earth could give Mrs. F. & myself more satisfaction than having you with us on the friendly familiar footing we passed the two months you were here last Summer. And that your too scrupulous mind may be perfectly and forever at rest on the score of obligation, we will take you in the manner you propose, at the rate of One Hundred Pounds[117] Pr. Annum, which we know will fully cover every expence you can possibly put us to. This includes the accomodations (such as they are) that you held before, or when at Haughland, what we then fixed on—with the same sort of table as formerly—Washing—and the command of a saddle Horse, to which latter convenience I must have you take more kindly than you did before. Tho' I have said Pr. Ann:, you must consider yourself as in a Coffeehouse with us as to the time of your removal. When you find it more agreeable or more necessary for you to be elsewhere than in the North, there must be no ceremony <on *hole*> your part, and on ours there will be nothing I am sure <than *hole*> regrett. {*space*} I have only now to mention that it is necessary <for *hole*> Mrs. F. to spend a month or two on the sea side after the middle or end of June to recover Strength from the use of the Bath & the Break. If you chose to do so too it is the simplest matter imaginable to add a Bedroom to her accomodations & you are both sett up. But if you preferr Haughland Cottage where I shall sleep and breakfas[t] the girls & we will carry on the system there while she is enjoying & encreasing her Stock of health, & some of us will be continually going down to see her. {*space*} Another thing is that the present tenants hold the Cottage by agreement to the 30th. day of April, & with some little repairs we may reckon it will / be the 10th. of May before we can be in possession.

There is nothing ^however^ in the world to hinder you to come down instantly, as your old room & closet will be ready for you, & you will find us jogging on exactly in the old style. {*space*} As to the proposal of tenanting the Cottage, I don't think that setting up a system of eating & drinking & servants would suit a person so unfixt as you yet are, but if you should be now or hereafter desirous to entertain

117. The equivalent value (2018) of the £1.00 had risen to £68.00, almost to the value of 1801.

it, I shall be most ready to accomodate you 'till you are permanently and better settled than there. The rent for furniture & all should be at £36 P^r ann: which as I take that money from Mr Reid for it, would save any scruple in the world that ^even^ You ^could^ possibly muster up. If you could, put a plan of Paris into your trunk.[118] I want to be acquainted with the leading points in it. What think you of the progress of your old tormentor.[119] Thank God he can't touch a hair of your head now. I cannot describe how cheerful I feel when that idea comes upon me. Love from Catherine Eliza[120] & all to you, & a speedy voyage!

As ever I. Forsyth

April 1815	*Forsyth collects his books from Elgin*
September 1815	*Forsyth and Isaac make an excursion to Staffa*
September 21, 1815	*Forsyth dies*
November 1815	*Isaac corresponds with Michael Anderson, a friendly bookseller of Edinburgh, about the publication of the second edition of* Fosyth's Italy

LETTER 33: MICHAEL ANDERSON TO ISAAC, NOVEMBER 4, 1815

Edinburgh 4 Nov: 1815

My Dear Sir,

I have at length got through our dilatory trade, but Blackwood has not behaved like a Gentleman—after keeping my Catalogue for days, has not only declined to make any offer, but he has biassed the minds of others, and they also decline to say what they will give—I had a long interview with two of them today, and after pledging my honour that their offer should be sacred, and never recalled, Messrs Brown & Black came the length of only £480—They seem anxious to have

118. This links with Isaac's request for French grammars for a friend. His French is none too good, and he seems to be contemplating the visit that eventually he did make. It prompts the suspicion that the good-doing Isaac has sometimes his own interests behind charitable endeavors. See how the Norwich Insurance queries lead him to think of investing for himself.

119. On the March 20, 1815, Napoleon entered Paris, beginning the "Hundred Days" rule, which ended with his abdication after the Battle of Waterloo and his exile to St. Helena.

120. Two of his three daughters. Ann, not yet able to talk in 1806 (*L* 11), would now be about seven years old but would not have known her uncle.

the Library, and say they have gone to the utmost stretch. They suggested that as they are to publish a catalogue for auction in six weeks, to publish your Books along with it, circulate it both in England & Scotland, and that you should have whatever your property brought on paying your proportion of expenses £10.10/-. I do not like this—your sterling gold would push off their base metal on <*hole* > the hurry of a moment it might bring nothing more than the tras<h *hole*> they however said that you could fix prices.—The Catalogue is sent to Mr Brown—I do not know its value, but I am of opinion, that in in the event of the offer in London not coming up to expectation, and that nothing more cane be made here the Library should be sold by itself here, by Ballantyne—print a catalogue, circulate it judiciously a genteel company would be brought together, and the value of this excellent collection might thus be obtained. We could affix prices at which they should not go below—I should see justice done, the money daily collected by myself at the conclusion of every sale and lodged in the Bank—The conduct of the Booksellers has led me to think of this, and if it failed there would be no deadly expenses concerned in proportion to our chance—I should like to hear from you when Mr Brown writes to you and in case that I may do any thing farther let me know what is the highest offer you get.

I ever am,

My Dear Sir,

Yours very faithfully

Michael Anderson

[UNNUMBERED] MICHAEL ANDERSON TO ISAAC (TWO SEPARATE PAGES), NOVEMBER 18, 1815

Isaac Forsyth
Bookseller
Elgin

dependence here—it is only when he perceives my indifference, that he gives the matter any consideration—I rather think that if Murray restricts his offer to a limited time you must close. The Book is excellent—I have read it, but unless the notes were translated it never will be so generally read as it deserves—it is, at any rate confined to the learned, and to conneiseurs in the fine arts—if you close with Murray—make it part of the bargain, that I shall print the Work—you can safely say, that from the Books you have seen of mine, that I'll do it as well as any man in London or Edinb—will get his proofs franked, and get him a fair bargain of Paper

&c and to the boot can give the Book greater than ordinary publicity by Extracts occasionally in my News Paper which circulates from the one end of the /[121]

I find that the work has been often in request here after the supply was gone—The Edition would clear more than £100 but the Booksellers are such a selfish contemptible set, they would set their faces against it unless interested.

121. A page seems to be missing here.

APPENDIX A

Works of Art Forsyth Saw

This list uses Forsyth's spelling of artists and his descriptive titles, except those in square brackets. Page numbers refer to the second edition of *Forsyth's Italy*.

General observations	**Pages**
Orders of columns	68, 153–155
Materials	131, 153
Restoration of palaces	141–142
Nature of architecture	165–167, fn
Design of palaces	170–172
Relievos sepulchral and monumental	232

Name of Artist	**Subject**	**Location**	**Page**
	ARCHITECTURE		
	Aqueducts	Rome: Esquiline, Campagna	133
	Arches, see also relievos		
	Bath	Rome	145
	Baths of Caracalla	Rome	150
	Baths of Diocletian	Rome	151
	Gates of Rome	Rome	175
Michelangelo	Capitol	Rome	206

(*continued*)

Name of Artist	Subject	Location	Page
	ARCHITECTURE		
	Arches, see also relievos		
	Caracalla's Circus	Rome	148
	Colosseum	Rome	142–145
	Pantheon	Rome	134–137
	Villa Albani	Rome	220
	Churches		
	Cathedral	Pisa	9–11
	Campo Santo	Pisa	12–14
	Leaning Tower	Pisa	1112
	Baptistery	Pisa	11
Brunelleschi	Cathedral	Florence	63–64
Michelangelo	de' Depositi [Chapel Princes]	Florence	66
Borromini	St. John Lateran	Rome	158
Honorius	St. Paul's	Rome	159
	Santo Stefano Rotondo	Rome	160
Michelangelo	St. Peter's Basilica	Rome	177–183
	Jesus	Rome	183
	S. Pietro in vincoli	Rome	185
	S. Martino ai Monti	Rome	185
	S. Pietro in Montorio	Rome	186
Bramante	Tempietto	Rome	186
Bernini	S. Bibiana	Rome	187
	[S. Maria della Concezione]	Rome	187
	Fountains		
	Navona, Trevi, Termi, Acqua Paola	Rome	174

Name of Artist	Subject	Location	Page
	DRAWING/ENGRAVING		
Michelangelo	Christ	Palazzo Buonarroti	69n
Michelangelo	Fortune	Palazzo Buonarroti	69n
Morghen	Last Supper of da Vinci		355
	FRESCO		
	[Triumph of Death]	Pisa: Campo Santo	13
	Herculaneum frescoes	Portici: Museum	288
	Pompeii Frescoes	Pompeii	307
Adimollo		Arezzo: Duomo	96
Adimollo	Rape of the Sabines	Siena	453
Adimollo		Siena: Dominican chapel	105
Andrea del Sarto	Madonna del Sacco	Florence: Santissima Nunziata	443
Andrea del Sarto	Dead Christ	Florence: Santissima Nunziata	444
Caracci (both)	ceilings	Bologna	328
Caracci (both)	ceiling	Rome: Palazzo Farnese	226
Caravaggio	Palazzi façades	Florence: nr Santa Croce	67
da Vinci	Last Supper	Milan: Dominican onvent	354
Euphranor	Twelve gods	Athens: Temple of Ceramcinus	355
Giulio Romano	Fall of the Giants	Mantua: Palazzo Te	349
Guercino	Hercules and Antaeus	Bologna	328
Guercino	Aurora	Rome: Villa Lodovisi	225
Guido Reni	Aurora	Rome: Palazzo Rospigliosi	225
Mengs	[Triumph of History]	Rome: Library, Vatican	202
Mengs	Mount Parnassus	Rome: Villa Albani	222
Mengs	Mount Parnassus	Rome: Villa Albani	429
Michelangelo	Conversion of St. Paul	Rome: Vatican	203

(*continued*)

Name of Artist	Subject	Location	Page
	FRESCO		
Michelangelo	Crucifixion of St. Peter	Rome: Vatican	203
Michelangelo	Last Judgement	Rome: Vatican	203
Perruzzi	Sibyl	Siena: Fonte Giusta	106
Pinturrichio	[Aeneas Piccolomoni]	Siena: Duomo library	104
Sodoma	Christ	Siena: Franciscan cloister	107
Santi di Tito	Christ dining with Pharisee	Florence: Santissima Nunziata	444
	ILLUMINATION		
Oderisi	Greek & Latin classics	Florence: Laurentian Library	47
	MOSAIC		
Duccio	Mosaics of Siena	Siena: Duomo	102
Meccarino	Mosaics of Siena	Siena: Duomo	102
Sosus	Four doves mosaic	Rome: Museum, Capitol	209
	PAINTING		
Greek artists	Madonnas	Florence: Galleria degli Uffizi	40
	Lord Cowper	Cortona: Etruscan academy	98
[Uccello]	John Hawkwood	Florence: Duomo	65
	Christian and Orphic	Rome: Catacombs	163
	Paintings of hell	Rome: Jesus & St. Ignatius	184
	Magdalen	Rome: Palazzo Doria	197
[Caravaggio]	Flight to Egypt	Rome: Palazzo Doria	198
Andrea del Sarto	Altarpiece of four saints	Vallombrosa: chapel	83
Andrea del Sarto	Macchiavelli	Rome: Palazzo Doria	197
Andrea del Sarto	portrait	Naples: Capo di Monte	269

Name of Artist	Subject	Location	Page
	PAINTING		
Bassano	Scriptural paintings	Rome: Palazzo Doria	196
Caracci, Annibale	Silk palliotto	Prato Vecchio: Sacro Eremo	88
Caracci, Annibale	Dead Christ	Rome: Palazzo Doria	196
Caracci, Annibale	Landscapes	Rome: Palazzo Doria	197
Caravaggio	Infant Christ	Prato Vecchio: Sacro Eremo	88
Caravaggio	St. Michael	Rome: S. Maria della Concezione	187
Caravaggio	Christ	Rome: Palazzo Giustiniani	194
Caravaggio	Faun	Rome: Palazzo Giustiniani	194
Caravaggio	St. Thomas	Rome: Palazzo Giustiniani	194
Caravaggio	St. Jerome	Rome: Palazzo Doria	197
Casolani	Flight into Egypt	Siena: San Quirico	106
Claude	Two beautiful examples	Rome: Palazzo Colonna	190
Claude	Two Landscapes	Rome: Palazzo Doria	198
D'Arpino	History of the kings	Rome: Museum, Capitol	213
da Vinci	St. John the Baptist	Naples: Palazzo di Francavilla	270
da Vinci	Joan II of Naples	Rome: Palazzo Doria	197
Domenichino	St. John the Divine	Rome: Palazzo Giustiniani	194
Domenichino	Landscapes	Rome: Palazzo Doria	197
Durer	Misers	Rome: Palazzo Doria	198
Guercino	Saints	Naples: Capo di Monte	269

(*continued*)

Name of Artist	Subject	Location	Page
	PAINTING		
Guido da Siena	Madonna	Siena: Dominican church	105
Guido Reni	St. Michael	Rome: S. Maria della Concezione	187
Guido Reni	Madonnas	Rome: Palazzo Colonna	190
Guido Reni	St. Paul & St. Anthony	Rome: Palazzo Giustiniani	195
Guido Reni	Judith	Rome: Palazzo Doria	196
Guido Reni	Blessed spirit soaring to Paradise	Rome: Museum, Capitol	214
Guido Reni	[St. Peter and St. Paul]	Bologna	328
Honthorst	Christ before Pilate	Rome: Palazzo Giustiniani	195
Honthorst	Surprising candlelights	Rome: Palazzo Doria	196
Lauretti	Infant republic	Rome: Museum, Capitol	213
Luca Giordano	Several paintings	Florence: Sta Maddelena de' Pazzi	446
Orcagna	Dante	Florence: Duomo	65
Palma	Last Judgment	Venice: Palazzo Ducale	338
Parmigianino	2 portraits [Antea, Galeazzo]	Naples: Capo di Monte	269
Perrugino	admired are gone	Cremona	350
Pietro da Cortona	Battle of Arbela	Rome: Museum, Capitol	213
Pietro da Cortona	Rape of the Sabines	Rome: Museum, Capitol	213
Pietro da Cortona	Sacrifice of Iphigenia	Rome: Museum, Capitol	213
Pietro da Cortona	Triumph of Bacchus	Rome: Museum, Capitol	213
Poussin	Massacre of the Innocents	Rome: Palazzo Giustiniani	195

Name of Artist	Subject	Location	Page
	PAINTING		
Poussin, Gaspar	Landscapes	Rome: Palazzo Doria	197
Raphael	St. John the Divine	Rome: Palazzo Giustiniani	194
Raphael	Bartolo and Baldi	Rome: Palazzo Doria	197
Raphael	Constantine & Maxantius	Rome: Vatican	204
Raphael	Attila	Rome: Vatican	205
Raphael	Heliodorus	Rome: Vatican	205
Raphael	Miracle at the Borgo	Rome: Vatican	205
Raphael	School of Athens	Rome: Vatican	205
Raphael?	Portrait	Naples: Capo di Monte	269
Rembrandt	Philosophers	Rome: Palazzo Doria	196
Salvator Rosa	St. Jerome	Rome: Palazzo Doria	197
Sassoferato	Holy Family	Rome: Palazzo Doria	196
Schidoni	2 dead Christs	Naples: Palazzo di Francavilla	270
Spagnolet	St. Jerome	Rome: Palazzo Doria	197
Spagnolet	Twelve prophets	Certosa: Church of convent	271
Teniers	Comic paintings	Rome: Palazzo Doria	198
Tintoretto	Paradise	Venice: Palazzo Ducale	338
Titian	Abraham	Rome: Palazzo Giustiniani	196
Titian	Landscapes	Rome: Palazzo Doria	197
Titian	Andrew Doria	Rome: Palazzo Doria	197
Titian	Jansenius	Rome: Palazzo Doria	197
Vanni	Descent from the Cross	Siena: San Quirico	105
Various	Portraits	Florence: Galleria degli Uffizi	41
Velasquez	Innocent X	Rome: Palazzo Doria	197

(*continued*)

Name of Artist	Subject	Location	Page
	PAINTING		
Veronese	Allegorical subjects	Venice: Palazzo Ducale	338
Veronese	Martyrdom of St. Justina	Padua: St. Justina	344
	RELIEVO		
	Amazons; Endymion; Andromeda	Rome: Capitol	226
	Meleager; Acteon; Esculapius	Rome: Villa Borghese	226
	Dedalus; Bellerephon; Paris; Archemorus	Rome: Palazzo Spada	227
	Arch of Titus	Rome: Forum	227
	Arch of Trajan	Rome: Forum	227
	Column of Trajan	Rome: Forum	228
	Arch of Constantine	Rome: Forum	230
	Arch of S. Severus	Rome: Forum	230
	Column of M. Aurelius	Rome: Forum	230
Algardi	[Leo the Great]	Rome: St. Peter	179
Bacciano	Farnese defeat of Flanders	Caserta: Palazzo	297
Canova	Honorific tablet	Padua: Hospital	345
Le Gros	St. Lewis Gonzaga	Rome: St. Ignatius	184
Michelangelo	Dead Christ and Virgin	Genoa: Albergo de Poveri	6
Hugford		Vallombrosa: Chapel	83
	SCULPTURE		
	Niobe	Florence: Galleria degli Uffizi	43
	Marsyas	Florence: Galleria degli Uffizi	43

Name of Artist	Subject	Location	Page
	SCULPTURE		
	Virgin	Loretto	321
	Farnese statues	Naples: Palazzo dei Studii	269
	Faun, Mercury, Canephora	Portici: Musuem	291
	Sanazzaro's tomb	Posilipo	275
	Laocoon; Apollo	Rome	230
	Apollo; Laocoon; Gladiator: Hercules	Rome	232
	Amazons	Rome: Capitol	161n
	M. Aurelius	Rome: Capitol	207
	Apollo	Rome: Museum, Capitol	207
	Faun	Rome: Museum, Capitol	207
	Meleager	Rome: Museum, Capitol	207
	Pyrrhus	Rome: Museum, Capitol	208
	Dying Gladiator, etc. (casts)	Rome: Museum, Capitol	209
	Furietti Centaurs	Rome: Museum, Capitol	209
	Busts of Emperors	Rome: Museum, Capitol	210
	Busts of Philosophers	Rome: Museum, Capitol	210
	Rome Triumphant	Rome: Museum, Capitol	212
	Coat of Hercules	Rome: Museum, Capitol	213
	Geese	Rome: Museum, Capitol	213
	Wolf	Rome: Museum, Capitol	213
	Minerva Medica	Rome: Palazzo Giustiniani	192
	St. Andrew	Rome: St. Peter	183
	St. Veronica	Rome: St. Peter	183
	Canopus	Rome: Villa Albani	222
	Apollo & Daphne	Rome: Villa Borghese	216

(*continued*)

Name of Artist	Subject	Location	Page
	SCULPTURE		
	Borghese Gladiator	Rome: Villa Borghese	216
	Hermaphrodite	Rome: Villa Borghese	216
	Silenus	Rome: Villa Borghese	216
	Seneca	Rome: Villa Borghese	217
	Germanicus; M. Agrippa; Tiberius; Corbulo; S. Severus; Geta	Rome: Villa Borghese	218
	Magistrates	Rome: Villa Borghese	219
	Pætus & Arria	Rome: Villa Lodovisi	224
	Papirius & mother	Rome: Villa Lodovisi	224
	Warrior	Rome: Villa Lodovisi	225
	Caracalla	Venice: Palazzo Grimani	340
	Marcus Agrippa	Venice: Palazzo Grimani	340
	Venus	Naples: Capo di Monte	269
	Venus	Palermo: Museum	426
Apollonius	Toro	Naples: Seaside	270
Bernini	Saint Bibiana	Rome: Santa Bibiana	187
Bernini	St. Jerome & Magdalene	Siena: Duomo, Chigi chapel	104
Canova	Tomb of Rezzonico	Rome: St. Peter	182
Canova	Creugas	Rome: Belvedere, Vatican	201
Canova	Graces et al	Rome	238
Canova	Psyche	Venice: Palazzo Manzilli [Mazzilli?]	339
Canova	Daedalus & Icarus	Venice: Palazzo Pisano	339
Giovanni da Bologna	Nettune	Bologna: Piazza del Gigante	327
Giovanni da Bologna	Michelangelo	Palazzo Buonarroti	69n
Michelangelo	Dead Christ	Florence: Duomo	69

Name of Artist	Subject	Location	Page
	SCULPTURE		
Michelangelo	Brutus	Florence: Galleria degli Uffizi	69
Michelangelo	Day & Twilight	Florence: Medici Chapel	69
Michelangelo	Madonna	Florence: Medici Chapel	69
Michelangelo	Victory	Florence: Palazzo Vecchio	69
Michelangelo	Moses	Rome: S. Pietro in vincoli	185
Michelangelo (restorer)	Lion tearing a Horse, etc.	Rome: Museum, Capitol	211
Periodi	Dead Christ	Padua: St. Justina	344

APPENDIX B

A Sequence for the Passages Omitted from the First Edition of *Forsyth's Italy*

All the canceled passages have titles, except for some pages on Cardinal York's brother (i.e., Charles Stuart, the Young Pretender). Murray shows these mostly by capitalization but uses italics where it is a subheading. There are three groups of passages arranged almost chronologically. The first group of canceled passages follows a chronological order, succeeded by a second group that returns in time to the beginning of the narrative and then follows a chronological order. A third group repeats this pattern. The titling and groupings suggest that this was Forsyth's work, looking toward the possibility of their return to the text for the second edition, with the first group being the most likely to go in.

The order of the passages has been determined by looking for junctures in the narrative, where they would follow on naturally. The first column shows the page number of the 1816 edition where a passage should be inserted. The next three columns separate the three sequences to show the groupings, giving each passage its page number in *1816* and identifying the first and last words of the passage within square brackets. A brief indication of contents follows. Index entries under "Forsyth's *Italy*" link passages in this table to discussions in the book. In many of these cases, there are substantial quotations.

Insertion page	First group	Second group	Third group
7		420–421 [GENOA . . . winds.] The local costume of women, a kind of shawl, compared to mantles. Laws regarding stilettos and assassination.	
7	357–361 [LEGHORN . . . my voyage.] F avoids mountain route of eastern Riviera, where bandits are. Reflections on German travelers. The story of how Prince Belmonte's wife assumed her husband was dead. The painting of the Virgin that flew of its own accord from Judea to Monte Nero. A long footnote on how saints are described in Virgil, Ovid, and Statius.		
15		422–423 [*University* . . . love of the new.] Pisa university suspends pro-French professors. The students favor revolution.	
23		421–422 [*Poets* Monti . . . e scelerenza.] The poet Monti as a turncoat, but some of his plays and poems are worthy of note.	
24			440–441 [PISA . . . has none.] Scotto, the richest man in Tuscany, and lowborn, is more worthy than the nobles. F visits the convent of St. Joseph. A list of Italian historians.
28		423–426 [CERTOSA . . . full of Faustinae.]. Magnificence and hospitality of a convent six miles from Pisa. The posturing aimlessness of rich nobles such as Cavaliere Seta and Marquis Bicchi.	
31		426 [LUCCA . . . of their community.] Lucca swarms with prostitutes, suggesting wives are more faithful than in Pisa.	

Insertion page	First group	Second group	Third group
39		426–427 [*Gallery* . . . stopped the dialogue.] Puccini sends art treasures such as the Venus—Raphael's, Titian's, and Correggio's—to Palermo away from French. How members of the audience dispute about Zanerini the actor's performance and are silenced.	
66			441–446 [FLORENCE . . . former failures forgotten.] *First draft of the passage printed.* Preaching in Florence. Charity to abandoned children. Asses (animal & human) bringing oil to church. Andrea del Sarto's *Madonna del Sacco*. Santi da Tito's *Christ Dining with the Pharisee*. Nuns' ideas of heaven. Pazzi family.
66			447–450 [*Good Friday* . . . just as before.] Drama of the Passion. Entry of the nuns. Revival of Holy Inquisition. One young man's political whim (Napleon's) restores the church.

(*continued*)

Insertion page	First group	Second group	Third group
70	362–386 [MANNERS OF FLORENCE . . . from the excise.] Secret abhorrence of the French, who bring a general breakdown in manners. Loss of national pride. Buonuomini di San Martino and the *Misericordia* assist the destitute. Florence more devout than Pisa. A miracle-working Madonna taken from bake-house by the archbishop to his "own shop" (duomo). The "Miracolo!" of an Annunciation painting with an angel whose eyes moved. It brings good sale of owner's wine. Parlor games. Lending out carriages and wives. Servants doubling as footmen and tradesmen. Six greatest Tuscans. Indelicacies and crudities of cicisbeism. Leopoldo's reforms before the Rights of Man declared.		
75		427 [DOCCIA . . . to the exquisite.] Superiority of English manufactures.	
76			446–447 [*Certosa* . . . St. John Baptist.] Forsyth taken to a monastery by Gius Baldi.
95		428 [AREZZO . . . ringleaders in the war.] *First draft of the passage printed.* Aretine defiance of French in 1799.	
98		428–429 [CORTONA . . . more easy one.] Priests took over the seminary of the Vagnotti.	
112	386–395 [SIENA . . . imitata figuram.] Siena's history: idle nobles, factious monks, industrious people; Ghibellines and Alexander III; Barbarossa; the Chigi (who threw a silver plate into the river). Devotion to blessed Virgin. General surrender of chastity. Drunken English with chamber pots. Offence caused by the naked posteriors of a statue.		

Insertion page	First group	Second group	Third group
112			450–453 [SIENA . . . variety of expressions.] Anna Rinieri's conversazione. Moncenni's daughter weds and makes advances to F's friend Brown. Count Vargas as president of the *Accademia Italiana. Collegio Tolomei.* Signore Spannochi. Ademollo's ceiling painting.
199		429 [ROME. *Vatican* . . . to furnish it.] Pius VI had various expedients to stock his gallery but did not destroy antiquities.	
219		429–430 [*Villas* . . . reclaimed from Braschi.] Continuation of remarks on restorers. Mengs's portraits of Muses. Pius VI thwarted of a million crowns from Lepri family and took revenge.	
235			453–454 [ROME . . . does the same.] Prince Marino pretends to be English to get in to the Palm Sunday service. Lord Bristol's atheistic talk as a bishop and obscene behavior with women.

(*continued*)

Insertion page	First group	Second group	Third group
237		430–431 [*Letters and Arts* . . . rightful owner.] Outburst against Carlo Fea. A note on Cicero's attack on Verres and many instances of stealing during the French looting.	
240	395–405 [ROME . . . visible on earth.] F will never describe Easter pomp but will not laugh at it. Supremely grand but too long. Vestments redeemed from pawn in Leghorn. Richness destroys sense of venerable. One pope exclaimed it easy to fool the public. Pius VII gentle and simple. Priest begged for poor and stole the money. Ruined character of Romans. Men are what government makes them. They are street fighters not soldiers and secretly post satires in public (pasquinades). Libertinage is a response to animal wants in a state of celibacy. Women used to wear the doctoral cap. Wretched state of all kinds of people, including a noble woman and an old priest.		
252			454–457 [FRASCATI . . . only as an agent.] F dines with Henry Benedict Maria Clementi, Cardinal York. Madame Cicciaporci's conversations with F.
255		431–434 [FRASCATI . . . offended his brother.] Sale of the villa and title of Bracciano. Charles Edward Stuart, York's brother, accomplished and rash. He returns to England, retires to Paris, decays in Italy. Departure of his mistress and wife. Reconciled with daughter.	

Insertion page	First group	Second group	Third group
256			454 [*Tivoli* . . . does the same.] A gentleman talks about a poisonous mushroom.
260		434 [TERRACINA . . . bankrupt schedules.] Braschi drained the marshes near Terracina and also the coffers.	
267			457–459 [NAPLES . . . now expatriated.] A friend at the Tuileries would reform the nobility. In Naples, Acton, aged sixty, married a girl of fourteen and tried to seize the estates of Monteleone.
268		435 [NAPLES . . . oppressor in Naples.] Decay of the local assembly.	
273	406–416 [NAPLES SOCIETY . . . mi diede.] Ceremony of the *Bacciamano* (kissing the hand) of Ferdinand IV of Naples / Ferdinand I of Two Sicilies. "Noblemen" everywhere. Farcical prodigality. Women court gallantry. A paradise inhabited by merry devils. A case of cannibalism. Bloodthirsty lazzaroni compared with similar Calabrians. Murder happens with impunity. An anecdote of a mattress-maker who was compelled to murder.		
276		439 [PHLEGREAN FIELDS . . . solecisms of our own.] *A fragment.* Italians better Latin speakers than the English.	
297		435 [CASERTA . . . who looked on.] *A fragment.* The visit of Bourbon royalty.	

(continued)

Insertion page	First group	Second group	Third group
319		435 [CIVITA CASTELLANA . . . made him prisoner.] *A fragment.* French catch an Austrian general at his devotions.	
325			459–460 [CESENNA . . . ancient grandeur.] *A fragment.* Three forums and Forli.
326		436 [FAENZA . . . can carry off.] Three forums. A canon of the church assists the French to take treasures.	
341		436–437 [VENICE . . . decorous old-maid.] Decline of goldsmiths and glassworks. Old lady faces down loose women.	
342			460 [VENICE . . . written ΔΟΥΛΚΙΞΙΜΩ.] The immoderate claims on Mauroceni's epitaph.
345		439 [PADUA . . . London for one.] *A fragment.* Astronomers send to buy a horizon from the London observatory.	
348		437–438 [VICENZA . . . tools were concealed.] Republican orator giving tall tales asked had he just come that day from China or Verona.	

Insertion page	First group	Second group	Third group
			461 [VERONA . . . interrupt our passage.] *First draft of the passage printed.* Arch of Gavi does not conform to Vitruvius's principles. Sentinels from both states "six yards asunder" are on each bridge.
352		439–440 [PAVIA . . . fame of Pavia.] Scientific quarrels of Spallanzani, Scopoli, and Grigorio Fontana.	
355		438–439 [MILAN . . . philosophical proposal.] City quieting down after the revolt against the pope. Woman announces she would exchange her maidenhead for his head.	
355			461 [MILAN . . . in the forum.] Du Pau's dog bit cheeses to the shape of Voltaire's profile.
356	417–419 [TURIN . . . and Volgari.] Description of the prospect of the Alps and river. Royal Palace. "Freekish" architecture of Guarini. Decline of silk manufactory.		
461			461 [GENERAL ITALY . . . and Berger.] *Note form.* Geographical statistics of Italy. Portraits of Italian poets left to Reynolds and Berger.

ACKNOWLEDGMENTS

To Nora Crook, I owe the edition of *Forsyth's Italy* I had published in 2001. In addition, she scrupulously read, challenged, and commented most helpfully on the drafts of this book. Without her interventions, neither book would exist, and I dedicate this one to her with grateful thanks.

Donald H. Reiman and the late Charles E. Robinson were encouragers of my edition. I owe them thanks for believing my research was worthwhile enough to continue, although I could not then see the direction to take. Discussions with the late Peter Cochran about Byron and Hobhouse were always stimulating. I wish he was still here to exchange more ideas. I had fruitful interchanges with Ben Colbert when he was writing *Shelley's Eye*. I was able to publish at length various lines of inquiry about Forsyth thanks to the space given me by Lilla Crisafulli in *Immaginando l'Italia* (Imagining Italy), by Alison Chapman and Jane Stabler in *Forum for Modern Language Studies*, and by Jennifer Speake in *Literature of Travel and Exploration*. The pieces I wrote for them helped shape the arguments I put in this book, and I am most grateful to them for helping me in this process.

Part of the pleasure of writing this book has been the assistance of many experts over the years, whom I wish to thank with great appreciation and to celebrate here. The Moray Local Heritage Centre, with the assistance of Graeme Wilson and his staff, acted as a springboard for my thinking about Forsyth's imprisonment and for writing this book. The later part of my research, using the resources of the Carl H. Pforzheimer Library to access prison literature relating to Napoleonic France and in particular that of James Lawrence and Joshua Done, was assisted by Doucet Devin Fischer and Elizabeth Denlinger, who doubled the pleasure of working there. Lia Guerra at the University of Pavia and Carla Garbarino at its museum generously helped me with locating Susini's anatomical waxworks there, and Anthony Mandal led me to the Palazzo Poggi in Bologna. Ursula Crook uncovered on the Web the Henry Hobson Richardson archive of architectural photographs.

ACKNOWLEDGMENTS

At Bucknell University Press, Greg Clingham encouraged me to submit my book to him and has been a welcoming publishing editor, succeeded by Pam Dailey. The two readers who gave their time and stimulating advice helped me shape the final version of the book. The care from the team of Rutgers and Scribe was exemplary and made me feel that they wanted to give my book the best chance of reaching a wide readership. Particularly I wish to mention the editors, Lauren Conkling, succeeded by Megan Grande; the cover designer Connie Timm; and the eagle-eyed Sam Martin, whose copyediting was extremely helpful.

NOTES

CHAPTER 1 THE HISTORICAL MOMENT OF *FORSYTH'S ITALY*

1. Joseph Forsyth, "Advertisement," *Remarks on Antiquities, Arts, and Letters during an Excursion in Italy, in the Years 1802 and 1803*, 2nd ed. (London: John Murray, 1816; repr., Newark, N.J.: University of Delaware Press, 2001). The pagination given parenthetically throughout this book, unless otherwise stated, is derived from the reprint edition, edited by Keith Crook.
2. Nora Gietz, "Tracing Paintings in Napoleonic Italy: Archival Records and the Spatial and Contextual Displacement of Artworks," *Artl@s Bulletin* 4, no. 2 (2016): 58.
3. Francis Haskell and Nicholas Penny, *Taste and the Antique: The Lure of Classical Sculpture* (New Haven, Conn.: Yale, 1991), 113, 111.
4. Haskell and Penny, 290.
5. John Chetwode Eustace, *A Classical Tour through Italy, an. MDCCCII* (1813), 6th ed. (London: J. Mawman, 1821).
6. [Francis Cohen (Palgrave)], review of *Le voyage en Italie*, by d'Aubin-Louis Millin, *Edinburgh Review* 29, no. 57 (November 1817): 191.
7. Unsigned review of *Observations on Italy*, by Bell, *Edinburgh Magazine* 17 (July 1825): 25.
8. Unsigned review of *Observations on Italy*, by Bell, *Edinburgh Magazine* 17 (July 1825): 36.
9. A selection of some of the authors to whom Forsyth alludes gives an idea of his range: classical writers like Juvenal, Cicero, the two Plinys, Livy, Horace, Martial, Ovid, and Virgil; Italian poets like Dante, Tasso, Bettinelli, Parini, Pignotti, Casti, Pindemonte, Alfieri, and Monti; Italian historians of art and antiquities like Vitruvius, Vasari, Vettori, Paoli, Maffei, Martorelli, Muratori, Venuti, Vasi, Visconti, and Soldani; and other writers whose works bore on the art of Italy, such as Winckelmann, Gibbon, Roscoe, Reynolds, Burke, and Paine.
10. This version, published in Paris, was taken from the 6th London edition. It formed volumes 202 and 203 of Baudry's series, *A Collection of Ancient and Modern Authors*.
11. Letters of the Forsyth brothers, unnumbered, November 18, 1815. Other letters are hereafter are referenced as *L* 1, *L* 2, and so on.
12. George Smith (1789–1846) "first began his working life as an apprentice to the Elgin bookseller and banker Isaac Forsyth. He migrated to London in 1812 and was initially employed by the publisher Charles Rivington, and subsequently became a clerk for John Murray at Albemarle Street." In 1816, he cofounded the famous publishing firm Smith, Elder & Co.,

which moved to 65 Cornhill, London, in 1824 (Sidney Lee, *Oxford Dictionary of National Biography*, s.v. "Smith, George" accessed June 20, 2019, https://www.oxforddnb.com/view/10.1093/odnb/9780192683120.001.0001/odnb-9780192683120-e-36138). He is referred to several times in Isaac's letters (see *L* 27, *L* 28).

13. Elizabeth K. Helsinger, *Ruskin and the Art of the Beholder* (Cambridge, Mass.: Harvard University Press, 1982), 313n. Helsinger discusses how the young Ruskin desired illustrations in guidebooks to accompany descriptions of landscapes. Forsyth felt the inadequacy of words alone: at the falls of Terni, he wrote, "At last came the roar of the Velino upon the cliffs—but this cataract, whether viewed at the tremendous chasm above it, at the verge of precipitation, or midway down at the belvedere in front—the evening sun painting an iris on the spray—the obscurity of the gulf below—the vista of the rich vale of Nera—all must have been so often described, that I leave them in silent admiration" (319). Of Naples, he wrote, "To describe its buildings I leave to the guide-books: its environs belong to the painter" (265).
14. [Henry Brougham?], review of *Italy*, by Forsyth, *Edinburgh Review* 22 (January 1814): 376. I refer to the author as "Brougham" here and throughout, though Brougham's authorship is not certain. *The Wellesley Index to Victorian Periodicals* (ed. Walter E. Houghton et al., 5 vols. [Toronto: University of Toronto Press, 1966–1989]) attributes the review to him, since he previously wrote the linked review of Eustace's *Classical Tour*, but with a query. The *Edinburgh* editors, Edwin Daniel Clarke and Francis Jeffrey, may also have had a hand in it.
15. [Brougham?], review of *Italy*, 376.
16. Unsigned review of *Italy*, by Forsyth, *British Critic* 7 (January 1817): 34.
17. Unsigned review of *Italy*, by Forsyth, *Monthly Review*, ser. 2, 89 (May–August 1819): 15.
18. Looking forward to 1847, we find Herman Melville paying a backhanded compliment to Forsyth's style. Annoyed by his sweeping judgment in favor of the Italian sonnet ("English poets cannot plead for the sonnet one successful precedent. Even the greatest of them all, Shakspere, Milton, Spenser, split on this rock and sank into common versifiers" [*1816*, 111]), Melville added a marginal note in his copy of the two-volume edition of 1824: "What pedantry is this! Yet its elegance all but redeems it. Forsyth is the most graceful of pedants" (Herman Melville, *Published Poems*, vol. 11 of *The Writings of Herman Melville* [Evanston, Ill.: Northwestern University Press and Newberry Library, 2009], 876).
19. Unsigned review of *Italy*, by Forsyth, *Monthly Review*, ser. 2, 89 (May–August 1819): 15.
20. Unsigned review of *Italy*, by Forsyth, *Monthly Review*, ser. 2, 89 (May–August 1819): 24.
21. George Gordon Byron, *Byron's Letters and Journals*, ed. Leslie A. Marchand, 13 vols. (London: John Murray, 1976), 3:49 (May 19, 1813), hereafter cited as *BLJ*.
22. Leigh Hunt, "Letters from Abroad I: Pisa," *Liberal*, no. 1 (1822): 106. The article was later reprinted in *The Autobiography of Leigh Hunt* (1850). Hunt is alluding to Forsyth's opinion here: "Music, divested of poetry, is but a sensual art, and, as such, should be classed with cookery and perfumery. Its direct object is to please one sense" (*1816*, 166n).
23. Hunt, "Letters from Abroad," 112, 114. Palgrave, in *Hand-Book for Travellers in Northern Italy* (London: John Murray, 1842), also dwells on the Campo Santo frescoes.
24. [Giovanni Rosini], *Lettere pittoriche sul Campo Santo di Pisa* [Letters about paintings in the Pisan Campo Santo] (Pisa: Tipografia della Società Letteraria, 1810).
25. Carlo Lasinio, *Pitture a fresco del Campo Santo di Pisa* [Fresco paintings in the Pisan Campo Santo] (Florence: Bernardini, 1828).

26. Lasinio's engravings became the stimulus for Rossetti's founding of the pre-Raphaelite brotherhood in 1848 and were reproduced in the popularization of the frescoes in the Eastlakes' revised version of Franz Kugler's *The Schools of Painting in Italy* (1851).
27. *BLJ* 5:221 (May 9, 1817).
28. *BLJ* 5:221, 224, 227 (May 9, 11, 12, 1817).
29. *BLJ* 7:182 (September 28, 1820).
30. *BLJ* 5:183 (September 29, 1820). See Jane Waldie, *Sketches Descriptive of Italy, in the Years 1816, 1817*, 4 vols. (London: John Murray, 1820).
31. Hereafter cited as *CHP* 4. Quotations from *CHP* are taken from vol. 2 of *Lord Byron: The Complete Poetical Works*, ed. Jerome J. McGann (Oxford: Clarendon, 1980), cited as *CPW*.
32. *BLJ* 5:251 (July 15, 1817).
33. *BLJ* 5:253 (July 20, 1817).
34. Stuart Curran, *Poetic Form and British Romanticism* (Oxford: Oxford University Press, 1986), 152.
35. Peter Vassallo, *Byron: The Italian Literary Influence* (London: Macmillan, 1984), 16.
36. *CHP* 4.904.
37. *CHP* 4.1319–1320.
38. Germaine de Staël, *Corinne*, trans. Sylvia Raphael (London; Penguin, 1998), 60.
39. *CHP* 4.1387–1390.
40. *CHP* 4.1420–1422.
41. *BLJ* 7:201 (October 12, 1820).
42. *BLJ* 5:233–234 (June 4, 1817).
43. Unpublished letter, John Cam Hobhouse to John Murray, December 7, 1817, John Murray Archive, National Library of Scotland, Edinburgh (hereafter Murray Archive), Acc.12604. This is cited by Peter Cochran at https://petercochran.files.wordpress.com/2009/02/07-venice-1816-1817.pdf (accessed October 18, 2018). He refers to Castel Onorato; the passage occurs in *1816*, 289–290.
44. The discovery of this unpublished letter was made by Peter Cochran and communicated to me privately.
45. *BLJ* 5:233 (June 4, 1817).
46. *BLJ* 7:210 (October 10, 1820).
47. Mary Shelley, review of *Journal of a Tour in Italy*, by J. P. Cobbett, *Westminster Review* 14 (January 1831): 178.
48. *BLJ* 7:132, 190 (July 17, 1820; October 1, 1820).
49. Peter Cochran documents Byron's fluctuating opinion of Napoleon in "Byron and Napoleon" (paper delivered at University of Gdansk, Poland, May 13, 2003), accessed October 18, 2018, http://www.newsteadabbeybyronsociety.org/works/downloads/byron_napoleon.pdf.
50. Byron, *Marino Faliero* 5.2.52–57, in *CPW* 4. Hereafter *MF*.
51. *MF* 5.2.93–94.
52. The following revises the account given in my introduction in my 2001 reprint of the second edition of *Forsyth's Italy*, xxi–xxix.
53. [Henry Brougham], review of *A Tour through Italy, Exhibiting View of Its Scenery, Its Antiquities, and It Monuments; Particularly as They Are Objects of Classical Interest and Elucidation: With an Account of the Present State of Its Cities and Towns, and Occasional Observations on*

the Recent Spoliations of the French, by John Chetwode Eustace, *Edinburgh Review* 21 (July 1813): 378.

54. [Brougham], 380, 417.
55. [Brougham], 411, 417.
56. [Brougham], 414.
57. [Brougham], 418.
58. Unsigned review of *Tour through Italy*, by Eustace, *Quarterly Review* 10 (October 1813): 242. The reviewer has not been securely identified. Reginald Heber, Robert Bland, Herman Merivale, and William Stewart Rose have been put forward as possibilities. See Jonathan Cutmore, *Quarterly Review Archive*, accessed October 18, 2018, https://www.rc.umd.edu/reference/qr/index.html. Cutmore establishes the actual publication date of the October number as December 18, 1813.
59. [Brougham?], review of *Italy*, 232, 248, 242.
60. [Brougham?], 243.
61. [Brougham?], 376.
62. [Brougham?], 380.
63. [Brougham?], 376.
64. [Southey, Robert], review of *Vita di Vittorio Alfieri, &c. Memoirs of the Life and Writings of Victor Alfieri*, by Victor Alfieri, and of *The Tragedies of Vittorio Alfieri*, translated by Charles Lloyd, *Quarterly Review* 14, no. 28 (January 1816): 365–366.
65. Unsigned review of *Classical Tour*, by Eustace, *Monthly Review* 74 (May–August 1814): 39.
66. Byron, *Don Juan* 1:1672, in *CPW* 5.
67. Unsigned review of *Classical Tour*, by Eustace, *British Critic* n.s. 1 (January–June 1814): 252.
68. Unsigned review of *Classical Tour*, by Eustace, *British Critic* n.s. 1 (January–June 1814): 263, 388, 393.
69. Unsigned review of *Classical Tour*, by Eustace, *British Critic* n.s. 1 (January–June 1814): 250, 400.
70. Unsigned review of *Classical Tour*, by Eustace, *British Critic* n.s. 1 (January–June 1814): 401, 399, 250, 400.
71. Unsigned review of *Italy*, by Forsyth, *British Critic* n.s. 7 (January 1817): 34.
72. Unsigned review of *Italy*, by Forsyth, *British Critic* n.s. 7 (January 1817): 42.
73. Unsigned review of of *Italy*, by Forsyth, *Anti-Jacobin Review* 52 (March–August 1817): 108, 126.
74. Unsigned review of of *Italy*, by Forsyth, *Anti-Jacobin Review* 51 (September 1816–February 1817): 589, 590.
75. Unsigned review of of *Italy*, by Forsyth, *Anti-Jacobin Review* 51 (September 1816–February 1817): 596.
76. Unsigned review of of *Italy*, by Forsyth, *Anti-Jacobin Review* 52 (March–August 1817): 125, 118–119.
77. John Stoddart, review of *Manfred*, *Day and New Times* (July 23, 1817); see Ralph Milbanke, *Astarte* (New York: Charles Scribner's Sons, 1921), 69. *The Day and New Times* "was notable for containing the most explicit public statement that linked Byron with the crime of incest" (Reiman, "Part B: Byron and Regency Society Poets," in *The Romantics Reviewed: Contemporary Reviews of British Romantic Writers*, ed. Donald H. Reiman [New York: Garland, 1972], 3:1106). I am grateful to Nora Crook, who drew this to my attention.

78. Unsigned review of *Childe Harold's Pilgrimage*, by Byron, *Quarterly Review* 19 (April–December 1818): 230–232.
79. *CPW* 2:262.
80. Unsigned review of *Historical Illustrations*, by Hobhouse, *British Critic* n.s. 12 (July–December 1819): 229.
81. Unsigned review of *Classical Tour*, by Eustace, *British Critic* n.s. 12 (July–December 1819): 227.
82. Unsigned review of *Childe Harold's Pilgrimage*, by Byron, *Edinburgh Review* 30 (June–September 1818): 88–120.
83. These appear in "An Essay on the Present Literature of Italy," an appendix to the *Illustrations*. This was "mainly written by Foscolo, but translated and polished by Hobhouse" (Valeria Vallucci, "A Little Italian Byron: Foscolo, Byron and Hobhouse in London," in *Byron in London*, ed. Peter Cochran [Newcastle, U.K.: Cambridge Scholars, 2008], 105).
84. Unsigned review of *Italy*, by Forsyth, *Monthly Review*, ser. 2, 89 (May–August 1819): 24.
85. Unsigned review of *Italy*, by Forsyth, *Monthly Review*, ser. 2, 89 (May–August 1819): 15.
86. Unsigned review of *Italy*, by Forsyth, *Monthly Review*, ser. 2, 89 (May–August 1819): 16, 19.
87. Frédéric Lullin de Chateauvieux, *Letteres écrites d'Italie en 1812 et 1813 . . .* [Letters written about Italy in 1812 and 1813 . . .], 2 vols. (Paris: J. Paschoud, 1816). Reviewed in the *Edinburgh Review* 28 (March 1817): 31.
88. [Frédéric Lullin de Chateauvieux], *Manuscrit venu de St. Hélène, d'une manière inconnue* [Manuscript that has come from St. Helena in an unknown way] (London: John Murray, 1817).
89. Eustace, *Classical Tour* (1821), 1: xli.
90. Unsigned review of *Italy*, by Forsyth, *Monthly Review*, ser. 2, 89 (May–August 1819): 15.

CHAPTER 2 FORSYTH'S PRISONS

1. These are to be found, respectively, on pages 441, 428, and 481 of the 1816 edition.
2. Letters quoted are referenced within the text as "(*L* 1)," "(*L* 2)," and so on.
3. Lazare Carnot, "Le Grand Carnot" (1753–1823), was a staunch republican. He made Napoleon general of the Italian campaign and became his minister of war but resigned in 1800. In that year, he was reelected as a member of the Académie des sciences, a division of the Institut de France, which was created in 1795 from the amalgamation of France's five learned *académies*, but I have not found confirmation (e.g., from the *Biographie universelle* [Universal biography]) that he was ever the Institut's president. In 1802, he was appointed a member of the Tribunat (the debating body of Napoleon's administration). His integrity and prestige ensured Napoleon's continuing respect.
4. James Forbes, *Letters from France Written in the Years 1803 and 1804*, 2 vols. (London: White, 1806), 2:264; John Goldworth Alger, *Napoleon's British Visitors and Captives 1801–1815* (Westminster: Constable, 1904), 224–226.
5. James Lawrence, *A Picture of Verdun*, 2 vols. (London, Hookham, 1810), 2:68–78.
6. Alger, *Napoleon's British Visitors*, 226.
7. Alger, 206.
8. Among the surviving service memoirs are those of Andrew Blayney, Jahleel Brenton, John Tregerthen Short, Thomas Williams, Donat Henchy O'Brien, and George Black. The

Reverend Robert Wolfe began as a civilian *détenu* but was appointed a chaplain by Brenton and served mainly at Givet, among imprisoned sailors.

9. Obituary of James Lawrence, *Gentleman's Magazine* 169 (February 1841): 205–206.
10. The 1900 *ONDB* entry by Richard Garnett for "James Henry Lawrence" incorrectly gave the dates of his imprisonment as beginning in 1808 "for a few years," which is corrected to 1803 in the revised version by Nigel Leask, but the date of escape is left indeterminate. In his own book, Lawrence speaks of "our detention" in 1803 and of composing odes for parties in 1804 and 1805 and of escaping in January 1809. Lawrence, *Picture of Verdun*, 1:9, 68, 109, 248; 2:188–211.
11. Alger, *Napoleon's British Visitors*, 194, 196, 269n.
12. Lawrence, *Picture of Verdun*, 1:61–62, 52.
13. Lawrence, 2:134.
14. Lawrence, 1:55, 78; 2:159, 165–166.
15. Lawrence, 2:174–175.
16. Lawrence, 2:175–176.
17. The actual dates, derived from letters between the brothers are as follows: Bitche from November 23, 1803, to April 20, 1806, is twenty-eight months, eight days. Verdun from April 20, 1806, to April 22, 1810, is forty-eight months, two days. Paris from April 22, 1810, to July 24, 1811, is fifteen months, two days. Valenciennes to concluding his book—from July 24, 1811, to June 1, 1812—is ten months, eight days. Rest of imprisonment in Valenciennes from June 1, 1812, to detention in Leipzig until October 19, 1813, is sixteen months, eleven days. Orleans and Blois from October 19, 1813, to end of April 1814 is six months, eleven days. Total is ten years, eleven months, four days.
18. Forbes, *Letters from France* 1:258; Lawrence, *Picture of Verdun*, 1:168.
19. Lawrence, *Picture of Verdun*, 1:43.
20. Seacome Ellison, *Prison Scenes; and Narrative of Escape from France during the Late War* (London: Whittaker, 1838), 74.
21. Ellison, 72–73.
22. Ellison, 75.
23. Ellison, 72–76.
24. Joshua Done, "Narrative of the Imprisonment and Adventures of Joshua Done, in Various Parts of France," *London Magazine* n.s. 1 (January 1826): 27.
25. Ellison, *Prison Scenes*, 85.
26. Lawrence, *Picture of Verdun*, 2:178.
27. Ellison, *Prison Scenes*, 112.
28. Identified via the letters. On his release, Forsyth stayed at Thomas Dax's house at 28 Queen Square, receiving a letter on June 2, 1814. Later, on March 27, 1815, Isaac sent a letter to Forsyth via George Smith at 23 Doughty Street (recently developed in the 1792 expansion of the Foundling Hospital and creation of Mecklenburgh Square, 1808–1825). In 1816, a Thomas Dax, solicitor, lived at 23 Doughty Street (Walter H. Godfrey and W. McB. Marcham, *King's Cross Neighbourhood (the Parish of St. Pancras), Part 4 of the Survey of London*, 52 vols. [London: London County Council, 1952], 24:53). Queen Square was a quarter of a mile west of this development.
29. Lawrence, *Picture of Verdun*, 134.
30. Isaac's introductory life has its own pagination shown by bracketed numbers, a sign of its late insertion. Murray registered *Italy* on May 31, 1816 ("Entering at S. Hall . . . Copy to Wm

Gifford," ledger B, folio 117, Murray Archive). The Murray's reception of the manuscript of Isaac's biography is endorsed "1816 April Forsyth Isaac Memdm for a Life of his Brother."

31. Alger, *Napoleon's British Visitors*, 218, records a request that "the garrison should be strengthened, the walls being so dilapidated that egress was easy." This probably overstates the case in order to exculpate those in charge, whose laxity and favoritism, based on bribery, made it easier for the escapes that Alger describes (*Napoleon's British Visitors*, 207–216).
32. Lawrence *Picture of Verdun*, 1:56.
33. Lawrence, 1:155, 157.
34. Forbes, *Letters from France*, 2:245.
35. Forbes, 2:254.
36. Lawrence, *Picture of Verdun*, 1:82, 67.
37. Lawrence, 1:67.
38. Lawrence, 1:233.
39. Lawrence, 1:271.
40. Lawrence, 2:103.
41. Lawrence, 1:73–75; 2:97; 1:115.
42. That Forsyth was far from unsociable can be deduced from his references to attending gatherings throughout *Italy* and from the frequent references to his (usually unnamed) friends, companions, or contacts. For example, he speaks of the opinion of "my excellent and learned friend P. Gandolfi" concerning a shower of stones (119); the palaces that are "facciate (said a friend of mine) con mobilia e quadri dietro" [171; facades . . . for furniture and pictures behind]; the road built by Pope Pius VI through the Pontine marshes "at enormous expense of human lives" called after him the "*Linea Pia* [pious route] (which an intelligent friend of mine calls the Linea Impia [*a made-up word*: impious route])" (259); Pompeian artifacts being removed from the site ("How shameful, said a friend to me . . . to remove any antiquities from the spot" [301]); the bridges in Venice that interrupt "the thread of talk" (332); the galleries where "while you linger . . . your friends are advancing into other rooms" (342); the prior of Certosa "to whom my friend Gius[eppe] Baldi introduced me" (447); the bride-to-be who "told my friend Brown . . . [she would] be glad to receive his addresses" after the wedding (451); the Irish gentleman who introduced him to Cardinal York (454); the occasion "a friend pointed out to me at the Tuillerie . . . so many wild sprigs of nobility" (457).
43. David M. Walker, *A Legal History of Scotland* (Edinburgh: T&T Clark, 1998), 5:566ff.
44. Walker, 5:532.
45. Lawrence, *Picture of Verdun*, 1:155.
46. More needs to be discovered about this network of friends and high officials. For notes on Lady Grant and General Le Febre, see the section entitled "Letters of the Forsyth Brothers."

CHAPTER 3 THE 1813 AND THE 1816 VERSIONS OF *FORSYTH'S ITALY*

1. Probably Forsyth was considered to have broken his parole and received unsympathetic treatment from officials who did not know him. See letter 21 about parole. According to Isaac's memoir, Forsyth was liked and respected by French officials who had contact with him (*1816*, 4–5).
2. Alger, *Napoleon's British Visitors*, 261–262.

3. An indication that Forsyth may have had inside knowledge from a private correspondent is the fact that Visconti's name does not appear on the title page of any edition of Venuti that I have seen. Indeed, it seems that he was not technically the editor of the second 1803 edition but made additions to part 1 of that work. The only corroboration that I have found of Forsyth's statement is an 1841 record: "Ridolfino Venuti '*Accurata e succinta Descrizione topografica di Roma* [Accurate and succinct topographical descriptions of Rome], Rome, 1763. This work has been edited by F. A. Visconti, in 1803, and by Stef. Piale in 1824, 2 vols, 4to" (advertisement in *Penny Cyclopaedia of the Society for the Diffusion of Useful Knowledge* [London: Charles Knight, 1828–1843], 20:103).
4. Letter, Isaac Forsyth to John Murray, November 10, 1829. Isaac had sent a letter mentioning it on March 28 when he was in London, requesting a quick response before he returned to Scotland. This second letter is the more detailed and contains the cast list. On receiving Murray's assent, he sent the manuscript on November 27, 1829. The entry in Murray's ledger starts on November 17 and, in the action column, says "sent to Mr Smyth Cornhill" with the date December 12. Only one entry in this column says "printed," so this may have been the return of the manuscript via a contact, or the passing of it on to another publisher for consideration. If "Mr Smyth" was a slip for "Mr Smith," either role would have been filled in 1829 by George Smith (1789–1846), referenced in chapter 1 note 12. He is referred to several times in Isaac's letters. I have found no further trace of *The Condottiero*. Forsyth had evidently studied the career of Cabrino Fondulo (1370–1425), the condottiero who became lord of Cremona, but the condottiero in Forsyth's play seems to be invented (see chapter 3).
5. That is, eight by five inches.
6. Cicero, *In Verrem* 2.4, 132.
7. "Pignotti," *Penny Cyclopaedia*, 18:153. This article records that Pignotti kept out of party controversy, but it includes an anecdote that gives some idea both of his wit and his political sympathies: "The poet and improvisatore [Francesco] Gianni one day observed to Pignotti with a sneer, that the university of Pisa reckoned several asinine doctors among its members. 'That may be,' retorted Pignotti, 'we have heard of Caligula making his horse a senator.' The repartee consists in this: Napoleon, had just made Gianni a senator of the kingdom of Italy, and the enemies of Napoleon used to nickname him Caligula, on account of some fancied resemblance between him and the medals of that emperor." Forsyth mentions the same Gianni and implies that he is a toady, who in his publications "gives thirteen dedications in a single duodecimo" (*1813*, 20).
8. I have not succeeded in locating a poem or part-poem (Pignotti's fables and novels are in verse) about the "art of robbing" in the seven collections of Pignotti's verse issued from 1809 to 1833.
9. A reference to Pignotti in this pen-portrait suggests that some of Forsyth's animadversions on Monti came from him. The portrayal of Monti as a corrupt turncoat resembles that drawn by Ugo Foscolo in Hobhouse's *Historical Illustrations* (423–449). The result led to enmity between Byron and Monti. Byron, at first an admirer of Monti, later called him the "Giuda di Parnasso" (Judas of Parnassus; *BLJ* 7:151 [August 7, 1820]). I am grateful to Nora Crook for pointing this out.
10. Faustin Hélie and Parisot, "Fabroni ou Fabbroni (Jean Valentin-Mathias)," in *Biographie universelle*, ed. Louis-Gabriel Michaud, 2nd ed., 45 vols. (Paris: Desplaces, 1843–1865), 13:311–314.
11. Hugh Honour, "Canova's Statues of Venus," *Burlington Magazine* 114 (1972): 658–670.
12. "Fabroni (*Jean-Valentin-Mathias*, baron)," in *Nouvelle biographie générale*, ed. M. Hoefer (Paris: Didot Frères, 1856), 16:974–975. This biographical dictionary changed its name from *Nouvelle biographie universelle* after the ninth volume.

13. Hélie and Parisot, "Fabroni ou Fabbroni," 13:312, expands on these intrigues. The *Biographie* asks who would have thought that after all his service to his country, Fabbroni would be deprived of the directorship. Protests in 1807 came from the Parisian intelligentsia in the Jardin des Plantes and through the *Journal de Paris*. It adds that Maria Luisa herself was deposed by Napoleon in 1807 and sent into exile. Maria Luisa was a Spanish infanta married to Louis, the Prince of Parma. Louis was used as a tool by Napoleon. He had been made to exchange Parma for the short-lived Kingdom of Etruria in 1801; after Louis died (1803), Maria Luisa was assigned a hostile French ambassador, Hector d'Aubusson, in 1806. She is not to be confused with Marie-Louise, Napoleon's second wife, who in the post-Napoleonic settlement of 1815 was awarded the Duchy of Parma, while Maria Luisa was awarded the Duchy of Lucca in compensation for Parma.
14. His high opinion is shared by W. N. Hargreaves-Mawdsley, *The English Della Cruscans and Their Time, 1783–1828* (The Hague: Martins Nijhof, 1967), 8–10.
15. These are detailed in my edition of 2001.

CHAPTER 4 TALKING TO ITALIANS

1. Ilaria Bignamini, "Grand Tour: Open Issues," in *The Grand Tour: The Lure of Italy in the Eighteenth Century*, ed. Andrew Wilton and Ilaria Bignamini (London: Tate Gallery, 1997), 32–34. Bignamini cites Cardinal Albani's successful courting of English tourists to come to Rome by persuading the Hanoverian Duke of York to visit Rome in 1764, despite the presence in Rome of the Stuart claimant to the British throne (otherwise known as the Young Pretender, who also claimed the title of Duke of York).
2. Alger, *Napoleon's British Visitors*, 24–25; Samuel Rogers, *The Italian Journal of Samuel Rogers*, ed. J. R. Hale (London: Faber, 1956), 56–57.
3. Rogers, *Italian Journal*, 67.
4. Eustace, *Classical Tour* (1821), 1:54.
5. *BLJ* 5:191; 6:65.
6. Henry Matthews, *The Diary of an Invalid*, 2nd ed. (London: John Murray, 1820), 112.
7. Eustace, *Classical Tour* (1821), 1:34.
8. Lacey Collison-Morley, *Giuseppe Baretti and His Friends* (London: John Murray, 1909), 286–288.
9. Jörg Garms, "The Journey," in *Grand Tour*, ed. Wilton and Bignamini, 93–94.
10. Wilton and Bignamini, *Grand Tour*, 107.
11. Eustace, *Classical Tour* (1821), 3:153.
12. That inn was actually at Coviliajo, near Pietra Mala. The gruesome events appear to have occurred in the 1780s. The story became well-known through Forsyth's account. Jane Waldie (*Sketches Descriptive of Italy, in the Years 1816, 1817*), Lady Morgan (*Italy*), and Anna Jameson (*Diary of an Ennuyée*) all describe its Gothic atmosphere, which, however, changed during the 1820s. The building still exists, much altered, and is now a nursing home.
13. Possibly at Rocca di Papa, which is close by to Campo di Annibale, where York built a convent in 1788 on top of the temple of Jupiter Latiaris (Augustus Hare, *Walks in Rome* [1871], 20th ed. [London: Kegan Paul, Trench, Trübner, 1913], 690).
14. Sismondi, *Histoire des républiques italiennes* [A history of the Italian republics], 2nd ed. (Paris: Treuttel & Würtz, 1818), 16:327 (chapter 125 in editions with continuous numbering). Sismondi published his sixteen-volume work serially between 1807 and 1818.

15. Sydney Morgan, *Italy*, 2nd ed. (London: Colburn, 1821), 2:204.
16. These two instances relate to *1816*, 71–73 and their notes. He also speaks of sharecropping (*mezzadria*) and *fattorie* [collective farms]. Forsyth thus gives first hand observations of what a later historian would call the increasing ruralization and hardship of Northern Italians (Gregory Hanlon, *Early Modern Italy, 1550–1800* [London: Macmillan, 2000], 326, 368ff.).
17. Forsyth's view is endorsed by Hanlon: "Leopold advocated what he called the 'scientific method' of governing; that is, he chose to gather information from many sources so that he would not have to rely on the observations of single individuals" (Hanlon, *Early Modern Italy*, 362).
18. "The great misfortune which nobles labour under is, in the first place, a bad education, and afterwards the want of a career" (Mary Shelley, *Rambles in Germany and Italy*, 2 vols. [London: Moxon, 1844], 2:110; original pagination as derived from *The Novels and Selected Works of Mary Shelley*, vol. 8, ed. Jeanne Moskal [London: Pickering, 1996]).
19. The word *accademia* was formerly applied to exhibitions of the art of improvisation, recitals, and did not mean exclusively a learned society or school of art.
20. Hobhouse to Murray, December 7, 1817.
21. A transference of Horace's tag "genus irritabile vatum" [quarrelsome race of poets] to scientists (*Epistolae* 2.2, 102).
22. Particularly noted by the online *Enciclopedia italiana* (Treccani) in the article "Santi, Giorgio," accessed June 21 2019, http://www.treccani.it/enciclopedia/giorgio-santi.

CHAPER 5 THE HIDDEN THOUGHTS OF JOSEPH FORSYTH

1. Peter Cochran links this to stanza 116 of canto 4 in *Childe Harold* ("Childe Harold's Pilgrimage Canto IV" on Peter Cochran's website, last modified November 2014, petercochran.files .wordpress.com/2009/03/childe_harold_4.pdf).
2. Giant king of the Teutons. The skeleton thought to be him was twenty-five feet tall.
3. Hobhouse, *Historical Illustrations*, 158n.
4. Fea held the position of *commissario delle antichità* [commissioner for antiquities] from 1801 to 1836. His predecessors included Ridofino Venuti and Winckelmann. The office was abolished in 1870. With Canova, he established control of the selling of remaining art treasures to wealthy foreigners.
5. Immediately after this outburst, there is another pointed note (left out of 1813) quoting from Cicero's attack on Verres and saying there were "hundreds" of cases of other stealing while the French looting went on.
6. L. C. D. [Stendhal], "On Italian Literature, No. II," *London Magazine* 14 (January 1826): 23.
7. "Forsyth Isaac Memorandum for a Life of His Brother," Isaac Forsyth to John Murray, April 1818, Murray Archive. Isaac's writing is a fair copy with few corrections in his hand and no other annotations.
8. Advertisement to the first edition, reprinted in *1816*.
9. Forsyth has prepared the reader to value the Pandects highly by noting that the University of Pisa was ranked with Bologna for its possession of these documents. Forsyth expects the reader to know about the Pandects ("this famous code"). David Hume had seen them as a catalyst for founding a system of jurisprudence. Forsyth takes issue with Hume's idea of where they were found (17).

10. [Charles Armitage Brown], "Vallombrosa, Camaldoli, La Verna," *New Monthly Magazine and Literary Journal* 14 (September 1825): 263.
11. I am grateful to Carla Garbarino at the museum of the University of Pavia for this information.
12. Enoch Cobb Wines, *Two Years and a Half in the Navy*, 2 vols. (Philadelphia: Carey & Lea, 1832), 2:42. Possibly the effect of English-speaking tourists and the diffusion of Forsyth's account among them caused the directors of the Gabinetto to forbid what had been normal thirty years before, making the process of visiting the Gabinetto into an initiation ceremony in which one man at a time only was allowed to view the inmost shrine of the secrets of gestation.
13. Fergus Robson, "French Soldiers in Italy, 1795–1815" (introductory text to the exhibition of www.mwme.eu, 2015), accessed October 18, 2018. https://www.mwme.eu/essays/french-soldiers-italy/Intro_Italy/index.html. This is an introductory essay to a large international project on *Making War, Mapping Europe: Militarized Cultural Encounters*, which has an online exhibition at www.mwme.eu.
14. The *Anti-Jacobin* reviewer was happy to be shocked by stories of the immodesty and immorality of Italian ladies, but took issue with this particular statement. He declared that women in general play a greater part in forming the characters of men than vice versa (Unsigned review of of *Italy*, by Forsyth, *Anti-Jacobin Review* 52 [March–August 1817]: 120).
15. A member of a noble Florentine family, particularly distinguished during the Renaissance. Giovanni Rucellai (1403–1481) was a wealthy patron of the arts; his son Bernardo (1448–1514), uncle to two popes, founded the Platonic Academy, which met in the gardens of his Florentine mansion. Bernardo's son, Giovanni di Bernardo (1475–1525), diplomat and man of letters, best fits the context, being also a priest who was closely associated with service to several popes in Rome.
16. Here, again, the *Anti-Jacobin* resoundingly objected, saying that virtue is not relative but absolute. However, determined to think well of the otherwise admirable author of *Forsyth's Italy*, the reviewer charitably supposed that the he merely meant to say that the faithful Italian wife was more *meritorious* (Unsigned review of of *Italy*, by Forsyth, *Anti-Jacobin Review* 52 [March–August 1817]: 122).
17. G. L. Craik, *The Pursuit of Knowledge under Difficulties, Illustrated by Female Examples* (London: Cox, 1847), 123–124, lists eminent women from the faculties of divinity, law, and medicine at Bologna in the Middle Ages and adds that the skills of "the treatment of diseases, and especially the cure of wounds" were not confined to the highborn, citing nuns such as Margaret and Pontia of Marcigni.
18. Her daughter, Giulia, became the lover of Stendhal.
19. The *Anti-Jacobin Review*—asserting the primacy of the role of the Church rather than government, local or national, in taking charge of poor relief—demurred at this conclusion and thought that it was too dismissive of the monks' charitable work. Perhaps, too, the reviewer was nervous about the leveling implication of Forsyth's phrase. If men of property were to be compelled to be public benefactors by taxing their luxuries, where would this policy end? He accused Forsyth of advancing an economic rather than a philosophical argument, deliberately missing Forsyth's point: he is concerned with practical, not abstract, justice (Unsigned review of of *Italy*, by Forsyth, *Anti-Jacobin Review* 51 [September 1816–February 1817]: 597–598).
20. Jean-Jacques Rousseau, *Discours sur l'origine et les fondements de l'inégalité parmi les hommes* [A discourse on the origin and causes of inequality within mankind] (1754; Amsterdam: Marc Michel Ray, 1755), 95.

21. "Assimilating a new sort of fact demands a more than additive adjustment of theory, and until that adjustment is completed—until the scientist has learned to see nature in a different way—the new fact is not quite a scientific fact at all" (T. S. Kuhn, *Structure of Scientific Revolutions* [Chicago: University of Chicago Press, 1976], 2:53).

22. Haskell says that the marble statues went from the Palazzo Farnese in Rome to Naples in 1800 and eventually to the Capo di Monte in 1805, after which portable items were taken to Palermo, before the French army came. The Farnese Hercules, which had been selected and of which Denon said, "Three times it had been earmarked for France," never in fact went to France (Haskell and Penny, *Taste and the Antique*, 76, 229). There is no more about Naples in the 1803 *Catalogo de' capi d'opera* of items taken from Italy. It does not mention Naples, except to say that later the Venus de Medici was yielded up: "La famosa Statua della venere de' Medici . . . fu anch'essa posteriorente all'epoca suddetta trasportata in Francia" (*Catalogo de' capi d'opera di pittura, scultura, antichità, libri, storia naturale, ed altre curiosità trasportati dall'Italia in Francia*, 2nd ed. Milan: Borsani [?1803 or after], 32; The famous statue of the Venus de Medici . . . was also after this time taken to France).

23. Samuel Johnson, *A Dictionary of the English Language in Which the Words Are Deduced from Their Originals and Illustrated in Their Different Significations by Examples from the Best Writers*, 6th ed., vol. 1 of 2 (London: Rivington et al., 1785), s.v. "Grace."

24. Johan Winckelmann, *Gedancken über die Nachahmung der griechischen wercke in der Malerei und Bildhauerkunst* (1755–1756). The quotation is from the excellent modern translation by Elfriede Heyer and Roger Norton, *Reflections on the Imitation of Greek Works in Painting and Sculpture* (La Salle, Ill.: Open Court, 1987), 21.

CHAPTER 6 VISUAL ARTS, ARCHITECTURE, AND LITERATURE

1. Joseph Addison, preface to *Remarks on Several Parts of Italy, &c. in the Years 1701, 1702, 1703* (London: Tonson, 1705).

2. Jonathan Richardson, *An Account of Some of the Statues, Bas-reliefs, Drawings and Pictures in Italy, &c. with Remarks. By Mr. Richardson, Sen. and Jun.* (London: J. Knapton, 1722).

3. John Breval, *Remarks on Several Parts of Europe: Relating Chiefly to the History, Antiquities and Geography, of Those Countries through which the Author Has Travel'd*; [. . .] *Illustrated with Several Maps* (London: Lintot, 1726); later published as *Remarks on Several Parts of Europe: Relating Chiefly to the Antiquities and History, Collected upon the Spot in Several Tours since the Year 1723* (London: Lintot, 1738).

4. Breval, preface to *Remarks* (1726).

5. The information here comes from "pulpito," *Catalogo Generale dei Beni Culturali*, accessed October 18, 2018, http://www.catalogo.beniculturali.it/sigecSSU_FE/dettaglioScheda.action?%5BBeni%20Culturali%5D&%7BBeni%20Culturali=%7D&keycode=ICCD2754728&valoreRicerca=&titoloScheda=pulpito&stringBeneCategoria=&selezioneSchede=&contenitore=&flagFisicoGiuridico=0. On the specific page given, a more complete description (*scheda completa*) may be downloaded.

6. Carmen Gómez-Moreno, "Giovanni Pisano at the Metropolitan Museum Revisited," *Metropolitan Museum Journal* 5:1972–1973. This gives a succinct account of the vagaries of Pisano's pulpit in an examination of some of its panels that are now in the Metropolitan Museum of New York.

7. Mariana Starke, *Travels on the Continent: Written for the Use and Particular Information of Travellers* (London: John Murray, 1820), 168. This work, updated several times under different titles, is the true ancestor of the Murray Guides. Starke's description of the pulpit is almost word for word taken from an earlier but slightly less clear description in her *Letters from Italy, between the Years 1792 and 1798* (1800), and it is reproduced in her later *Travels on the Continent between the Years 1824 and 1828* (London: John Murray, 1828). Her eyewitness evidence is not mentioned in Gómez-Moreno's account ("Giovanni Pisano").
8. H. H. (Henry Hobson) Richardson, seqs. 4, 14, 15, 16, *Photographs Collected by Henry Hobson Richardson, 1870–1885 (Inclusive)*, photographs of Architecture in Italy, volume HHR218_22, Frances Loeb Library, Harvard University Graduate School of Design, accessed June 3, 2017, https://iiif.lib.harvard.edu/manifests/view/drs:52784172$3i. The image "seq. 4" shows the pulpit against a pillar and with a curtain around its supports. Three others—seqs. 14, 15, 16—show columns with brocatello and bas-relief images. They do not appear to be of purple-red porphyry (which would be dark in these sepia images), and the shown carvings are not gross. I am grateful to Ursula Crook, who drew this resource to my attention.
9. At a first reading of Forsyth's criticism of the pulpit, I thought that he might be referring to Pisano's naked Herculean figure of Fortitude, which is in the present reconstruction one of the capital figures supporting the pulpit. Within the tightly controlled symbolism of Pisano's masterwork, it was in "keeping" with the other Christian iconography. If it had been included in Chiarissimo Fancelli's reworking, it would have lost the meaning that it had had, and might well have incurred Forsyth's strictures. However, the Hercules was probably not seen by Forsyth. Nor is the nakedness of the Hercules likely, in itself, to have prompted him to call it a "gross design."
10. James Elmes, "Encaustic," in *General and Bibliographical Dictionary of the Fine Arts* (Chiswick, U.K.: Tegg, 1824).
11. The British Museum at that time would not have served that purpose. It was in its infancy and consisted largely of a repository of literature from the Cotton and Harleian bequests.
12. "Verses flowing smoothly along, so that the critical nail glides unjarred over the joinings" (Persius, *Saturæ* 1.312, translated by G. G. Ramsay in *Juvenal and Persius*).
13. There is an outside possibility Forsyth read it in the original German, given Isaac's mention of German books in his library. But his castigation of Fea for the fault of coming "to edit Winkelman with the spirit of an enemy" (430) suggests that he had read Fea's version, if no others. The first complete translation into English (1849–1873) was made by the Boston scholar G. Henry Lodge, from which my quotations are taken.
14. Johannes Winckelmann, *The History of Ancient Art*, trans. G. Henry Lodge, 4 vols. (Boston: Osgood, 1880), 1:107.
15. Paetus was a Roman commanded to commit noble suicide by the emperor Claudius. He fell on his sword only after his wife, Arria, had given the lead, saying, "O Paetus, it does not hurt."
16. The statue group, now in the Museo Nazionale Romano, is thought to represent neither; it is at present called the Ludovisi *Gaul Killing Himself and His Wife*.
17. Winckelmann, *History*, 2:244.
18. His enthusiasm draws him to allude to Dante: "flaming porphyry, Red as the blood that gusheth from a vein" (Dante, *Purgatorio* 9.101–102, translated by Ichabod Charles Wright).
19. Ennio Visconti, *Sculture del palazzo della Villa Borghese detta Pinciana* [Sculptures in the palace of the Villa Borghese, known as the Pincian], 2 vols. (Rome: Fugini, 1797), 2:52–53.

20. See also, "Butcher'd to make a Roman holiday" *CHP* 4.1267.
21. See Camille, comte de Tournon, *Études statistiques sur Rome et la partie occidentale des états Romains* [Statistical papers on Rome and the western sector of the Roman states] (Paris: Treuttel & Würtz, 1831).
22. John Parker, *The Flavian Amphitheatre Commonly Called the Colosseum at Rome: Its History and Substructures Compared with Other Amphitheatres* (London: John Murray, 1876), 32.
23. The plate section after page 68 comprises about two thirds of the book but is unpaginated.
24. Samuel Johnson, *Mr Johnson's Preface to His Edition of Shakespeare's Plays* (London: Tonson, 1765), lx.
25. Hobhouse to Murray, December 7, 1817.
26. Shelley, *The Tower of Famine*, in *The Complete Poetical Works of Shelley*, ed. Thomas Hutchinson (Oxford: Clarendon Press, 1904), 694, probably with Forsyth's phrasing in mind.
27. William Griswold and Linda Walk-Simon, *Sixteenth-Century Italian Drawings in New York Collections* (New York: Metropolitan Museum of Art, 1994), 25.
28. For example, Ruskin attacked both artists in *Modern Painters*. He mentioned "works devoid of art and decency, as that Susannah of Guido, in our own gallery," and in a footnote to the text, he deplored "the coarseness, mindlessness, and eclecticism of Guido." He criticized "Guercino's Hagar, in the Brera Gallery at Milan, [as] partly despicable, partly disgusting, partly ridiculous." When he revised the text in 1883 for a second edition, Ruskin added an endnote endorsing his comment on Guercino's *Hagar* as "extremely right" (John Ruskin, *Modern Painters*, 2nd ed. [London: Allen, 1900], 2:122, 162n1, 126, 259n146).
29. Bernard Berenson endorsed his 1907 dismissal of Reni in 1952, saying his (Berenson's) volume "still seems to fulfil its purpose." Guido belongs to one of the "ages of bad taste," which Berenson calls "the Eclectics"; they are "worthless" (*The Italian Painters of the Renaissance* [London: Phaidon, 1952], xii, 86, 203).
30. George Richardson, *Iconology; or, A Collection of Emblematical Figures*, 2 vols. (London: Scott, 1779).
31. E. H. Gombrich, *Gombrich on the Renaissance*, vol. 2, *Symbolic Images* (London: Phaidon, 1985), 12.
32. Jean Seznec, *The Survival of the Pagan Gods*, trans. Barbara Sessions (New York: Harper, 1961); Edgar Wind, *Pagan Mysteries in the Renaissance* (London: Faber, 1958). Wind takes the view that the great artworks do follow more precisely the "exactly relevant texts" (187) and advises us to beware of the fallacy of "a robust common sense in the interpretation of images" (190).
33. L. C. D. [Stendhal], *Journal d'Italie*, ed. Paul Arbelet (Paris: Calmann-Lévy, 1911), 187.
34. *Catalogo de' capi d'opera*, 5.
35. Richardson, *Account of Some Statues*, 266.
36. Richardson, 272.
37. Tobias Smollett, *Travels through France and Italy*, 2 vols. (1776; London: R. Baldwin, 1778), quoted in letter 33.
38. Joshua Reynolds, "Discourse XV" in *Discourses on Art*, ed. Robert R. Wark (New Haven, Conn.: Yale,1981).
39. Moses descended from the mountain of Sinai with the Ten Commandments and his face radiant from his encounter. The Hebrew word for this was translated either as "shining" or "horned." It was a syncretic tradition to accept both interpretations of a heroic figure rather than reconcile them. Another example would be of the constellation of Perseus holding

Medusa the Gorgon's head and also a bearded demon's head, which gives rise to the Arabic name of Algol to the star still shown in our map of the stars. Seznec in *The Survival* gives the example of Perseus (180) and describes how Apollo acquired, through different interpretations of his attributes, "scattered features" that were "necessarily lacking in unity" (178).

40. Smollett, *Travels*, 27.

41. Eustace, *Classical Tour* (1821), 1:321.

42. William Cowper's preface to *The Task* (first published in 1785, and collected in a "new edition" of his poems in 1798) tells of its inspiration: "A lady, fond of blank verse, demanded a poem of that kind from the Author, and gave him the SOFA for a subject" ("The Task, in Six Books," in *Poems by William Cowper of the Inner Temple in Two Volumes*, vol. 2 [London: J. Johnson, 1798]). The first book of the six-book poem is called *The Sofa*.

43. These portraits in paper and cheese are also, in their humble way, lost artworks, though specimens of the first may still exist. This is evidently the same Du Pau of Geneva who showed "Mrs ***, later Countess of ***," his "clair de lune decoupures, a mixture of painting and cutting out," on her visit to Geneva in 1786, and who "cut [her] out some likenesses in card, a talent that he possesses to perfection" ("Journal of the Late Countess of ***," in *The Sketch Book of the South* [London: Edward Churton, 1835], 217, 236).

BIBLIOGRAPHY

Addison, Joseph. *Remarks on Several Parts of Italy, &c. in the Years 1701, 1702, 1703*. London: Tonson, 1705.

Alger, John Goldworth. *Napoleon's British Visitors and Captives 1801–1815*. Westminster: Constable, 1904.

Alighieri, Dante. *The Purgatorio of Dante*. Translated by Ichabod Charles Wright. New edition, revised and corrected. London: Longman, Rees, Orme, 1845.

Anti-Jacobin Review; True Churchman's Magazine; and Protestant Advocate: or, Monthly, Political, and Literary Censor. Unsigned review of *Remarks on Antiquities, Arts, and Letters, during an Excursion in Italy, in the Years 1802 and 1803*, by Joseph Forsyth, 2nd ed. 51 (September 1816–February 1817): 585–602; and 52 (March–August 1817): 105–26.

Bannermen Mackintosh, Herbert. *Elgin Past and Present*. Elgin, U.K.: J. D. Yeadon, 1914.

Berenson, Bernard. *The Italian Painters of the Renaissance*. London: Phaidon, 1952.

Breval, John. *Remarks on Several Parts of Europe: Relating Chiefly to the Antiquities and History, Collected upon the Spot in Several Tours since the Year 1723 and Illustrated by Upwards of Forty Copper Plates, from Original Drawings*. London: Lintot, 1738.

———. *Remarks on Several Parts of Europe: Relating Chiefly to the History, Antiquities and Geography, of Those Countries through which the Author Has Travel'd; as France, the Low Countries, Lorrain, Alsatia, Germany, Savoy, Tyrol, Switzerland, Italy and Spain. Illustrated with Several Maps, Plans, and above Forty Copper Plates*. London: Lintot, 1726.

British Critic and Theological Quarterly Review n.s. Unsigned review of *Historical Illustrations of the Fourth Canto of Childe Harold: Containing Dissertations of the Ruins of Rome; and an Essay on Italian Literature*, by John Hobhouse, 2nd ed. 12 (July–December 1819): 23–40.

———. Unsigned review of *Remarks on Antiquities, Arts, and Letters, during an Excursion in Italy, in the Years 1802 and 1803*, by Joseph Forsyth, 2nd ed. 7 (January 1817): 32–48.

———. Unsigned review of *A Tour through Italy, Exhibiting View of Its Scenery, Its Antiquities, and It Monuments; Particularly as They Are Objects of Classical Interest and Elucidation: With an Account of the Present State of Its Cities and Towns; and Occasional Observations on the Recent Spoliations of the French*, by John Chetwode Eustace. 1 (January–June 1814): 246–263; 386–401.

[Brougham, Henry]. Review of *A Tour through Italy, Exhibiting View of Its Scenery, Its Antiquities, and It Monuments; Particularly as They Are Objects of Classical Interest and Elucidation: With an Account of the Present State of Its Cities and Towns, and Occasional Observations on the Recent Spoliations of the French*, by John Chetwode Eustace. *Edinburgh Review* 21, no. 42 (July 1813): 378–424.

[Brougham, Henry?]. Review of *Remarks on Antiquities, Arts, and Letters, during an Excursion into Italy, in the Years 1802 and 1803*, by Joseph Forsyth. *Edinburgh Review* 22, no. 44 (January 1814): 376–385.

[Brown, Charles Armitage]. "Vallombrosa, Camaldoli, La Verna." *New Monthly Magazine and Literary Journal* 14 (September 1825): 261–266, 346–352. Signed B.

Byron, George Gordon. *Lord Byron: The Complete Poetical Works*. Edited by Jerome J. McGann. 7 vols. Oxford: Clarendon, 1980–1993.

———. *Byron's Letters and Journals*. Edited by Leslie A. Marchand. 12 vols. London: John Murray, 1973–1982.

Catalogo de' capi d'opera di pittura, scultura, antichità, libri, storia naturale, ed altre curiosità trasportati dall'Italia in Francia. 2nd ed. Milan: Borsani [?1803 or after].

Chateauvieux, Frederic Lullin de. *Lettres écrites d'Italie en 1812 et 1813* [. . .]. 2 vols. Paris: J. Paschoud, 1816.

———. *Manuscrit venu de Sainte-Hélène, d'une manière inconnue*. London: John Murray, 1817.

Cochran, Peter. "Byron and Napoleon." Paper delivered at University of Gdansk, Poland, May 13, 2003. newsteadabbeybyronsociety.org/works/downloads/byron_napoleon.pdf.

[Cohen, Francis (Palgrave)]. Review of *Le voyage en Italie*, by d'Aubin-Louis Millin. *Edinburgh Review* 29, no. 57 (November 1817): 191–217.

Colbert, Benjamin. *Shelley's Eye: Travel Writing and Aesthetic Vision*. Aldershot, UK: Ashgate, 2005.

Collison-Morley, Lacey. *Giuseppe Baretti and His Friends*. London: John Murray, 1909.

Cowper, William. "The Task, in Six Books." In *Poems by William Cowper of the Inner Temple in Two Volumes*, vol. 2, 1–243. London: J. Johnson, 1798.

Craik, G. L. *The Pursuit of Knowledge under Difficulties, Illustrated by Female Examples*. London: Cox, 1847.

Curran, Stuart. *Poetic Form and British Romanticism*. Oxford: Oxford University Press, 1986.

Done, Joshua. "Narrative of the Imprisonment and Adventures of Joshua Done, in Various Parts of France." *London Magazine* n.s. 4 (January 1826): 26–37.

"The Double 'ff' or Capital 'F.'" *Notes and Queries: A Medium of Inter-communication for Literary Men, Artists, Antiquaries, Genealogists, Etc*. 12, no. 305 (September 1): 169–170.

Edinburgh Magazine and Literary Miscellany. Unsigned review of *Observations on Italy*, by John Bell. 17 (July 1825): 25–36.

Edinburgh Review or Critical Journal. Unsigned review *Childe Harold's Pilgrimage. Canto the Fourth*, by George Gordon Byron. 30 (June–September 1818): 87–120.

Ellison, Seacome. *Prison Scenes; and Narrative of Escape from France during the Late War*. London: Whittaker, 1838.

Elmes, James. *General and Bibliographical Dictionary of the Fine Arts*. Chiswick: Tegg, 1824.

Eustace, John Chetwode, *A Classical Tour through Italy, an. MDCCCII*. 6th ed. London. J. Mawman, 1821.

———. *A Classical Tour through Italy*. Vols. 202 and 203 of *A Collection of Ancient and Modern Authors*. Paris: Baudry, 1837.

"Fabroni (*Jean-Valentin-Mathias*, baron)." In *Nouvelle biographie générale depuis les temps le plus reculés jusqu'a nos jours avec les reseignements bibliographiques et l'indication des sources a consulter*, edited by M. Hoefer (Jean Chrétien Ferdinand), 46 vols.,16: 974–976. Paris: Firmin Didot Frères,1856. Title changed to *Nouvelle biographie générale* after volume 9.

Forbes, James. *Letters from France Written in the Years 1803 and 1804*. 2 vols. London: White, 1806.

Forsyth, Joseph. *Remarks on Antiquities, Arts, and Letters during an Excursion in Italy, in the Years 1802 and 1803*. London: Cadell & Davies, 1813.

———. *Remarks on Antiquities, Arts, and Letters during an Excursion in Italy, in the Years 1802 and 1803*. 2nd ed. London: John Murray, 1816.

———. *Remarks on Antiquities, Arts, and Letters during an Excursion in Italy, in the Years 1802 and 1803*. Repr. of 2nd ed. Edited by Keith Crook. Newark, N.J.: University of Delaware Press, 2001.

Gietz, Nora. "Tracing Paintings in Napoleonic Italy: Archival Records and the Spatial and Contextual Displacement of Artworks." *Artl@s Bulletin* 4, no. 2 (2016): 54–69.

Godfrey, Walter H., and William McBeath. Marcham. *King's Cross Neighbourhood (the Parish of St. Pancras), Part 4 of the Survey of London*. 52 vols. London: London County Council, 1952.

Gombrich, E. H. *Gombrich on the Renaissance*. Vol. 2, *Symbolic Images*. London: Phaidon, 1985.

Gómez-Moreno, Carmen, "Giovanni Pisano at the Metropolitan Museum Revisited." *Metropolitan Museum Journal* 5 (1972): 51–73.

Grant, John, and William Leslie. *A Survey of the Province of Moray; Historical, Geographical, and Political*. Aberdeen, U.K.: Isaac Forsyth, 1798.

Griswold, William, and Linda Walk-Simon. *Sixteenth-Century Italian Drawings in New York Collections*. New York: Metropolitan Museum of Art, 1994.

Hanlon, Gregory. *Early Modern Italy, 1550–1800*. London: Macmillan, 2000.

Hare, Augustus. *Walks in Rome*. 1871. 20th ed. London: Kegan Paul, Trench, Trübner, 1913.

Hargreaves-Mawdsley, W. N. *The English Della Cruscans and their Time, 1783–1828*. The Hague: Martins Nijhof, 1967.

Haskell, Francis and Nicholas Penny. *Taste and the Antique: The Lure of Classical Sculpture*. New Haven, Conn.: Yale, 1991.

Hélie, Faustin, and Parisot. "Fabroni ou Fabbroni (Jean Valentin-Mathias)." In *Biographie universelle, ancienne et moderne: ou, histoire, par ordre alphabétique, de la vie publique et privée de tous les hommes qui se sont fait remarquer par leurs écrits, leurs actions, leurs talents, leurs vertus ou leurs crimes*, edited by Michaud, Louis Gabriel, 2nd ed., 45 vols., 13: 311–314. Paris: A. T. Desplaces, 1843.

Helsinger, Elizabeth. *Ruskin and the Art of the Beholder*. Cambridge, Mass.: Harvard University Press, 1982.

Hobhouse, John. *Historical Illustrations of the Fourth Canto of Childe Harold*. 2nd ed. London: John Murray, 1818.

Honour, Hugh. "Canova's Statues of Venus." *Burlington Magazine* 114 (1972): 658–672.

Hunt, Leigh. "Letters from Abroad I: Pisa." *Liberal*, no. 1 (1822): 97–120. [4 numbers only.]

Ingamells, John. *A Dictionary of British and Irish Travellers 1701–1800*. New Haven: Yale, 1997.

Johnson, Samuel. *A Dictionary of the English Language in Which the Words Are Deduced from Their Originals and Illustrated in Their Different Significations by Examples from the Best Writers*. 6th ed. 2 vols. London: Rivington et al., 1785.

———. *Mr Johnson's Preface to His Edition of Shakespeare's Plays*. London: Tonson, 1765.

"Journal of the Late Countess of ***." In *The Sketch Book of the South*, 187–276. London: Edward Churton, 1835.

Kugler, Franz. *The Schools of Painting in Italy*. Edited by Sir Charles L. Eastlake. Translated by Lady Eastlake. 2 vols. London: John Murray, 1851.

Kuhn, Thomas S. *The Structure of Scientific Revolutions*. 2nd ed. Chicago: University of Chicago Press, 1976.

Lasinio, Carlo. *Pitture a fresco del Campo Santo di Pisa*. Florence: Bernardini, 1828.

Lawrence, James. *A Picture of Verdun*. 2 vols. London: T. Hookham, Jun., and E. T. Hookham, 1810.

MacAndrew, Isaac Forsyth. *Memoir of Isaac Forsyth, Bookseller in Elgin 1768–1859, by His Grandson Major-General Isaac Forsyth MacAndrew, Bengal Staff Corps*. London: Kegan Paul, Trench, 1889.

Matthews, Henry. *The Diary of an Invalid; Being the Journal of a Tour in Pursuit of Health in Portugal, Italy, Switzerland and France in the Years 1817, 1818 and 1819*. 2nd ed. London: John Murray, 1820.

Melville, Herman. *Published Poems*. Vol. 11 of *The Writings of Herman Melville*. Edited by Robert C. Ryan et al. Evanston, Ill.: Northwestern University Press and Newberry Library, 2009.

Monthly Review or Literary Journal. Unsigned review of *Classical Tour through Italy*, by John Chetwode Eustace. 74 (May–August 1814): 35–44.

Monthly Review or Literary Journal, Enlarged. Unsigned review of *Remarks on Antiquities, Arts, and Letters, during an Excursion into Italy, in the Years 1802 and 1803*, by Joseph Forsyth, 2nd ed., and of *A Journey to Rome and Naples, Performed in 1817; Giving an Account of the Present State of Society in Italy; and Containing Observations on the Fine Arts*, by Henry Sass. Series 2, 89 (May–August 1819):15–25.

Morgan, Sydney [Lady Morgan]. *Italy*. 2nd ed. 3 vols. London: Henry Colburn, 1821.

Palgrave, Francis. *Hand-Book for Travellers in Northern Italy*. London: John Murray, 1842.

Parker, John. *The Flavian Amphitheatre Commonly Called the Colosseum at Rome: Its History and Substructures Compared with Other Amphitheatres*. London: John Murray, 1876.

Penny Cyclopaedia of the Society for the Diffusion of Useful Knowledge. 27 vols. London; Charles Knight, 1828–1843.

Persius. "Satire 1." In *Juvenal and Persius*, edited by T.E. Page, translated by G.G. Ramsay, Loeb Classical Library ed., 316– 331. London: Heinemann, 1928.

Quarterly Review. Unsigned review of *Childe Harold's Pilgrimage. Canto IV*, by Byron. 19 (April–December. 1818): 215–232.

———. Unsigned review of *A Tour through Italy, Exhibiting a View of Its Scenery, Its Antiquities, and It Monument, Particularly as They Are Objects of Classical Interest and Elucidation*, by John Chetwode Eustace. 10, no. 19 (October 1813): 222–250.

Reiman, Donald H., ed. *Part B: Byron and Regency Society Poets*, 5 vols. *The Romantics Reviewed: Contemporary Reviews of British Romantic Writers*, 9 vols. in 3 parts. New York: Garland Publishing, 1972. Reprint, Abingdon, Oxon: Routledge, 2016.

Reynolds, Joshua, "Discourse XV." In *Discourses on Art* ed. Robert R. Wark, 265–282. New Haven, Conn.: Yale, 1981.

Richardson, George. *Iconology; or, A Collection of Emblematical Figures*. 2 vols. London: Scott, 1779.

Richardson, Jonathan. *An Account of Some of the Statues, Bas-reliefs, Drawings and Pictures in Italy, &c. with Remarks. By Mr. Richardson, Sen. and Jun*. London: J. Knapton, 1722.

Rio, Alexis-François. *De la poésie chrétienne dans son principe, dans sa matière et dans ses formes*. 2 vols. Paris: Debécourt; Hachette, 1836.

Ripa, Cesare. *Iconologia di Cesare Ripa Perugino*. 3 vols. Venice: Tomatini, 1593.

Rogers, Samuel. *The Italian Journal of Samuel Rogers*. Edited by J. R. Hale. London: Faber, 1956.

Rosini, Giovanni. *Lettere pittoriche sul Campo Santo di Pisa*. Pisa: Tipografia della Società Letteraria, 1810.

Rousseau, Jean-Jacques. *Discours sur l'origine et les fondements de l'inégalité parmi les hommes*. 1754. Amsterdam: Marc Michel Ray, 1755.

Ruskin, John. *Modern Painters*. 2nd ed. 6 vols. London: Allen, 1900.

Seznec, Jean. *The Survival of the Pagan Gods*. Translated by Barbara Sessions. New York: Harper, 1961.

Shelley, Mary. *Rambles in Germany and Italy*. 2 vols. London: Edward Moxon, 1844.

———. *Travel Writing*. Vol. 8 of *The Novels and Selected Works of Mary Shelley*. Edited by Jeanne Moskal. London: Pickering, 1996.

Shelley, Percy Bysshe. "The Tower of Famine." In *The Complete Poetical Works of Shelley*, edited by Thomas Hutchinson. Oxford: Clarendon Press, 1904.

Sidney, Philip. *The Countess of Pembroke's Arcadia*. Edited by E. A. Baker. London: Routledge, 1921.

Sismondi, J. C. L. Simonde de. *Histoire des républiques italiennes du moyen âge*. 2nd Paris edition. 16 vols. Paris: Treuttel & Würtz, 1818.

Smollett, Tobias. *Travels through France and Italy*. 2 vols. London: R. Baldwin, 1778.

[Southey, Robert]. Review of *Vita di Vittorio Alfieri, &c. Memoirs of the Life and Writings of Victor Alfieri*, by Victor Alfieri, and of *The Tragedies of Vittorio Alfieri*, translated by Charles Lloyd. *Quarterly Review* 14, no. 28 (Jan. 1816): 333–68.

Staël, Germaine de. *Corinne; ou, l'Italie*. 1807. Edited by Simone Balayé. Paris: Gallimard, 1985.

———. *Corinne ou l'Italie*. Translated by Sylvia Raphael. London: Penguin, 1998.

Starke, Mariana. *Travels on the Continent: Written for the Use and Particular Information of Travellers*. London: John Murray, 1820.

Stendhal [Henri Beyle]. *Journal d'Italie*. Edited by Paul Arbelet. Paris: Calmann-Lévy, 1911. Signed L. C. D.

Sturm-Lind, Lisa. *Actors of Globalization: New York Merchants in Global Trade, 1784–1812* Leiden, Netherlands: Brill, 2018.

Tournon, comte de, Camille. *Études statistiques sur Rome et la partie occidentale des états Romains*. Paris: Treuttel & Würtz, 1831.

Vallucci, Valeria. "A Little Italian Byron: Foscolo, Byron and Hobhouse in London." In *Byron in London*, edited by Peter Cochran. Newcastle, U.K.: Cambridge Scholars, 2008.

Vassallo, Peter. *Byron: The Italian Literary Influence*. London: Macmillan, 1984.

Visconti, Ennio. *Sculture del palazzo della villa Borghese detta Pinciana*. 2 vols. Rome: Fugini, 1797.

Waldie, Jane. *Sketches Descriptive of Italy, in the Years 1816, 1817; with a Brief Account of Travels in Various Parts of France and Switzerland*. 4 vols. London: John Murray, 1820.

Walker, David M. *A Legal History of Scotland*. Vol. 5 of *The Eighteenth Century*. Edinburgh: T&T Clark, 1998.

Wilton, Andrew, and Ilaria Bignamini, ed. *The Grand Tour: The Lure of Italy in the Eighteenth Century*. Exhibition catalogue. London: Tate Gallery, 1997.

Winckelmann, Johannes. *Gedancken über die Nachahmung der griechischen wercke in der Malerei und Bildhauerkunst* (1755–1756). With English text, *Reflections on the Imitation of Greek Works in Painting and Sculpture*. Translated by Elfriede Heyer and Roger C. Norton. La Salle, Ill.: Open Court, 1987.

———. *The History of Ancient Art*. Translated by G. Henry Lodge. 4 vols. in two. Boston: Osgood, 1880.

Wind, Edgar. *Pagan Mysteries in the Renaissance*. London: Faber, 1958.

Wines, E[noch] C[obb]. *Two Years and a Half in the Navy; or, Journal of a Cruise in the Mediterranean and Levant On Board of the U.S. Frigate Constellation in the Years 1829, 1830, and 1831*. 2 vols. Philadelphia: Carey & Lea, 1832.

Young, Robert. *Annals of the Parish and Burg of Elgin*. Elgin, U.K.: Printed for the Author, 1879.

INDEX

F refers to Forsyth throughout.

ABOUT THE AUTHOR

DR. KEITH CROOK taught for many years at Anglia Ruskin University, Cambridge, specializing in eighteenth-century literature, where he is now an Honorary Fellow. His main publications are on Samuel Johnson and Swift. He published the standard scholarly edition of Joseph Forsyth's *Italy* in 2001.